About Island Press

Since 1984, the nonprofit organization Island Press has been stimulating, shaping, and communicating ideas that are essential for solving environmental problems worldwide. With more than 1,000 titles in print and some 30 new releases each year, we are the nation's leading publisher on environmental issues. We identify innovative thinkers and emerging trends in the environmental field. We work with world-renowned experts and authors to develop cross-disciplinary solutions to environmental challenges.

Island Press designs and executes educational campaigns, in conjunction with our authors, to communicate their critical messages in print, in person, and online using the latest technologies, innovative programs, and the media. Our goal is to reach targeted audiences—scientists, policy makers, environmental advocates, urban planners, the media, and concerned citizens—with information that can be used to create the framework for long-term ecological health and human well-being.

Island Press gratefully acknowledges major support from The Bobolink Foundation, Caldera Foundation, The Curtis and Edith Munson Foundation, The Forrest C. and Frances H. Lattner Foundation, The JPB Foundation, The Kresge Foundation, The Summit Charitable Foundation, Inc., and many other generous organizations and individuals.

The opinions expressed in this book are those of the author(s) and do not necessarily reflect the views of our supporters.

A Road Running Southward

John Muir, circa 1870. Courtesy of the NPS, John Muir National Historic Site, JOMU 3519.

A Road Running Southward

FOLLOWING JOHN MUIR'S JOURNEY
THROUGH AN ENDANGERED LAND

Dan Chapman

◖ **ISLAND**PRESS | Washington | Covelo

The findings and conclusions in this publication are those of the author and should not be construed to represent any official US Government determination or policy.

Library of Congress Control Number: 2021946477

All Island Press books are printed on environmentally responsible materials.

Manufactured in the United States of America
10 9 8 7 6 5 4 3 2 1

Keywords: John Muir, the South, walk, dispatches, endangered, Sierra Club, national park, botany, environment, sprawl, species, biodiversity, coal ash, mountains, Appalachian, climate change, Chattahoochee, natural resource, Savannah, sea level rise, invasive species, pollution, aquifer, Florida, development, wilderness

Contents

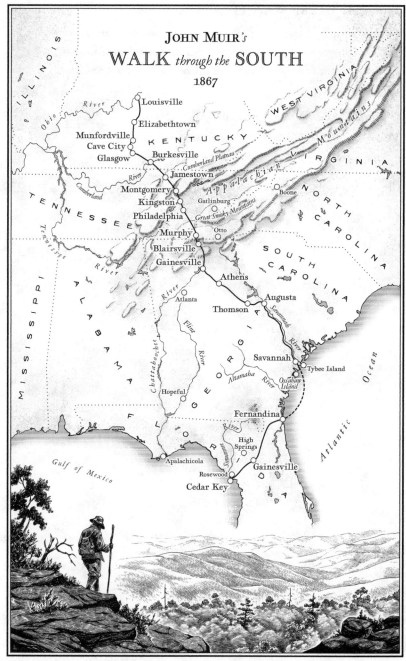

JOHN MUIR's
WALK *through the* SOUTH
1867

ILLINOIS

Ohio River

Louisville

Elizabethtown

KENTUCKY

Munfordville
Cave City
Glasgow

Burkesville

Cumberland Plateau

Cumberland River

Jamestown

Montgomery

Kingston

Gatlinburg

Great Smoky Mountains

Appalachian Mountains

WEST VIRGINIA

VIRGINIA

Boone

NORTH CAROLINA

TENNESSEE

Tennessee River

Philadelphia

Murphy

Otto

Blairsville

Gainesville

Athens

SOUTH CAROLINA

MISSISSIPPI

ALABAMA

River

Atlanta

Flint River

Chattahoochee River

Augusta

Savannah River

Thomson

GEORGIA

Savannah

Altamaha River

Tybee Island

Ossabaw Island

Hopeful

Gulf of Mexico

Apalachicola

FLORIDA

River

Fernandina

High
Springs

Rosewood

Gainesville

Cedar Key

Atlantic Ocean

Ghosts, Skeeters, and Rye

I could not possibly have been placed in circumstances more highly favorable for study and exploration than those which I now enjoy. I am free from the distractions constantly arising in civilized life from social claims. Nature offers unceasingly the most novel and fascinating objects for learning.
—Alexander von Humboldt

Savannah, Georgia — By the time he reached this colonial city in the throes of Reconstruction, John Muir had walked more than seven hundred miles in thirty-eight days, guided by little more than divine inspiration, boundless curiosity, and a love of plants. Tired, hungry, and broke, he wandered the cobblestoned streets and the swampy outskirts of town in search of a place to sleep.

He ended up at Bonaventure Cemetery. It changed his life, and America's relationship with nature.

Bonaventure was a private cemetery on the grounds of an old cotton plantation, a bucolic refuge along the Wilmington River with live oaks festooned in Spanish moss. The bluff afforded stunning views of the salt marsh with cordgrass that magically changed colors as the day unfolded. Bald eagles, snowy white egrets, and monarch butterflies dotted the sky. It was mid-October and fall had yet to reach Savannah.

"The rippling of living waters, the song of birds, the joyous confidence of flowers, the calm, undisturbable grandeur of the oaks, mark this place as one of the Lord's most favored abodes of life and light," Muir wrote in *A Thousand-Mile Walk to the Gulf.*

He fashioned a small shelter of moss and sparkleberry bush and spent a half-dozen nights in Bonaventure. Each day he hiked three miles into town along a crushed shell road to the express office, where he hoped a package from his brother containing $150 awaited. He survived on breakfast crackers and water from a "coffee-colored stream" outside the cemetery's gate. Each day he grew fainter. Bonaventure, though, invigorated Muir's mind and made the twenty-nine-year-old wanderer reconsider long-held notions of life, death, nature, and man's twisted relationship with all three.

Why, he wondered, are humans considered more important than birds, bees, or bluets? Weren't animals a "sacred fabric of life and well-being," worthy of preservation and not to be killed for fashion, sport, or whim? The death of plants, animals, and men are all part of life's natural cycle and God's plan. Yet Muir intuited that nature would ultimately get crushed by man if not preserved. Flora and fauna of all sizes need space—untrammeled forests, mountain ranges, ocean preserves, wildlife refuges—so their lives can proceed apace without undue human interference. Nature requires "the smallest transmicroscopic creature that dwells beyond our conceitful eyes and knowledge," Muir wrote. Humans, too, need room to roam.

The budding environmentalist also began to realize at Bonaventure that there was more to life than collecting plants.

Never was Muir happier than outside the industrial grime and incessant clamor of the city. The Civil War's destruction and ensuing decay that he had witnessed while crossing Kentucky, Tennessee, North Carolina, and Georgia en route to Savannah and, ultimately, Florida solidified, for him, the preeminence of the natural world. Indeed, many of Bonaventure's newer residents—generals, colonels, and privates—offered silent testimony to man's capacity for awfulness. So-called civilization left a lot wanting; not so with nature, Muir believed.

Muir's environmental, ethical, and philosophical beliefs that undergird the American conservation movement took hold at Bonaventure. Ironically, the "father" of the national parks, conscience of the environmental movement, cofounder of the Sierra Club, and passionate defender of all things wild owes much of his life's work and reputation to the dead.

"His transformational moment began with his experience at St. Bonaventure," a biographer wrote.

That was enough for me. It was time for a visit.

I leave Atlanta, my wife, Bita, and sons Sammy and Naveed on a warm October morning. It rains sporadically as my Subaru chugs south to Macon, then east to Savannah. My goal is to spend the night in Bonaventure as close to Muir's "hidden spot in a dense thicket" as possible. I'd reported from Savannah a hundred times before and on occasion played tourist in the cemetery. The parklike layout is magnificent, with boulevards and paths bordered by towering oaks leading to the marsh, as is the craftsmanship of the tombs. Poet laureate Conrad Aiken's gravesite includes a marble bench inscribed with the epitaph "Cosmos Mariner Destination Unknown." The plot for songsmith Johnny Mercer ("Moon River," "Days of Wine and Roses") also includes a bench etched with his likeness. Little Gracie Watson, the cemetery's most beloved denizen, died at age six from pneumonia. Visitors leave toys and stuffed animals alongside the iron gate that surrounds her tomb and life-sized statue. Legend has it that tears of blood flow from Gracie's eyes if her presents are removed.

I'd earlier messaged the cemetery supervisor for permission to camp one night in Bonaventure. Permission denied. I'd be breaking the law and arrested for trespassing as if I were a common vagabond simply seeking a quiet night's rest. Just like Muir.

I arrive late in the afternoon in time for a bit of reconnaissance. I stop first at the cemetery office. I ask a volunteer about the cemetery's layout circa 1867. She knows why I'm asking.

"What do people think about Muir these days?" I prod.

"Nobody cares," she says. "Nobody knows who he was."

Undaunted, I scurry to the area where the little-renowned naturalist, in the South at least, likely camped. The mostly well-tended cemetery gives way to a tangle of live oaks, loblolly pines, southern magnolias, dwarf palmettos, and opportunistic vines along the river which doubles as the Intracoastal Waterway. The mosquitoes are voracious, covering open skin the minute I stop to take notes. Muir, too, felt the wrath of "a lot of hungry, stinging mosquitoes," yet he dismissed the little buggers as mere nuisances. Biographers, though, attribute Muir's near-death from malaria possibly to Bonaventure's mosquitoes. At the time, scientists thought pestilent air caused jungle fever. I'm quite certain that if Muir had known the truth about mosquitoes he wouldn't have been as enraptured with Bonaventure. Would his philosophy of the importance of *all* creatures have changed, too?

While I'm keen to replicate Muir's journey as faithfully as possible, authenticity goes only so far. I search for neighboring spots to camp, away from the bluff. Little Gracie's tomb is nearby, but damned if I'm going to sleep near her. As it grows dark, I discover a chain-link fence bordering the cemetery's northern edge where, in a few hours, I'll begin my adventure.

Bonaventure, established in 1846 as Evergreen Cemetery, was a "rural" or "garden" cemetery with exquisitely planted trees and bushes surrounding marble crypts, sculptures, and headstones. Its seventy acres were carved from a plantation nearly ten times as large and owned variously by Mullrynes, Tattnalls, and Habershams, all prominent Savannah clans. Local lore has it that the manor house caught fire in the late 1700s during a dinner party. The servants carried the table and chairs outside and the fête continued as the house burned. A toast ended with crystal glasses smashed against an oak tree and, on quiet nights, as the story goes, the sound of shattering glass can still be heard in Bonaventure.

Muir passed the ruins of the plantation house on his daily walk into town to claim his money. Although General William Tecumseh Sherman had spared Savannah the torch (and presented the city to President Lincoln as a Christmas present), poverty and rot ruled the land.

"The ragged desolate fields, on both sides of the road, are overrun with coarse rank weeds, and show scarce a trace of cultivation," Muir wrote in *A Thousand-Mile Walk*. "Rickety log huts, broken fences, and the last patch of weedy rice-stubble are left behind."

James Oglethorpe sailed from England in 1733 and established the colony of Georgia with the loftiest of intentions: religious freedom; a prohibition against slavery; an agrarian utopia. The Revolutionary War and cotton, with its pernicious demand for slave labor, scuttled Oglethorpe's plans. Savannah was a bustling port town, thirty miles upriver from the Atlantic Ocean, with rivers and canals bringing cotton, timber, and indigo to its wharves. In 1793, Eli Whitney built a cotton gin at Mulberry Grove Plantation just west of town, revolutionizing production, industrializing the South, and turbocharging Savannah's development.

In 1860, Savannah's population neared twenty-three thousand. Muir, like millions of fellow Midwesterners and Northerners who have since sought reinvention in the balmy and booming South, was truly a man ahead of his time. Savannah today is a microcosm of New South success. A healthy mix of industry, tourism, military, higher education, retirees, and global trade, the Hostess City of the South tallies 150,000 residents. It's the fastest-growing metropolitan area in Georgia. The port of Savannah is the nation's fourth busiest. Record numbers of tourists descend upon the antebellum, European-styled National Historic Landmark district with its abundance of oak-shaded squares and Victorian mansions. John Berendt, in *Midnight in the Garden of Good and Evil*, describes Savannah as "the most remarkable, winsome, beautiful town I'd ever seen in America. . . . It's like *Gone With the Wind* on mescaline. They walk imaginary pets here, and they're all heavily armed and drunk."

I figure that a popular sports bar about a mile from the cemetery is a safe, unobtrusive spot to leave my car overnight. I shoulder my knapsack, pull my Braves cap tight, and, head lowered, walk briskly to Bonaventure. I'd spent the previous week in Florida chasing Hurricane Michael, showering little, and shaving less. I look the part of the hobo searching for a place to sleep; hard stares from residents of the working-class Victory Heights neighborhood confirm my shady appearance.

An oak-lined blacktop runs alongside Bonaventure. It is dark beyond the city's vapor-light glow and threatening rain. The wind-tousled moss dangling from tree limbs adds to the spookiness. I follow the road to the marsh, hop the fence, and enter Muir's "Eden of the dead," as biographer James B. Hunt put it. It's quiet except for the chorus of frogs, the susurrus of distant traffic, and the whine of mosquitoes.

I don't see a soul, living or dead. The prospect of a long night outdoors amidst the deceased bestirs some dread. I'd boned up the day before—foolishly, in hindsight—on Bonaventure ghost stories. The phantom "hell hounds" that roam the cemetery. The angelic statues that glare at passersby. The sounds of distant laughter and shattering glass. Little Gracie with her bloody tears.

Intent on facing my demons, I detour to Gracie's tomb en route to Muir's campsite. As my eyes grow accustomed to the dark, the contours of the headstones and the mausoleums, the towering trees, and the pebbled walkways come into focus. Everything is bathed in dark gray light. Gracie, in her Sunday dress and buttoned boots, still sits straight and motionless. Nary a drop of blood sullies her chubby cheeks.

I find Muir's sleeping spot. The mosquitoes haven't mellowed. I move on, wandering the cemetery and looking for signs of life. Seeing none, I begin to relax. This "weird and beautiful abode of the dead," as Muir called it, is peaceful and safe.

I circle the cemetery and, tired from an hour's walk, pick out a dry spot under a grand oak and a postcard-perfect palm. I lean against George Gemunden's crypt in Section E, Lot Four, and unscrew the cap from my flask of rye whiskey. According to the cemetery's registry, Gemunden died in 1888 at age seventy-six. I later Googled him, but found nothing. I assume he was a German immigrant and, from the looks of his well-appointed tomb, most likely a successful businessman.

I take another sip of rye and channel my inner Muir, but not in a creepy, seance-y way. I picture him, like me, staring vacantly skyward and thinking Big Thoughts. But then I hear fireworks in the distance, sirens in the city, and the drone of a freighter's horn on the Savannah River. It starts to rain. So much for an epiphany.

I pack up and seek a larger crypt with enough of an overhang to keep me dry. I espy an imposing mausoleum at one end of a grassy plaza with an obelisk at the other. But, just then, I see a woman running. I freeze. She doesn't move either, suspended in mid-stride. My heart thumps. My eyes narrow. She's frozen. In fact, she's attached to a low marble riser. Julia Denise Backus Smith was a runner, a beauty queen, a city commissioner, and a "prominent member of Savannah society" who committed suicide in 2003. A closer look reveals that her bronzed likeness has oxidized into an eerie-looking green color. I was right to be freaked out.

Nonetheless, I scurry past Julia and opt for the Tiedeman family crypt. At least five Tiedemans—four named George—are buried in Section A, Lot 122. George Washington Tiedeman was a grocer and a banker and, as mayor of Savannah in the early 1900s, managed the purchase of Bonaventure for the city.

I lean back and sip the whiskey. It nears midnight. The rain stops. The breeze quickens, dispersing the bugs. A three-quarter moon peaks from the clouds and illuminates the graveyard in a pleasing, otherworldly way. I'm at peace, happy as one of the clams found in the marsh along the nearby Bull River.

I return to my Muir reverie. My mood soon sours, though. The Big Thoughts are all Bad Thoughts on the state of Southern conservation and how "the temple destroyers, devotees of ravaging commercialism," as Muir said, keep screwing things up. It's hot, stuffy, and unnaturally warm even for coastal Georgia. Halloween's a week away, but it feels like Independence Day. The mosquitoes are surely in midsummer form. Even the azaleas, some of which naturally bloom in the fall, give off an unseasonably weird vibe.

October 2018, it turns out, is one of the warmest Octobers on record across Georgia's coastal plain, as much as six degrees above normal. The South, overall, has gotten nearly two degrees warmer since 1970. It could get as much as seven degrees hotter by 2100. Summer seems to last from April to November around here.

The seas surrounding nearby Tybee Island, where I spent an eventful Hurricane Matthew two years earlier, have risen ten inches since 1935. They could rise another three feet by century's end and swallow one-third of the funky-touristy beach town, which juts out into the Atlantic Ocean.

Tall, dead oak trees resembling the bones of giants rise from the marsh just north of Bonaventure, ghost-forest victims of a rising sea's surge of salt water. A billion-dollar river-deepening project for the port of Savannah allows even more salt water to push farther upstream and harm the delicate ecosystem that sustains crustaceans, fish, and shore-birds. Meanwhile, the beaches of Wassaw and Ossabaw, barrier islands below Savannah, get eaten away by ever-higher tides.

Muir, before reaching Savannah, passed "through the river country of Georgia" and "was intoxicated with the beauty of these glorious river banks." He would cry in his beer today. Most of the state's rivers have been dammed, industrialized, and heavily polluted. Augusta, up the Savannah River that Muir walked along, is a mash of power plants, paper mills, quarries, sewage-discharge stations, and chemical factories. The lower Savannah has been straightened, deepened, and dredged for two hundred years, with disastrous results for flora and fauna. Georgia, Alabama, and Florida have been fighting for thirty years over the low-flow Chattahoochee River, much to the detriment of farmers, fishers, kayakers, sturgeon, mollusks, and oysters. Warmer temperatures, and more frequent droughts, will only exacerbate the region's water wars.

Muir watched "large flocks of butterflies" flit merrily across Bonaventure, but I saw none during my stay. A freshwater snail, the beaverpond marstonia, was the latest Georgia critter to go extinct, in 2017. The hairy rattleweed, an endangered piney woods perennial, barely hangs on in two nearby coastal counties. Piping plovers, wood storks, Kirtland's warblers, and other threatened or endangered birds are disappearing from Georgia's barrier islands. Loggerhead sea turtles, a Georgia favorite adorning license plates and bumper stickers, lay their eggs along the beaches only to succumb to higher tides, nonnative wild hogs, or the bright lights of sprawling beachside communities that lure newborns to their death.

Ninety million acres of stately longleaf pine forests and nourishing savannah grasses once filled the coastal plains stretching from Virginia through Georgia and all the way to Texas. Only four million acres remain today, the rest disappearing under the woodsman's ax, the farmer's plow,

and the developer's bulldozer. The forests have been replaced by plantations of row upon monotonous row of slash and loblolly pine that grow
quickly and profitably. The red-cockaded woodpeckers, eastern indigo
snakes, and gopher tortoises that once thrived under the longleaf canopy struggle to survive.

It's a similar story with the forests of the Piedmont and the Appalachian mountains that Muir traversed en route to Bonaventure. European
settlers hunted the bison, deer, bear, elk, and beavers to near-extinction before decamping for greener pastures farther west. Then came the
timber companies that stripped bare the mountains and plains, filling
the streams with critter-killing sediment. Sprawling cities and five-acre
"ranchettes" chewed up mile upon mile of virgin land. And feckless,
money-minded officials in Washington and Southern capitals abetted
the region's ecological demise.

I take another sip. There's more.

Invasive plants and animals run roughshod over the South. The majestic chestnuts disappeared from the mountains in the early twentieth
century, thanks to an imported Asian fungus. The sap-sucking wooly
adelgid, another Asian import, has about wiped out hemlocks in the
Appalachians. Watch out for laurel wilt, yet another arboreal mass mur-
derer, which hopped off a cargo ship in Savannah fifteen years ago and
now targets red bay and, more recently, sassafras trees with deadly alacrity.

The Spanish brought pigs with them to Florida in the late 1500s,
and these newcomers bred in the wild like, well, rabbits. Sows can have
two litters per year, with as many as a dozen piglets per litter. They eat
everything: crops, mice, worms, snakes, acorns, roots, sea turtle eggs.
Wild hogs have now invaded thirty-eight states.

When Muir finally got his money, he jumped a steamer to Florida—
the poster child for nature gone bad. No major state has grown faster
the last hundred years, as evidenced by the paucity of condo-free shorelines and the degradation of its slow-flowing rivers, natural springs,

Everglades ecosystem, and coastal waters. The abundance of invasive, weird, and biologically harmful plants and animals—eight-foot-long monitor lizards, Cuban tree frogs, wetlands-killing melaleuca trees, deer-swallowing Burmese pythons—keeps Carl Hiassen in business. A sprawl-inducing superhighway threatens the Big Bend area, the untrammeled corner of the Florida Panhandle where Muir's trek ended.

The local Sierra Club met in Savannah the day I arrived and demanded action to combat climate change. A week earlier, the world's top climate scientists warned that it might be too late to avoid the apocalypse. Meanwhile, the World Wildlife Fund was finishing a report that said populations of mammals, birds, fish, and reptiles had decreased 60 percent since 1970. And beaches up and down Florida's coasts were closed due to a toxic algal bloom known as "red tide."

It's getting late and I'm getting tired. I don't have the energy, nor the stomach, to rehash all the environmental carnage perpetrated by Donald Trump and his regulation-gutting minions at EPA, Interior, Agriculture, and Justice. I do, though, think of my two boys and the future I'm leaving them, and it saddens me.

Muir slept his first night at Bonaventure under an oak tree and atop a grave. I sleep under an oak tree and alongside the many George Tiedemans. At 12:45 a.m., I cap the whiskey, wrap myself in a thermal blanket, and fall fast asleep.

I awake in a much better mood despite a cold front moving through during the night, chilling my achy bones. I'm also a bit fuzzy-headed from the rye.

But the sky lightens beyond the grassy plaza and a few early birds pick up a song. Muir had a similar awakening on his first morning in Bonaventure.

"When I awoke, the sun was up and all Nature was rejoicing," he wrote. "I arose refreshed, and looking about me, the morning sunbeams pouring through the oaks and gardens dripping with dew, the beauty displayed was so glorious and exhilarating that hunger and care seemed only a dream."

I stand, do some desultory jumping jacks for warmth, and head for the promontory overlooking the river. The sun crests the marsh, its brilliant orange orb changing to bright yellow as it climbs the cerulean sky. The spartina grass turns from black to gray to tan to gold. Mullet jump up out of the river and return with a splash. A white egret languorously prowls the shoreline. A fisherman hurries his Boston Whaler seaward.

I sit on a bench and vow to think Happy Thoughts this time. There is much of the Southeast's natural world to be thankful for. It is, pound for pound, the nation's most naturally eclectic and biodiverse region, with blue-green mountain ranges, Piedmont forests, mysterious swamps, and coastal marshes all swathed in a blanket of greenery. The rivers, including the Wilmington and Savannah, are much cleaner than they were fifty years ago, thanks to robust federal legislation and dedicated nonprofit action. Coal plants from here to the Midwest dump fewer tons of carbon dioxide into the Southern skies; many are closing. Millions of acres in the southern Appalachians and along the Gulf have been protected. The alligators below and the bald eagles above rebounded nicely with the advent of the Endangered Species Act and the prohibition of DDT. Serious conservation efforts are being made to save the red-cockaded woodpecker, the gopher tortoise, and the eastern indigo snake. Migratory birds descend in robust numbers upon the barrier islands of St. Catherines, Sapelo, Wolf, and Little St. Simons.

Nonprofits, along with state and federal agencies, withstand enormous development and political pressures, and paltry appropriations, to expand habitat essential for the survival of at-risk flora and fauna. In 2021, Florida dedicated $400 million for conservation, wildlife corridors in particular. Georgia voters three years earlier overwhelmingly approved the use of sales tax money for land conservation, state parks, hiking trails, and water protection. Fort Stewart, about thirty miles from where I sit, and other Southern military bases play little-known yet critical roles in the protection of threatened and endangered species and the creation of wildlife corridors that crisscross the coastal plain.

Just about everybody along the coast, Democrat and Republican alike, understands and fears sea-level rise. They know that the tides rise higher, barrier islands shrink, streets flood, and entire communities like Tybee may one day succumb to the relentless sea. Some will even blame man-made greenhouse gases for the rising temps. They may not be convinced that warmer temperatures and oceans fuel catastrophic storms, but they're coming around. Meanwhile, their elected officials require that new homes, sidewalks, and water-treatment facilities be built on higher ground.

So there is cause for hope. Muir, himself, even while fighting pangs of hunger and despair, never lost sight of nature's beauty. "In the morning everything seemed divine," he wrote on his third day at Bonaventure, and it's hard to disagree.

A few days later, Muir left the cemetery for good. His money had arrived. He sated his hunger with gingerbread and then a more traditional breakfast. He sailed that afternoon on the *Sylvan Shore* for Fernandina, Florida. One hundred and sixty miles remained before his Southern sojourn would end. Bonaventure, though, changed Muir, and America.

I head towards town. It's a beautiful Sunday morning with a hint of fall. Joggers and dog-walkers roam Bonaventure. I stop at the cemetery's bathroom and, hobo-like, avail myself of the amenities. I stroll leisurely to my car, head held high this time.

CHAPTER 1
Who Is John Muir?

I used to climb to the top of one of the huge chinaberry trees, which guarded our front gate, and look out over the world. The most interesting thing that I saw was the horizon. It grew upon me that I ought to walk out to the horizon and see what the end of the world was like.

—Zora Neale Hurston, *Dust Tracks on a Road*

Atlanta, Georgia — Any deep dive into understanding John Muir's rebellious life leads to one overriding conclusion: He was a hippie.

The shaggy, poetry-spouting, draft-dodging Bohemian thumbed his nose at conventional wisdom, religious orthodoxy, and societal mores. He defied his father, disavowed his early Christian upbringing, and made a lifetime habit of questioning authority. Muir shredded the nineteenth-century maxim that all progress is good progress. He didn't trust The Man—or, in his words, "Lord Man"—and society's money-first mentality. Confronted early on with good jobs and a bourgeois life, Muir recoiled. And then went hiking.

Nature was his bag. He was the proverbial "wild child" who never lost his love for adventure. An early advocate of Flower Power, Muir believed that all of God's flora and fauna were worthy of preservation and were no less valuable than us bipeds. Universal peace and quiet was his thing. The dude even loved weed(s). Plus, he up and did some crazy stuff, like climbing a tall tree in a storm to experience life in all its cosmic glory.

Yet Muir remained a Bible-toting prude who blanched at relations with the opposite sex. His encounters with African and Native Americans were less than enlightened, even downright racist. As a boy, he was cruel to animals. Marriage was more of a convenience than an affair of the heart. His all-natural piety grated on less-devoted disciples of wildness.

Muir eventually embraced mainstream society, raised a loving family, got rich, and trod the corridors of power. He realized that his articles and books, leadership of the Sierra Club, and lobbying of the mighty served the budding conservation movement better than his musings on flowers and glaciers. Still, it was Muir's status as an unassailable truth-sayer preaching the back-to-nature gospel to an increasingly jaded, yet eager, American audience that would prove to be his most enduring legacy.

John Muir was born April 21, 1838, in Dunbar, Scotland. He was the third of eight children and the first boy. His father, Daniel, had moved to the North Sea port town to recruit soldiers for the British army. He married a woman who inherited a prosperous grain and feed store. She died within a year. Daniel then married Ann Gilrye, whose father, a meat merchant, opposed their marriage. Ann loved nature, gathered flowers, wrote poetry, enjoyed music and painting. Daniel, a religious zealot, forbade idolatry of any kind and prohibited music, dancing, jokes, or pictures on the walls. Meals were spartan and taken in silence. Ann even felt compelled to drop her cross-stitching. Daniel, though, did allow one pleasure: an Eden-inspired backyard garden with high walls and locked gates. It also served to keep his children from wandering off into hedonic nature. Or so he thought.

"When I was in Scotland I was fond of everything that was wild, and all my life I've been growing fonder and fonder of wild places and wild creatures," reads the beginning of Muir's *The Story of My Boyhood and Youth*. "I loved to wander in the fields to hear the birds sing, and along the seashore to gaze and wonder at the shells and seaweeds, eels and crabs in the pools among the rocks when the tide was low; and best of all to watch the waves in awful storms."

By many accounts, Muir was a typically rambunctious Scottish kid. The ruins of Dunbar Castle were a playground and a training ground for rock climbing. Boys challenged each other to fistfights and cross-country races. He relished walks with his grandfather into the countryside to eat apples and figs and marvel at birds, mice, and other creatures. Muir dreamed of voyages to France, India, Australia, and America. He also enjoyed dogfights and the slaughter of pigs. He threw stones at cats and, with a brother, tossed one feline from the top story of their house onto the ground below—"a cruel thing for even wild boys to do," as Muir acknowledged decades later.

The Scots' characteristic dourness, coupled with Daniel's oppressive piety, relentless Bible study, and fondness for the switch, drained much of the joy from Muir's early childhood. So when Daniel, dissatisfied with the Church of Scotland's supposed religious leniency, told the family on February 18, 1849, that they were emigrating to America, young John was ecstatic.

The next morning, John, aged eleven, Sarah, thirteen, and David, nine, took the train with their father to Glasgow for the ship to America. Six weeks later, after joyful hours spent on deck with endless ocean vistas and shanty-singing sailors, the Muirs landed in New York City, ferried up the Hudson River to Albany, traveled the Erie Canal by packet boat to Buffalo, and steamed across Lake Michigan to Milwaukee. They paid a farmer thirty dollars to carry them a hundred miles by wagon into the hinterlands, where they soon settled on eighty acres of virgin land and open forest near the Wisconsin River. Their nearest neighbors were four miles away. Soon, though, the region would fill with fellow Britishers and afford Daniel a ready audience for his circuit preaching. The Muirs built a temporary shanty and set about carving a farm, and a new life, out of the Wisconsin wilderness. By fall, they had constructed a fine-looking, eight-bedroom home to welcome the rest of the Muir family.

The natural bounty surrounding Fountain Lake farm amazed Muir: whippoorwills, jack snipes, and sandhill cranes; love-struck frogs and snapping turtles; Winnebago Indians; ferocious thunderstorms; strawberries, dewberries, cranberries, and huckleberries.

"The sudden plash into pure wildness—baptism in Nature's warm heart," he wrote. "Here, without knowing it, we still were at school; every wild lesson a love lesson, not whipped but charmed into us."

Work, though, proved grueling. Muir's first job was to burn the brush that had been cleared for the planting of wheat, corn, and potatoes. A year later, he was put to the plow, a boy of twelve whose head barely cleared the handles. The brothers fetched water, chopped wood, and fed the animals before breakfast. Fall harvest required seventeen-hour days. Winters were spent shelling corn, fanning wheat, making ax handles, sorting potatoes. Daniel would allow only a few sticks of wood for the morning's fire, guaranteeing that his family would shiver around the stove while putting feet with chilblains into wet socks ("causing greater pain than a toothache") before hurrying to their chores.

John missed but one day of harvest that first decade, and only because he had pneumonia. "We were all made slaves through the vice of over-industry," he wrote.

The soil was exhausted within five years. Daniel bought another farm three years later, named it Hickory Hill, and set John to work digging a well ninety feet deep. He nearly died of asphyxiation from the carbon dioxide vapors that filled the bottom of the hole.

Daniel prayed that his eldest son would follow in his pious footsteps. Daily Bible lessons resulted in John's rote mastery of the New Testament, and three-fourths of the Old, by age eleven. Any misquote was met with a whipping. The burning of brush afforded John's father countless opportunities to warn his sinful children of hellfire and eternal damnation. Daniel belittled virtually every nonreligious endeavor that John undertook. James B. Hunt, a Muir biographer, writes that father and son "were locked in mental and theological combat."

Daniel left his children free to enjoy Sunday afternoons, the Fourth of July, and January first. They made the most of it. The fields, woods, and streams were cathedrals of learning and mystery that piqued John's ceaseless sense of wonder. Ducks, loons, and millions of passenger pigeons filled the skies. A few stray pine boards were transformed into a boat to better catch pickerel, sunfish, and perch. The boys hunted muskrats. They learned to swim by imitating frogs (and almost drowning).

Too busy on the farm, the kids didn't go to school. Yet John, by age fifteen, grew hungry for knowledge. He sold squirrel and muskrat pelts to buy algebra, geometry, and grammar books. He borrowed the works of Walter Scott, William Shakespeare, and John Milton from neighbors despite his father's admonition that the "Bible was the only thing required on earth." Mungo Park, a Scottish explorer, enthralled Muir with tales of Africa. Alexander von Humboldt, the German naturalist, introduced him to Latin America. Muir would steal minutes at lunch or before bed to read. Daniel ordered John to bed promptly at eight, but said he could get up as early as he wanted. John woke at 1:00 a.m. to read or tinker. He became quite the inventor. With bits of leather, metal, and whittled wood, John made water wheels, locks, clocks, thermometers, barometers, and hygrometers. He built a self-starting sawmill and a bed that stood its occupant upright at an appointed hour via a clock, pulleys, and counterweights. Daniel considered the inventions nonsense, but word of the crazy contraptions spread across the countryside.

John, unsure of what to do with his life, stayed on the farms until he was twenty-two. A Scottish neighbor, wowed by the inventions and sympathetic to the boy's harsh home life, told John about the upcoming Wisconsin state fair with its display of scientific inventions. On a September morning, in 1860, John left home. Daniel offered no money. John pocketed the gold sovereign his grandfather had given him upon leaving Scotland a decade earlier and headed to Madison.

The fair changed Muir's life. His clocks, thermometers, and self-rising bed wowed the judges and earned him a ten-dollar prize and accolades in the local newspaper as "An Ingenious Whittler." Two boys helped Muir demonstrate the bed's mechanics. One was the son of Ezra and Jeanne Carr, who became mentors and confidantes and steered Muir's intellectual journey over the next two decades.

Muir recalled that he was "desperately hungry and thirsty for knowledge and willing to endure anything to get it," yet he couldn't afford college. Once the fair ended, he traveled to Prairie du Chien with another exhibitor to help build steam-powered iceboats that could sail across the frozen Mississippi River. He lived in a boardinghouse whose occupants played parlor games where kisses were exchanged. Muir rebuked the players by quoting Scripture.

Bored by the foundry work, Muir returned to Madison after three months. He scratched up the money to attend the University of Wisconsin by selling some of his bedsteads, addressing circulars in an insurance office, and caring for horses.

Muir followed his own course of study, which precluded earning a degree in four years. He took classes in chemistry (from Ezra Carr), math, physics, Greek, Latin, botany, and geology. A fellow student introduced him to the wonders of flowers and trees, and Muir took every opportunity to explore the countryside in search of plants to collect and catalogue.

He survived on bread, mush, and the occasional potato. His family sometimes sent ten or twenty dollars. His funky bed would get him up in the morning for a day of classes, studies (Muir would climb a basswood tree overhanging the campus lake with book in hand), botanizing, and work. The farm boy with an unkempt beard "was already acquiring a reputation for amiably eccentric social behavior," writes biographer Stephen Fox.

Muir was rootless and restless, uncertain who he was and what he wanted to be. The times, too, were unsettling. The Civil War had begun. Muir witnessed military training at Camp Randall, which also housed Confederate prisoners. The draft began in 1862. Immigrants who, like Muir, didn't consider themselves American rioted against compulsory military service. (Muir didn't become a US citizen until he was sixty-five.) War was also contrary to Muir's religious faith. His violent upbringing, at the hands of his father, further cemented Muir's pacifism.

He left the university in 1863 after the spring semester, planning to attend medical school at the University of Michigan in the fall. A botanical journey down the Wisconsin River valley into Iowa came first, though. "I was only leaving one University for another, the Wisconsin University for the University of the Wilderness," Muir wrote.

A year later Muir crossed into Canada and disappeared into the woods and swamps around Lake Huron. One boggy day, with the sun setting and hunger rising, he stumbled across a rare botanical find—*Calypso borealis*. Muir, ecstatic, called the swamp orchid "the most spiritual of all the flower people I had ever met." Forty-five years later he reminisced that only meeting Ralph Waldo Emerson, and a few other notables, was more memorable than discovering *Calypso*. Muir related his discovery to a former professor who sent it along to the *Boston Recorder*. It was Muir's first published work.

The orchid infused Muir's budding philosophy of nature. "Are not all plants beautiful?" he wrote. "Or in some way useful? Would not the world suffer by the banishment of a single weed? The curse must be within ourselves."

Muir was questioning the anthropocentric ideal that anything not human or made for the benefit of man wasn't important, useful, or worthy. Everything in the universe, Muir was beginning to believe, had a purpose. This signified a break from the Christian creed that nature must be subservient to man, a far-out discovery that would be reinforced during Muir's Southern trek.

Muir continued his Canadian walkabout acting "like a fugitive," according to biographer Fox. Later, embarrassed by his draft dodge, he glossed over his two-year stint in Canada, as did some of his biographers and disciples. Muir soon met up with younger brother Dan, who had already fled the country, and found work at a mill in Meaford, Ontario, that made handles for rakes and brooms. They lived in a boardinghouse run by Campbellites, members of the same strict religious order as their father. John slept little, worked long hours, and improved the factory's productivity enough to be offered a partnership. He was, as usual, conflicted. Doctor? Inventor? Machinist? Professor? Scientist? Explorer?

He rekindled an epistolary relationship with Jeanne Carr. "How intensely I desire to be a Humboldt!" he wrote. Carr, a Vermont-born botanist in her own right, pushed the young wanderer to find God in nature. She told him what to read, encouraged him to write, and sent his work to East Coast publishers. She eventually introduced him to Emerson and other leading lights, as well as to his future wife, Louisa Strentzel. Nobody outside of family so influenced the young Muir's life. He called Jeanne his "spiritual mother." "She had opened his whole being to a physical and spiritual relationship with nature," writes Donald Worster, another Muir biographer.

In March 1866, a winter storm sent fireplace embers onto the mill's roof. Gone was the factory, a large inventory of wooden handles, and Muir's dream of returning to college. The owners couldn't pay the three hundred dollars they owed Muir. He returned to the States—the war was over—and settled in Indianapolis with a job at a manufacturer of wheels, spokes, and carriage parts. The factory-versus-forest struggle continued to gnaw at his soul. Soon, disaster would resolve matters.

Muir threw himself into the job at Osgood, Smith & Co. with characteristic intensity. He started as a sawyer at ten bucks a week, but quickly advanced to supervisor of all machinery at eighteen a week. He teased his inner Humboldt with Sunday-afternoon excursions into the surrounding oak and hickory forests with paper and pen in hand. Back at work, his boss encouraged him to improve the factory's design and production, a task Muir relished. On March 6, 1867, the tinkerer was shortening a belt when a file slipped and ricocheted into his right eye. His cornea was pierced. He couldn't see out of the eye. He staggered back to the boardinghouse, where his left eye went dark, too. He feared he would never again witness nature's beauty.

"You have, of course, heard of my calamity," Muir wrote to Jeanne Carr. "The sunshine and the winds are working in all the gardens of God, but I—I am lost. I am shut in darkness. My hard, toil-tempered muscles have disappeared, and I am feeble and tremulous as an ever-sick woman."

William Frederic Badè, literary executor of Muir's estate and an early president of the Sierra Club, said that the accident ended Muir's indecisiveness over a career path. "He concluded that life was too brief and uncertain, and time too precious, to waste upon belts and saws, that while he was pottering in a wagon factory, God was making a world;

and he determined that, if his eyesight was spared, he would devote the remainder of his life to a study of the process," Badè wrote. "Thus the previous bent of his habits and studies, and the sobering thoughts induced by one of the bitterest experiences of his life, combined to send him on the long journey."

Muir would walk the South. Within a month his eyesight had returned. He journeyed to Wisconsin to set his affairs in order—which family member would inherit what if he died in Georgia, Florida, or Brazil. The life of a wandering botanist did not appeal to his father, however. Daniel likened his son's proposed journey to "walking in the paths of the Deevil." He made John pay for his summer's room and board. Incensed, John responded: "You may be sure it will be a long time before I come again."

He didn't return until twenty years later, as his father lay dying.

In 1864, President Lincoln signed legislation transferring forty thousand acres, including the Yosemite Valley, to the state of California to be set aside for public recreation. Towering waterfalls, granite cliffs, ancient sequoias, deep valleys, and flower-filled meadows were the already popular preserve's calling cards. Many consider the alpine refuge high in the Sierra Nevada as the country's first national park. Muir would eventually consider Yosemite home. "I should like to live here always. It is so calm and withdrawn while open to the universe in full communion with everything good," he wrote in *My First Summer in the Sierra*. "No words will ever describe the exquisite beauty and charm of this mountain park—Nature's landscape garden at once tenderly beautiful and sublime."

He first visited the Yosemite Valley in 1868 upon completion of his Southern journey. A year later, Muir joined Billy the shepherd, Carlo the St. Bernard, and 2,050 sheep in the valley below the towering Sierra mountains. He helped Billy and Carlo corral the "hoofed locusts," as Muir disdainfully called them, and push them higher into the hills in search of green pastures. However, with a block of bread and a notebook tied to his belt, Muir was largely free to wander, botanize, geologize, sketch, rhapsodize about nature, taunt bears, and tempt fate.

They left on June 3 for the headwaters of the Merced and Tuolumne Rivers, up through the tawny foothills and the pine forests to the High Sierra. Everything natural was a gift from God, Muir believed. He extolled the "sacred fern forests." In a field of lilies, Muir found it difficult to keep up with the herd "while such lovely plant people are standing preaching by the wayside."

Every species served a purpose, even if Lord Man couldn't profit by it. Lizards were "lowly, gentle fellow mortals, enjoying God's sunshine and doing the best they can in getting a living." He rhetorically questioned the need for poison oak and ivy before concluding that "like most other things not apparently useful to man . . . it might have been made for itself." Sitting atop Yosemite's North Dome, Muir marveled at the lowly grasshopper: "Cosmic redlegs, the mountain's merriest child, seems to be made up of pure, condensed gayety," he wrote alongside a sketch of a jumping grasshopper. "The Douglas squirrel is the only living creature that I can compare him with in exuberant, rollicking, irrepressible jollity."

He reserved special praise for the mountains. "Nevermore, however weary, should one faint by the way who gains the blessings of one mountain day," Muir wrote; "whatever his fate, long life, short life, stormy or calm, he is rich forever."

One morning, while perched on a ridge between the two riverbeds, Muir was overcome by emotion: "Exhilarated with the mountain air, I feel like shouting this morning with excess of wild animal joy." All around were sugar pines and silver firs, lilies and larkspurs, lupines and columbines—"noble plants . . . Nature's darlings." Muir was especially enraptured by the towering cumulus clouds ("fleeting sky mountains"), which daily at noon unleashed cleansing rains.

The higher he climbed, the more he studied glaciers. At ten thousand feet, the smooth slabs of granite with parallel striations indicated the direction the ice sheets had once flowed. Muir likened the immense protuberances of rock to God's temples and cathedrals. He struggled for superlatives in describing Yosemite. "Sublime domes and cañons, dark upsweeping forests, and glorious array of white peaks deep in the sky, every feature glowing, radiating beauty that pours into our flesh and bones like heat rays from fire," he wrote. "Never before had I seen so glorious a landscape, so boundless an affluence of sublime mountain beauty."

Muir ambled through the valley for three weeks, from granite dome to sequoia forest to thundering waterfall, while the sheep fattened on nearby meadows. Worster, the biographer, says that Muir "experienced, in the fullest sense yet, a profound conversion to the religion of nature. His Sierra summer awakened the deepest and most intense passion of his life, a long moment of ecstasy that he would try to remember and relive to the end of his days."

There were moments of self-induced terror as well. In search of the best view, Muir crab-walked alongside Yosemite Creek just before it plunged to the valley floor a half-mile below. He slipped on "an immense snow and ice cliff" before righting himself "just on the brink of a yawning ice gulf." He tracked a five-hundred-pound bear to within a dozen yards before the bear let him know that he wasn't amused.

Muir also burnished his budding conservation ethos. He despised "the crawling sheep-cloud" that devoured the flowers and grasses. He lambasted the gold miners who blasted the roads and dammed the streams. A deforested hillside was an unholy abomination. Fishermen sought "pleasure in the pain of fishes struggling for their lives." Not even tourists en route to Yosemite were spared: "A strange show they made, winding single file through the solemn woods in gaudy attires, scaring the wild creatures, and one might fancy that even the great pines would be disturbed and groan aghast."

In early September, the rancher who had employed him, Patrick Delaney, returned his sheep to the valley. Muir wanted "to stay here all winter or all my life or even all eternity." Delaney, supposedly, convinced Muir that greater things awaited down the mountain. "Mr. Delaney," Muir wrote in *My First Summer in the Sierra*, "declares I'll be famous some day, a kind guess that seems strange and incredible to a wandering wilderness-lover with never a thought or dream of fame while humbly trying to trace and learn and enjoy Nature's lessons."

Muir's lifelong perturbations—steady employment vs. nature study, community vs. solitude, city vs. country—returned once he was off the mountain. Money woes simplified matters. He soon fashioned a reasonable life–work balance. Muir was hired by proprietor James Hutchings to fix up the Upper Hotel in the Yosemite Valley. Muir built himself a small cabin at the base of Yosemite Falls with a hammock suspended from the rafters and a stream running through one corner. Ferns poked through the floorboards. A sawmill was refashioned to turn pine trees into boards for the hotel and new tourist cabins. He ate bread, drank tea, read Emerson, and ambled through the backcountry on his free time. He guided tourists on nature walks. He also struck up a friendship with Mrs. Elvira Hutchings.

She was two decades younger than her husband, with three young children and a boatload of resentment toward Mr. Hutchings. She wrote poetry, played the guitar, and wandered alone through the valley. She and Muir picked flowers and shared a love of nature. Her husband left for Washington to contest an ownership claim in Yosemite. Muir was left in charge of the family that snowy winter. Fox, the biographer, writes that "it would have been remarkable if something had *not* hap-pened" between Muir and Elvira. On the other hand, Worster claims that Elvira loved Muir, but her feelings went unrequited: "He was too much of a spiritual prude and too sensible a man to return the desperate affections of such a sad case."

Perhaps. But, as Fox notes, Muir eventually regained control of letters he wrote to Jeanne Carr discussing Elvira, and he destroyed them.

The Carrs moved to California in 1869, Ezra to teach at the new Uni-versity of California in Oakland and Jeanne to, among other endeav-ors, boost Muir's naturalist-writer career. She acted as literary agent, prodding Muir to write and sending his manuscripts to newspaper and magazine publishers. Muir's wilderness wanderings and adventure sto-ries were printed in *Overland Monthly*, *Harper's*, and *Scribner's*, earning up to two hundred dollars per piece. One of his most popular articles recounted a windstorm near the Yuba River, where he climbed a hun-dred-foot Douglas spruce to experience Mother Nature's fury. "We all travel the milky way together, trees and men," Muir wrote.

Ralph Waldo Emerson, the philosopher and poet who led the Tran-scendentalist movement, visited Muir in Yosemite in 1871. He offered the budding eco-prophet a teaching position at Harvard University. Muir turned down his idol, preferring instead to remain in his Sierra sanctuary. "I am hopelessly and forever a mountaineer," he wrote. "And I care to live only to entice people to look at Nature's loveliness."

That same year, the Smithsonian Institution requested reports on Muir's mountain ramblings. He happily obliged. Already an expert bot-anist, Muir now focused on the Earth and its geologic history. With ice ax, felt hat, and hobnailed boots, Muir climbed and studied California's tallest mountains, including Mounts Shasta and Whitney. He deduced that the Ice Age never really ended and that glaciers had shaped the Yosemite Valley, a theory at odds with conventional wisdom, which held that the valley floor sank due to some cataclysmic event. Josiah Whitney, the state's geologist, reportedly derided Muir as an "ignoramus" and "mere sheepherder."

Sixty years later the US Geological Survey confirmed Muir's science.

In 1873, Muir, a much-changed man, moved to San Francisco. The Sierra remained his "true home," but Muir lived the rest of his life in or near cities. He shared the fine homes of friends and fraternized with educators, painters, politicians, and poets. Jeanne Carr introduced him to John Strenzel, a doctor and horticulturist with a 2,600-acre fruit orchard in Martinez, near Oakland. Carr's real intention was to introduce Muir to Dr. Strenzel's daughter, Louisa, or Louie, a lover of botany, astronomy, and current events. She was nine years younger than Muir, but unmarried with prospects diminishing. He proposed five years later. And then went to Alaska. They married a year later. And then Muir went to Alaska. Biographers suggest the marriage was practical, not romantic: a fancy home; steady income; two daughters; and a "scribbler's den."

Alaska promised a wilder wilderness adventure than the Sierra. Glaciers—and whales, wolves, bears, salmon, soaring mountains, and raging seas—were everywhere and offered a living classroom for the study of Earth's history. Tlingit tribesmen and S. Hall Young, a missionary, joined Muir on a two-hundred-mile canoe trip from the Alaska panhandle to the icy north. "From cluster to cluster of flowers he ran," Young wrote of Muir, "falling on his knees, babbling in unknown tongues, prattling a curious mixture of scientific lingo and baby talk, worshiping his little blue-and-pink goddesses."

His second Alaska adventure produced his most popular story, "Stickeen," about Young's little black dog—"so small and worthless," Muir wrote—which almost died during one of the explorer's heedless adventures. Muir and the mutt were facing "glaciers full of deadly crevasses" in the midst of an arctic storm when confronted with an icy cavern fifty feet across and hundreds of feet deep. Muir managed to cut steps in the ice wall, shimmy over a narrow, icy ridge, cut steps into the wall on the other side, and climb out. "Never before had I been so long under deadly strain," Muir wrote. Stickeen was paralyzed with fear, unwilling to follow. Finally, in the waning light, the dog jumped down the steps, over the ice bridge, and up the other side into Muir's waiting arms. "Our storm-battle for life brought him to light, and through him as through a window I have ever since been looking with deeper sympathy into all my fellow mortals."

The arctic explorer made another trip to Alaska before settling into seven years of domestic life. He managed the day-to-day operations of the family orchard and vineyard in the Alhambra Valley, planted money-making Bartlett pears and Tokay grapes, and rebuilt the homestead. His second daughter, Helen, was born. Muir wrote little. He yearned for the mountains, yet he adapted well to the role of landed gentry. "This is a good place to be housed in during stormy weather, to write in, and to raise children in, but it is not my home. Up there is my home," he said, motioning toward the Sierra.

Muir would soon return home. In the summer of 1888 he ventured north to Lake Shasta, the Columbia River, Mount Rainier, and the Puget Sound. He was struck by the beauty—and the environmental damage inflicted by overgrazing, deforestation, and newcomers. "The wedges of development are being driven hard," Muir wrote, "and none of the obstacles or defenses of nature can long withstand the onset of this immeasurable industry.

The botanist, glaciologist, and conservationist of increasing renown added preservationist to his environmental portfolio. Muir wrote a series of articles, *The Treasures of Yosemite*, for the influential *Century Magazine*, blasting tourism and development in the park. He proposed a federal reserve encircling the state-owned (and poorly managed) Yosemite, where logging and grazing would be outlawed.

With money no longer a worry, Muir devoted his time to educating the world about the wonders of nature and the dangers of greed. He advocated the protection of forests and the benefits of annual pilgrimages into the woods. He lambasted mining, logging, hunting, and the industrial pollution of waterways. Worster labels Muir's outdoor philosophy "a more enlightened utilitarianism." And by the 1890s, the nation was ripe for Muir's back-to-nature gospel after a decade of society-shattering industrialization and Gilded Age cynicism. In the early nineties, Congress created three national parks in California, including Yosemite, with Muir assuming the role of chief preservation cheerleader.

In May 1892, Henry Senger, a philologist at Berkeley, approached Muir about creating an alpine club *à la* the Appalachian Mountain Club. The Sierra Club was born with Muir as the unanimous choice to be president, a post he'd hold for the rest of his life. Muir, who wanted "to do something for wildness and make the mountains glad," instantly assumed the role of irreproachable prophet of the budding conservation movement.

By then the Progressive Era was in full swing, and Muir would solder the nation's social and political activism onto the struggle between preservationists, who wanted land and waterways protected, and conservationists, who believed that forests and rivers should also further the nation's economic growth. Yet it became abundantly clear by the mid-nineties that the growth-at-all-costs mantra was poisoning America. The forests were clear-cut, the waterways polluted. Palls of smoke from burning coal shrouded cities. Irresponsible or ignorant farming techniques eroded fields and ruined streams. Virtually all the larger mammals—wolves, elk, deer, bear, bison, otter—had been hunted to near-extinction. Birds that were a nuisance to farmers (carrier pigeons), adornments for hats (snowy egrets), or dinner for hunters (wood ducks) disappeared. Even the glaciers that Muir so loved were retreating as the climate warmed. "A bleak future of timber, water, and wildlife depletion seemed to be the fate of the nation, unless conservationists could seize the day," Worster writes.

Gifford Pinchot, the Yale-educated forester, politician, and first chief of the US Forest Service, embodied the working-forests ethic and proved a very effective foil for Muir. Friendly at first—Muir and Pinchot once camped along the rim of the Grand Canyon—both looked to the federal government to safeguard the nation's wild places. Pinchot, though, favored a more prosaic role for the federal lands that didn't outlaw logging, grazing, or hydropower. Most Western pols, and President Teddy Roosevelt, agreed. Muir, however, took to *Harper's* and other publications to boost the preservationist cause and harangue what he later described as "these temple-destroyers, devotees of ravaging commercialism." As he wrote in *Our National Parks*, published in 1901: "Thousands of tired, nerve-shaken, over-civilized people are beginning to find out that going to the mountains is going home; that wildness is a necessity; and that mountain parks and reservations are useful not only as foundations of timber and irrigating rivers, but as fountains of life."

Muir's concern over his fellow man's physical and mental well-being didn't extend to Native Americans or African Americans. Indians were "strangely dirty . . . half-happy savages," Muir wrote in *My First Summer*. He referred to Blacks as lazy "Sambos," and, while crossing a river in Kentucky, as "little Nig" and "little Afric." He dropped the n-bomb in letters and drafts of manuscripts throughout his life. In 2020, the Sierra Club apologized for Muir's "deeply harmful stereotypes" and the organization's "substantial role in perpetuating white supremacy."

In 1903, President Roosevelt asked Muir to guide him through Yosemite. Without aides, the two outdoorsmen spent four days trekking through the forests on horseback, camping in the snow, and ogling Bridalveil Fall, El Capitan, and other natural delights. "I never before had so interesting, hearty, and manly a companion," Muir wrote. "I fairly fell in love with him."

Said Roosevelt, "John Muir talked even better than he wrote."

All the while, the naturalist was cajoling the president into expanding the park's federal boundaries in order to curtail the rampant logging and mining across the Yosemite Valley. Roosevelt would eventually oblige, but not before Muir had lobbied Sacramento legislators on nine separate occasions and convinced railroad baron Edward Harriman not to oppose the Yosemite legislation. It was one of Muir's crowning achievements. The man who'd drawn up the boundaries of Yosemite National Park, cofounded the Sierra Club to protect it, and spent decades lobbying in print and in person to preserve it, could rightly bask in the glow of national renown.

But not for long.

San Francisco muckety-mucks wanted to build a reservoir in the park's Hetch Hetchy Valley to provide an ample amount of fresh water for the city. Mayor James Phelan sought water rights to the Tuolomne River in 1901 and again in 1905. Each time he was denied. Muir, with strong backing from the Sierra Club rank and file, considered the proposed reservoir unnecessary and said supporters showed "a perfect contempt for Nature." Muir charged that Phelan, Pinchot, and "mischief-makers and robbers of every degree from Satan to senators [were] trying to make everything dollarable." Worster writes that "saving the American soul from a total surrender to materialism was the cause for which he fought. The Sierra Nevada had been his first and would be his last stand."

Public opinion, though, was decidedly not on Muir's side. The devastating 1906 earthquake and fire convinced many that the city's water supply was insufficient. Muir was labeled elitist and out of touch, overly concerned about faraway forests that most city dwellers had neither time nor money to visit. Even John Burroughs, a friend and one of the nation's foremost nature writers, grew irritated by Muir's relentless harangues. "I love you though at times I want to punch you or thrash the ground with you," Burroughs wrote in a letter.

San Francisco voters overwhelmingly approved the dam by referendum in 1908. President Woodrow Wilson didn't give final federal approval until 1913, but Muir had lost the battle. The war, though, was just beginning. "His passion for nature had ignited a conservation movement across the country that was political, religious, aesthetic, and moral in scope, one that would fight on against the hydra-headed developers for generations to come," Fox writes.

Hetch Hetchy wore Muir out. He retired to his empty Martinez home—Louisa had died in 1905—and the "long, tiresome, endless job" of writing books. In December 1914, needing to flee the damp northern California winter, Muir visited daughter Helen in the Mojave Desert. He hoped to celebrate the holidays with Sierra Club members at the newly named Muir Lodge in Santa Anita Canyon. But pneumonia set in. Helen sent her father to the California Hospital in Los Angeles, where he died on Christmas Eve. The headline of the obituary in the *Los Angeles Times* read, "Earth He Loved Reclaims Him. John Muir, Apostle of the Wild, Is Dead."

CHAPTER 2

A New South Reckoning

A civilization which destroys what little remains of the wild, the spare, the original, is cutting itself off from its origins and betraying the principle of civilization itself.

—Edward Abbey, *The Journey Home: Some Words in Defense of the American West*

Louisville, Kentucky — On September 1, 1867, John Muir took the Jeffersonville, Madison, and Indianapolis railroad to the banks of the Ohio River. He crossed into Kentucky the next morning and into the "the big social establishment of Louisville." It was a bustling city of one hundred thousand people under the military rule of Union troops. And so began Muir's "thousand-mile walk." Although it wasn't really a thousand miles—more like nine hundred, with a hundred-mile boat ride. No matter. The great adventure had begun.

He wouldn't tarry in Louisville. He disliked cities of any size. Besides, Muir had a near-messianic desire to commune with nature. "I steered through the big city by compass without speaking a word to any one," he wrote. "My plan was simply to push on in a general southward direction by the wildest, leafiest, and least trodden way I could find, promising the greatest extent of virgin forest."

Muir sported a bushy beard with longish brown hair tucked beneath a flat-brimmed hat. He wore sturdy shoes, gray trousers, a jacket, and a shirt with money concealed in a hidden pocket. A black, rubberized backpack contained a change of underwear, soap, towel, comb, and brush. There were books: a collection of Robert Burns's poems; *Paradise Lost* by John Milton; a whopping five-pound New Testament; and a botanical text by Alphonso Wood. He also carried a homemade plant press—a contraption of wire-gauze sheets, leather straps, buckles, and blotting paper—for drying the leaves, flowers, and grasses he intended to pick and ship home. A small, leather-bound notebook with lined pages would serve as a journal. On the inside flap, the twenty-nine-year-old adventurer wrote: "John Muir, Earth-planet, Universe." It was encircled and underlined.

The man with an ambivalence towards nationality, and, for that matter, questions about his own identity, "was setting out in a joyful mood of freedom," writes biographer Donald Worster.

And why not? He was young, White, single, freed from a factory job, and recuperated from serious injury. An overbearing father and strict religious upbringing lay five hundred miles away in Wisconsin. A pleasant jaunt (or so he thought) through verdant forests and rolling hills beckoned. "He felt driven to lead the life of an outlaw toward society," says Worster.

And the South would be his frontier, a New World in which to discover himself. Eventually, millions of people from the North and Midwest would follow Muir to the Southern promised land of economic opportunity and temperate climes. In that sense Muir was a true pioneer.

He was also largely clueless about the South. "This will be a journey I know very little about," Muir confided to Jeanne Carr.

The South was hot, semi-tropical, and malaria-ridden. Its people were largely poor, uneducated, and struggling to recover from the Civil War. General Sherman and colleagues had laid waste to the South's cities, factories, and railroads. Nearly three hundred thousand Southerners had died in the Lost Cause—including one of every four White men between the ages of twenty and twenty-four. One-third of the region's population were newly freed slaves with a tenuous hold on what de Tocqueville considered America's "exceptional" democracy.

James B. Hunt, who chronicles Muir's trek in *Restless Fires*, writes that "Muir was ill-prepared for the rigors of the walk." He considered it merely a warm-up for his true ambulatory adventure—South America. "Had he fully known the practical obstacles to his health, his personal safety, and his physical well-being," notes Hunt, "one wonders whether he would have made the journey at all."

Muir, though, like the war-torn South itself, eventually made it. He survived run-ins with desperadoes, hunger, fatigue, malaria, and self-doubt to reach the Gulf Coast of Florida. The region he left behind, though, took longer to find its footing.

The farm and the forest fueled the South's rebirth. By 1880, Georgia produced a record six million bales of cotton. Hardwoods from the Appalachians, and softwoods from the coastal plains, built the cities from New York to New Orleans. Northern carpetbaggers and Southern boosters, including Henry Grady, the editor of the *Atlanta Constitution*, and Booker T. Washington, the African American educator, extolled the region's cheap labor, abundant natural resources, and pliant elected officials. The southern Piedmont soon eclipsed both New England and old England as textile capital of the world. The power companies dammed the region's rivers to provide electricity to the mills and factories that turned the South into a manufacturing powerhouse. New Yorker Willis Carrier made the summertime South tolerable with the invention of air conditioning. The precursor to the Centers for Disease Control in Atlanta eradicated the malarial scourge by swabbing five million homes with DDT.

The two World Wars proved both boon and burden to a region that witnessed incredible economic growth while losing tens of thousands of men overseas. The Great Depression, boll weevil, and shoddy farming methods crippled the cotton industry. Jim Crow and the KKK sent six million Blacks northward.

The twin evils of war and depression, though, created a dependency on the federal government that sustains the region's economy to this day. Powerful politicians brought billions of dollars in public works projects—the Tennessee Valley Authority, Savannah River Site, highways, bridges, drained swamps, straightened rivers—and military bases to the South. Local officials lavished free land and tax breaks on any domestic or foreign corporation looking for low-wage workers and lax environmental rules. Southern governors shared Dwight D. Eisenhower's belief that economic growth required ribbons of asphalt stretching from coast to coast. Auto-mobility brought hordes of Northerners and Midwesterners to the South for vacation, employment, retirement, or reinvention.

Transportation, as much as cheap land and labor, made the modern South. Louisville is a prime example of the power of propulsion, whether it's a horse treading the bluegrass, a riverboat plying the mighty Ohio, or an SUV rolling off an assembly line. The River City (or Derby City, Falls City, Gateway to the South) owes much of its existence to the Falls of the Ohio, where the river drops twenty-four feet over limestone ledges. Riverboats discharged passengers and cargo above the falls and gathered them up again two miles downriver before continuing on to the "Mighty Mississippi" and points south and west. Meriwether Lewis met William Clark here in 1803 before their historic expedition to the Pacific Ocean. Flat-bottomed boats have run the two rivers from Pittsburgh to New Orleans for two hundred years.

Central Kentucky has always been horsey country, its wholesome grasses and permissiveness toward gambling fueling a billion-dollar industry as well as Louisville's Kentucky Derby identity. Three interstate highways meet in Louisville, putting two-thirds of the country's consumers within a day's drive. Ford builds SUVs at one factory in Louisville, trucks at another. CSX, Norfolk Southern, and Canadian Pacific run trains through town. UPS operates an air force from Louisville that ships packages to more than two hundred countries.

The city more than doubled its population in the last two decades (thanks largely to a merger with Jefferson County), adding a whopping 350,000 residents. (Only two other cities, Elk Grove, California, and McKinney, Texas, grew proportionately faster.) Still, Greater Louisville carries the dubious distinction of having the most exurban—fast-growing, semi-rural, less-populated—counties in the nation. Thirteen of them, according to the Brookings Institution. Not Los Angeles. Not Atlanta. Little ole' Louisville. And one of those counties, Crawford, across the river in Indiana, is further distinguished by having the country's highest percentage of commuters who leave for work before six in the morning. The metropolitan region, overall, also has the highest percentage of people—83 percent—who commute by themselves. These people like their cars.

Louisville, of course, isn't the biggest or fastest-growing Southern city. It ranks as only the twenty-ninth largest in the United States. But, as the first Southern stop along a Midwesterner's journey, Louisville offers the traveler a preview of the region's growth and popularity.

Six of the top ten fastest-growing states—Texas, Florida, North Carolina, Georgia, Tennessee, South Carolina—are in the South. Nearly 40 percent of the country lives here.

The South's gain is the North's, and the Midwest's, pain. Georgia, for example, is the nation's eighth most populous state, with eleven million residents. The Peach State, as well as North Carolina, leapfrogged Michigan in population the last decade. Florida surpassed New York in 2014. Only California and Texas tally more residents than the Sunshine State's twenty-two million. Only Texas grows faster. Florida adds nine hundred people every day.

And it's only going to get better. Or worse, depending on your perspective. The South, overall, grows 40 percent faster than the rest of the country. Or, looked at another way, there were only five million people living in the five states that Muir crossed in 1867. Today, fifty-five million live here. And just about every one of them owns a car or a pickup. The car is king, and without one, or two, or three vehicles, the Southern family doesn't move. Cars beget highways which beget suburbs which beget sprawl which beget a host of environmental ills. A generation ago, metro Atlanta chopped down fifty acres of tree canopy every day. Florida, today, loses ten acres of natural land to development each *hour*. Edward Abbey, the author, critic, iconoclast, and stalwart defender of Western lands, labeled sprawl the "iron glacier." (As an aside: I once had a managing editor who forbade me from using the word *sprawl*, fearing that our dwindling number of readers who lived twenty miles from Atlanta's downtown core would find the term pejorative and, thereby, cancel their subscriptions. I tried to sneak it past copy editors every chance I got. Abbey would've approved.)

My eyes popped out when I read a 2014 article in the scientific journal *PLOS ONE*. "The Southern Megalopolis: Using the Past to Predict the Future of Urban Sprawl in the Southeast U.S." is the rare academic report—well-researched, quite readable, and scary as hell. It's written by a bunch of ecologists and biologists at the US Geological Survey and North Carolina State University and focuses on the nine southeastern states (not Texas) sandwiched between the Atlantic and the Gulf. It's the world of multicar families who live in ever-more-distant suburban or exurban enclaves behind gates and along cul-de-sacs. Four-, six-, and even eight-lane highways connect one urban node to the next with a mess of office parks, warehouses, gas stations, storage units, and Piggly Wigglys in between.

The report paints a particularly frightening picture of the Piedmont region, stretching from Raleigh through Charlotte to Atlanta, with the overall urban footprint nearly tripling in size by 2060. Why? Because of the lure of the New South boomtowns, the car-friendly culture, and the proximity to the mountains and seas. The so-called Piedmont Megaregion would become an uninterrupted, four-hundred-mile ribbon of concrete with Interstate 85 as its spine. Metro Atlanta alone would stretch from Alabama to South Carolina. In 2014, about 7 percent of the Southeast was covered in concrete. By 2060, 18 percent will be. A map of the futuristic landscape accompanies the report. On it, Atlanta looks like an angry fever blister anchoring the southwestern end of the corridor with smaller, yet equally angry red and yellow splotches (Greenville, Charlotte, Greensboro, Durham, Raleigh) running to the northeast. The editors fail to credit Hieronymus Bosch for the map.

The man in the corner of the coffee shop stares at me as I walk in. He looks familiar in a crazy-uncle kind of way. Bushy white eyebrows. Red suspenders. Round, wire-rimmed glasses. A tam-o'-shanter with red pompom atop his head.

I move closer.

"John Muir, I presume?"

He nods.

There's only one thing missing.

"Where's the beard?"

"I used a fake beard."

John Muir is, actually, Dick Shore, the South's most famous Muir impersonator or, as Dick prefers, interpreter. I stopped in Lexington on my way to Louisville to meet Dick. What better way to get in the true Muir spirit than by talking with a guy who's been channeling the Scottish naturalist for thirty years?

Dick fully embraces the Muir persona, affecting a brogue and regaling audiences in Kentucky, California, New Zealand, and beyond with poignant tales of the wayfarer's life and lessons. More than thirty thousand people have witnessed Dick's performances.

I found him via the Kentucky chapter of the Sierra Club.

"Yes, I am the resident Kentucky Muir Expert," Dick promptly e-mailed back.

We arranged to meet at the Chocolate Holler coffee shop in downtown Lexington. It was soon evident that he relishes the opportunity to talk Muir with a fellow aficionado. The actor, after all, craves the limelight. But Dick also wants to share the wisdom of Muir and why his environmental philosophy, and ecological ethos, are especially relevant today.

"Muir confronted the same forces we confront today—the fools who think they can 'dollarize' everything in nature, like the logging, mining, and energy industries in particular," Dick says. "But there was also a gentleness and sense of kinship with nature and wild creatures which we would do well to copy. People seek a hero and a champion, which is why they seek Muir."

Dick, eighty-one, grew up in Bakersfield, California, and as a boy camped in Muir's beloved Sierra Nevada. He graduated from the College (now University) of the Pacific, which today houses the largest collection of Muir-abilia—letters, journals, sketches—in the world. He got a PhD from Duke (zoology) and an MBA from the University of Toledo, and "somehow along the way," he says, "I picked up a very strong ecological ethic." A career as an industrial engineer ended in 1999. He's been a Sierra Club life member for thirty years.

Dick learned of Muir's Southern journey during a visit to the library in Elizabethtown, Kentucky, a town Muir passed through. He married his love of the eco-prophet and of the outdoors (teaching classes on edible plants, for example) with a latent thespian urge, to craft a distinctive Muir. An after-dinner performance at an Elderhostel gathering near Fort Knox kick-started his career.

"The world was in bad shape, with plagues here, droughts there, and people dying everywhere. It was a grim picture," Dick tells me before draining his tea. "People needed to hear a hopeful story. They needed to hear Muir. Those of us who have heard or read Muir have the opportunity, perhaps the obligation, to make sure his words were not spoken in vain."

The raconteur can't decide on his favorite Muir tale. Bonaventure Cemetery? The mutt Stickeen? Muir's escapades as a lad in Scotland? His first "interview" with a bear in the High Sierra? "It's a little like asking somebody who their favorite child is," says Dick, who wrapped up his Muir career in 2017. "It's really difficult to choose. The *Thousand-Mile Walk* has so many lovely stories that help us see our kinship with the rest of creation: the rocks and the streams; the flowers and the trees; the bears and the bees; all these wee creatures; the least ones, our brothers and sisters."

I listen, enthralled, for two hours. But I want to reach Louisville by nightfall. Dick, too, is fading. He hops on his bicycle, tam-o'-shanter firmly in place, and pedals off. But not before answering one last question.

"Muir might recognize some of these Southern places, outside the cities, the oldest portions of Bonaventure Cemetery, perhaps a few places in Kentucky that have remained off the well-beaten path," Dick surmises. "But he would object vigorously to the worship of growth.

He would be alarmed at the massive urbanization and investment in roads and highways paved with concrete, tar, and gravel. I think he would assert that sometimes more is not better."

It's gray and cold, twenty-seven degrees, as I eyeball Louisville from the Indiana side of the Ohio River. An early winter storm threatens the South. Few are foolish enough to brave these harsh conditions on a Saturday morning in January. But I, unlike Muir, don't have the luxury of waiting for gentler weather.

After leaving Dick I hustled to Louisville, eager to get an early-morning start on Muir's Southern trek. Construction and Friday afternoon traffic turned the one-hour drive into two. I stayed at a crummy motel in Jeffersonville and tried to block out the whir of Interstate traffic.

I, unlike Muir, can walk across the river on a bridge. The Big Four railroad trestle, with soaring steel trusses softened by the tinkling of piped-in classical music, reopened to walkers, joggers, and bikers in 2013. Jeffersonville fashioned a lovely park on its side of the river, complete with brew pub and pavilion. A sign touts a Tree Walk through town where seventy different species of native and nonnative trees—including a dozen of Muir's favored oaks—can be found and appreciated. John James Audubon ran a general store nearby and sketched swallows, woodpeckers, buntings, and hawks along the Ohio in the early 1800s.

I step onto the bridge. My Muir journey begins. But I don't feel anything in particular, no adrenaline rush of expectation or groundswell of emotion that a momentous undertaking is finally under way. Mostly, I feel cold. The wind rushing through the river valley cuts through my fleece pullovers. An occasional jogger lumbers past dutifully offering a "Good Morning" accompanied by a cloud of steam. My fingers grow numb as I take notes.

I cross the half-mile bridge quickly, observe the tangle of Louisville's buildings and highways, and scurry back to Jeffersonville and my warm car. Feeling returns to my fingers ten minutes later.

By then I'm recrossing the river on US 31, heading straight for the concrete and steel maw of downtown Louisville. Far below, a tugboat pushes a half-dozen coal barges toward the Mississippi. Only now do I remember that the Ohio River is considered one of the nation's most polluted waterways. An inauspicious start to my environmental voyage. Nonetheless, I relish my drive-by tour of Louisville which, like most mid-sized Southern cities, boasts of its specialness even as it yearns for bigger things.

As river traffic dwindled, Louisville remade its economy with transportation, food and drink, and health care. It is, supposedly, the nation's largest repository of "aging-care" businesses: hospitals, nursing homes, insurance companies, and health-care corporations. Yum Brands, which owns Kentucky Fried Chicken, Pizza Hut, and Taco Bell, is headquartered here and splashes its name across the basketball arena overlooking the river. Downtown boasts a slew of bourbon distilleries and the Louisville Slugger Museum & Factory. Nearby sits the Muhammad Ali Center, a museum dedicated to the life of Louisville's favorite son. "Favorite," that is, until the world's greatest boxer began expounding upon Islam, the Vietnam War, and racism. He called Louisville "one of the greatest cities in America." He also said "so-called Negro people in Louisville are treated like dogs." Court-ordered busing in the mid-seventies desegregated the schools and tamped down the racial unrest that plagued many American cities. Yet Breonna Taylor was shot and killed by Louisville cops during a botched raid in 2020.

Like most Southern urban strivers, Louisville shoulders bigger-city pretensions and believes itself, incorrectly, on a par with Nashville or Indianapolis. Louisville, though, does have Churchill Downs—the Valhalla of American thoroughbred racing—and I head that direction after my quick tour of downtown.

I take South Third Street past the hospital district, some public housing, and the historic Old Louisville neighborhood with its Victorian
mansions. Ballfields for the University of Louisville unfurl on the left
and, then, the twin-spired home of the Kentucky Derby on the right.
It's billed as the Greatest Two Minutes in Sports, a Louisville tradition
since 1875, famous for mint juleps, big hats, and springtime bacchanal.
But let's let another (questionably) favorite son of Louisville describe the
scene on race day. In a 1970 magazine piece entitled *The Kentucky Derby
Is Decadent and Depraved*, Hunter S. Thompson wrote:

> Just pretend you're visiting a huge outdoor loony bin. Thousands of
> raving, stumbling drunks, getting angrier and angrier as they lose
> more and more money. By mid-afternoon they'll be guzzling mint
> juleps with both hands and vomiting on each other between races.
> The whole place will be jammed with bodies, shoulder to shoul-
> der. It's hard to move around. The aisles will be slick with vomit;
> people falling down and grabbing at your legs to keep from being
> stomped. Drunks pissing on themselves in the betting lines. Drop-
> ping handfuls of money and fighting to stoop over and pick it up.

The gonzo journalist grew up in a stucco bungalow in East Louisville near Cherokee Park, one of many greenswards designed by Frederick Law Olmsted. Thompson and Olmsted each left twisted legacies
behind in Louisville. Thompson hightailed it out of town for the air
force instead of serving a jail sentence for throwing beer bottles through
the windows of a former teacher's house. He returned a couple of times
to dip his poison pen into Louisville's well of social and racial relations.
Olmsted created a system of wonderful parks linked by tree-lined boulevards intended for "pleasure traffic," not commercial use. His grand
plan, though, eventually grew tattered and traffic-choked as the parks
fell into disrepair. It didn't help that "urban renewal" in the 1960s

pushed Interstate 64 through two of Olmsted's major parks, including Cherokee. Louisville has since added thousands of acres of green space and rebranded itself as the City of Parks.

I continue southward out of town trying to divine Muir's route. *A Thousand-Mile Walk* offers clues.

"After passing a scatterment of suburban cabins and cottages I reached the green woods and spread out my pocket map to rough-hew a plan for my journey," Muir wrote. He mostly stuck to the turnpikes and farm-to-town roads. He walked twenty miles the first day. The forest enveloped him and "the great oaks seemed to spread their arms in welcome."

"I have seen oaks of many species in many kinds of exposure and soil, but those of Kentucky excel in grandeur all I had ever before beheld," Muir said. "They are broad and dense and bright green. In the leafy bowers and caves of their long branches dwell magnificent avenues of shade, and every tree seems to be blessed with a double portion of strong exulting life."

He spent his first night in Shepherdsville "in a rickety tavern." In the morning, Muir "escaped from the dust and squalor of my garret bedroom to the glorious forest."

Muir's route from Louisville, today, follows the same urban-to-suburban-to-exurban-to-rural trajectory found in every Southern state. Outer Louisville is home to the usual assortment of fast-food joints, gas stations, strip malls, affordable subdivisions, mobile home parks, and circa-1980 churches with big lawns and bigger parking lots. Tractor-trailer cabs sit in the occasional front yard. A cement plant, a wood pallet maker, a junkyard. Dixie Bowl ("the BEST ENTERTAINMENT VALUE in Louisville") beckons along the Dixie Highway, aka US 31. Train tracks run parallel to the road. Gone are the wide expanses of forests and grasslands. The US Forest Service predicts that as much as twenty-three million acres of trees—equivalent to all of the forests in Kentucky *and* South Carolina—will be lost to development across the

South by 2060. Beyond the cities, the South is getting nibbled to death. Everybody wants a "ranchette" on their slice of rural heaven, it seems. Munfordville, where Muir spent his second night in a log schoolhouse, advertises one- to five-acre lots with utilities already in place. Ridge lines in north Georgia atop what Muir labeled the "most luxuriant forest" are lined with upscale "cabins" featuring wraparound porches and three-car garages. Developers build mini–horse farms along the sinewy streams that Muir crossed in the Atlantic coastal plain. Eight of the top ten states in the country losing farmland to exurban sprawl are in the South, according to the American Farmland Trust. Kentucky (tenth) lost 200,000 acres during this century's first fifteen years.

The loss of green space is the greatest environmental scourge effecting the rural South today. But don't take my word for it. Here's what the witty authors of *The Southern Megalopolis* wrote: "History suggests humans, in contrast to ants and slime molds, rarely optimize growth, particularly when multiple objectives such as profit, equity, and ecological integrity come into conflict."

The impact of sprawl on nature-loving man is sad. The impact on flora and fauna, especially in the richly biodiverse South, is catastrophic. Birds, bees, frogs, turtles, snakes, bears, and deer migrate through forests, fields, and marshes in search of the next best spot to live and love. Yet the species-rich lands are clear-cut for housing tracts or row-cropped corn. Wetlands are filled with little regard for the unique habitats favored by bog turtles and pitcher plants. Survival for at-risk, threatened, and endangered species depends on an animal or plant's ability to seek greener pastures, especially as the temperatures warm and the rains disappear (or intensify). Australian and Canadian researchers published a study in 2018 claiming that urban sprawl, and new farms, are mainly to blame for driving species toward threatened or endangered status. Their work bolsters other reports singling out habitat destruction as Enemy Number One of flora and fauna.

"The changes we project would have significant and lasting effects on the region's ecosystems," the 2014 *Megalopolis* report reads. "The increasingly fragmented natural landscape would reduce habitat availability, suppress natural disturbance processes (such as wildfires), hinder management actions that come into conflict with urban areas, and likely eliminate existing corridors. (And) urban sprawl will also, almost certainly, influence the ability of species to respond to climate change."

The critters aren't the only ones suffering. Less pasture, woodland, and wetland translates into poorer water quality. Erosion increases with fewer trees. More concrete means rainwater can't seep into the ground and fill aquifers. It also leads to heavy runoff during storms, which inundates, and pollutes, streams and causes flash floods. (My basement flooded three times in two years.) Fewer forests, fields, and peat bogs means less carbon is sucked out of the atmosphere, fueling a warmer climate.

Disappearing green spaces also threaten other so-called ecosystem services, which the National Wildlife Federation classifies "as any positive benefit that wildlife or ecosystems provide to people. The benefits can be direct or indirect—small or large." Milkweed, for example, sustains butterflies and bees in prairies and pastures. Roaring streams attract trout-fishing enthusiasts. Scientists discover new medicines in the wild. Backpackers groove on forested trails. Nature, studies show, nurtures psychological health. Three-quarters of Americans say contact with nature is very, or extremely, important for their health and emotional outlook.

Can we put a price tag on nature, then? Robert Costanza tried. In a seminal 1997 report in the British journal *Nature*, the cofounder of the International Society of Ecological Economics pegged the value of the world's ecosystems at thirty-three trillion dollars a year. In 2011, Costanza recalculated and set the new value at $125 trillion, a sizable sum considering that the world's entire GDP at the time was seventy-five trillion.

Critics scoff at any attempt at putting a dollar value on nature like it's some sort of commodity to be bought and sold. Environmentalists recoil at the cost–benefit analysis of something as intrinsically wonderful as a saltwater marsh or the trill of a dark-eyed junco. Nature, after all, is like love. Money can't buy it.

Yet Costanza, who analyzed the economic value of seventeen different ecosystem services, made people think. These services are critical to a functioning, livable Earth. They support mankind's welfare and, therefore, should be considered public goods. It costs a lot of money to make up for their absence. Consider the lowly insect, for example. Bees and other bugs fertilize our crops for free, so, without them, we'd have to pay armies of workers to brush pollen on fruits and nuts. German researchers estimated the non-bug cost to agriculture at more than two hundred billion dollars a year. Closer to home, the Georgia Forestry Foundation placed the ecosystem value of the state's twenty-two million acres of private forest at thirty-eight billion dollars a year.

In *John of the Mountains*, Muir wrote, "In God's wildness lies the hope of the world." Surely, now, in 2022, with the horror of a global pandemic hopefully fading, Southerners have learned valuable lessons about the importance of Mother Nature and our responsibility to treat her right. At least, I'd like to think so.

I wanted to test my post-pandemic hypothesis of hope on somebody smart who ponders the big, existential questions like "Whither Southern ecology?" and "Has the cul-de-sac met its match?" Adam Terando came immediately to mind.

Adam is the lead author of the pithy *Southern Megalopolis* report. He's a research ecologist with the US Geological Survey in Raleigh, where he explores the interplay between ecosystems, land use, and climate change. I called him upon my return from Kentucky to learn what's changed since 2014. I wished I hadn't.

"I don't see much difference," Adam says. "This is still an attractive region with a favorable climate and the Atlantic Ocean and the mountains nearby. You have lots of jobs, and those jobs are attracting more jobs. It's a virtuous cycle in terms of fostering a strong economy. But, consequently, there's a lot more urbanizing going on. As housing gets more expensive closer to town, people continue to move further and further out where the affordable housing is. State departments of transportation want to accommodate that demand, so they build more highways which then makes it more feasible to build further and further out."

Case in point: Chatham Park, an under-construction, seventy-five-hundred-acre colossus of twenty-two thousand homes a half hour's drive west of Raleigh, North Carolina. The town's vision: "We're creating way more than buildings and roads."

Adam isn't so sure.

"They're taking up a huge amount of land that's currently rural, either forested or farmland, and they're platting out a whole new town," he says. "It's the same lack of imagination we've had for seventy years. Our entire transportation and housing systems are oriented around the automobile. Multiple generations of people have grown up with a certain idea of what it means to be in a city, which is really like being in a suburb or car-burb. Changing that mindset is like turning a big ship."

Adam lives in an apartment in downtown Raleigh near his office at North Carolina State University. He walks to grocery stores, parks, and restaurants. A bike-share program affords cheap, carbon-free transportation. For a boy who grew up on an Illinois farm, Adam believes *real* cities can save the natural world. Southerners, though, have a twisted view of nature.

"Our relationship with nature is very selective and values a certain aesthetic above all others," he says. "Why, for example, do we have big, green lawns? Those loblolly pines in our backyards? People think of both of those as 'nature.' And our suburbs are built and marketed in such a way as to give the appearance of a greater resonance with forested ecosystems and nature. But they are not. There is such a disconnect with true nature."

But if we don't know what nature is, how can we save it?

"Maybe your Mr. Muir would have an answer for that," Adam says.

CHAPTER 3

The South's Incredible Biodiversity Is Threatened and Endangered

The word *cavern* does not convey any idea of this immense space; words of human tongue are inadequate to describe the discoveries of him who ventures into the deep abysses of earth.
—Jules Verne, *Tales of Daring Voyages and Discoveries*

Cave City, Kentucky — It took Muir four quick-footed days to reach Mammoth Cave. It took me four meandering hours as I tootled along in my Subaru trying to imagine what Muir saw a century and a half earlier. It wasn't easy.

Muir "escaped to the woods" beyond Elizabethtown and into the "magnificent flowing hill scenery." He spoke admiringly of "gangs of woodmen engaged in felling and hewing the grand oaks for market." He passed through Munfordville, the scene of a Civil War skirmish along the Green River won by Confederate troops five years earlier. At Horse Cave, Muir took a ten-mile detour west to Mammoth Cave. "I was surprised to find it in so complete naturalness," he wrote before trashing the "paltry artificial gardens" surrounding the main hotel.

Muir didn't stay long. He didn't even go underground to witness the awe-inspiring caverns and cathedrals of limestone that stretch for miles in every subterranean direction. Mammoth would soon become one of the nation's top tourist spots, joining the Grand Canyon and Niagara Falls while attracting visitors from all over the world. But the "father of the national parks" didn't have time for what's now known as Mammoth Cave National Park.

Muir, uncharacteristically, was acting more like a typical American tourist than a soulful naturalist. Americans have long had a schizophrenic relationship with the natural world. They ooh and aah over the beauty of a mountain range, sandy seashore, or underground cavern. Yet they like to tart up their natural experiences with "artificial" attractions and all the auto-accessible amenities that can be squeezed in. It's as if they expect to be bored by wilderness so they stock up on sensory-numbing entertainment before, or after, their visit.

The fun starts in Munfordville along the same Dixie Highway where "Kentucky's Stonehenge," a pint-sized, ersatz replica of the prehistoric English masterpiece, awaits. Just down the road, in Cave City, the Wigwam Village motel and its fifteen concrete teepees arrayed in a half-circle entice travelers keen on a night of Instagram memories. No shortage of good times awaits the traveler on the run-up to Mammoth's main entrance: Dinosaur World; Raven's Cross Haunted Village; Big Mike's Rock Shop; and the Kentucky Action Park (with miniature golf, zip line, trampolines, and bumper cars).

Visitors have explored Mammoth Cave for millennia. Native Americans mined six miles of the cave as long ago as five thousand years, according to archaeological discoveries teased from gourds, cloth, pottery, and petroglyphs. A much-disputed legend has it that a hunter named John Houchins shot at a black bear along the Green River at the turn of the nineteenth century. Houchins missed, but he found an entrance to the cave. It wasn't long until the caverns were being mined by slaves for the saltpeter needed to make gunpowder. It was another slave, Stephen Bishop, bought in nearby Glasgow, whose explorations turned the central Kentucky cave into an international sensation. Bishop crossed the Bottomless Pit by ladder bridge with lantern firmly affixed between jaws to discover Echo River, Roaring River, and Mammoth Dome, which he labeled "a grand, gloomy, and peculiar place." By 1850, stage coaches from Lexington and steamboats from Bowling Green were delivering thousands of tourists annually to the ever-growing network of caverns. Tourism, abetted by the railroad and the automobile, proved profitable, and acrimonious. Owners of nearby caves—Colossal, Long, Crystal, Great Onyx—weren't above warning travelers that Mammoth was flooded and closed when neither was true.

Mammoth began losing its charm by the turn of the twentieth century and visitation soon dropped by two-thirds. Maintenance suffered, the buildings grew worn, and the privately held grounds were denuded of timber and wildlife. War and the Depression didn't help, though legions of Civilian Conservation Corps workers built new roads, cabins, trails, and an elevator to the cave's Snowball Room. For years conservationists had clamored for national parks east of the Mississippi River. Finally, in 1926, President Calvin Coolidge signed legislation creating Mammoth National Park, contingent upon donation of the land to the federal government. It took fifteen years, and the wholesale removal of hundreds of families, farmhouses, barns, churches, and schools, but Mammoth joined Shenandoah and the Great Smoky as the South's first national parks.

Kentucky, and the rest of the South that Muir crossed, is a geomorphologist's dream. A half-dozen very different geographic regions run from central Kentucky to coastal Florida. Muir first crossed the Bluegrass and Knobs regions of rolling hills, hardwood forests, and lush meadows leading to the Cumberland Plateau. Next up were the Appalachian Mountains of Tennessee and North Carolina with their six-thousand-foot peaks and mix of deciduous and coniferous forests. He descended through the ridge-and-valley region of Georgia into the Piedmont of lazy rivers, pine trees, and cotton fields. Muir crossed the coastal plain and its near-impenetrable swamps and longleaf pine stands. The Atlantic and Gulf coasts, with their marshes, estuaries, and beaches, offered the rambling man the most resplendent repositories of flora and fauna. No other thousand-mile walk in the United States crosses such a richness of habitats.

The South's natural bounty is owed to many factors. Glaciers halted their southern surge at the Ohio River valley, yet they drove plants and animals farther south across the Appalachians. Once the glaciers receded, the hills, dales, and streams filled with a mix of southern and northern plants fostering "enormous biological diversity," according to *Precious Heritage*, a compendium of the nation's ecology. Abundant rains fuel the biodiversity. Certain southern Appalachian hilltops, for example, receive a rainforest-like ninety inches a year. The Atlantic and Gulf coasts, with a healthy mix of fresh and salt water, produce some of the world's most fecund breeding grounds for birds, fish, and crustaceans. In fact, the Southeast is one of the world's hotspots of biodiversity.

Like birds? Well, more than 90 percent of the nation's bird species live or pass through the region.

What about fish? Nearly two-thirds of all US species of fish live in the Southeast's streams and estuaries, yet the region comprises only 17 percent of the nation's land mass. And more than a quarter of the area's freshwater species are found nowhere else in the world.

Trees and flowers your thing? One of every three plant species nationwide resides in the Southeast, with various ecosystems rivaling the Amazon or the Congo in biodiversity.

Mussels? More than 90 percent of all US freshwater mussel species—and 40 percent of the world's—inhabit Southeastern rivers and streams.

Crayfish? Almost half of the world's crawdads, some 250 different species, call the Southeast home.

Salamanders? More types of sallies live here than anywhere else in the world, including the otherworldly and slimy hellbender, which can grow up to two feet long.

Evidence of this biological uniqueness abounds nearby. Look no further than the unheralded Conasauga River. Seventy-six species of fish live in the stream that flows one hundred miles through northwest Georgia and a sliver of Tennessee. That's more species than the Columbia and Colorado rivers combined, yet its watershed is only one one-hundredth the size of those mighty Western rivers. Three of the Conasauga's fish are threatened or endangered. Six of the mussels are, too, including the wonderfully named Coosa moccasinshell and Georgia pigtoe. Only the tropics can match that level of bivalve biodiversity.

Then there are the few and fabulous mountain bogs, pint-sized wetlands sandwiched between the hills, pastures, blacktops, and railroad tracks of southern Appalachia. The bogs are home to mountain sweet pitcher plants (endangered), swamp pinks (threatened), and bog turtles (threatened), North America's smallest terrapin.

And the Green River itself, with 151 species of fish and 71 types of mussels, is the nation's fourth most biologically diverse river. Forty-three species are endemic—found nowhere else in the world—to the Green, including darters, beetles, crayfish, pseudoscorpions, and the Kentucky cave shrimp.

More than four hundred species of plants and animals are endemic to the southern Appalachians. The Nature Conservancy says no other place in North America is as bountiful.

And few spots around the globe tally as many critters and plants at risk of extinction. The US Fish and Wildlife Service lists 437 threatened or endangered species in the Southeast region. Only the massive Western region, which encompasses tropical Hawaii and Samoa as well as rainy Oregon and Washington, counts more (588). In fact, five of the top ten states (Florida, Alabama, Tennessee, Georgia, and North Carolina) with the most T&E species are in the Southeast. If you add Texas and Virginia, that makes seven of ten.

The South's biodiversity, though, is under attack, particularly its water-borne bounty. The Environmental Protection Agency reports that more than half of the streams in the southern Appalachians are "in poor biological condition." The ecological damage done to the Conasauga, Green, Tennessee, Chattahoochee, Savannah, St. Johns, Suwannee, and virtually every other Southern river, is heart-rending. Alabama's Coosa River, for example, used to be one of the most biologically diverse rivers in the world. It now holds the dubious distinction, according to the World Wildlife Fund, as the North American river with the most freshwater extinctions—thirty-eight—of the twentieth century.

In 2010, the Center for Biological Diversity (CBD) sued the Fish and Wildlife Service demanding that 404 aquatic, riparian, and wetland species in the Southeast be listed as threatened or endangered. "Nowhere is this extinction crisis more apparent than in the southeastern United States, where the combination of an incredibly rich fauna, pervasive threats, and few existing protections are leading to the demise of hundreds of aquatic species," the petition read. CBD warned that "extinction is looming" for 28 percent of the region's fishes, 48 percent of its crayfishes, and 70 percent of its mussels.

A year later, the nonprofit and the Service settled the suit with the federal conservation agency pledging to determine whether 374 species need listing. Progress has been slow. Dozens of the proposed species have yet to be fully vetted. A Trump administration hostile to the environment, and in bed with the coal, oil, and gas industries, reworked the landmark Endangered Species Act to make it harder to list plants and animals as threatened or endangered, and easier to remove them. (The Biden administration reversed course.) Fish and Wildlife, during the Trump years, added only twenty-five species to the T&E list. The Obama administration listed 360. It was one gut kick after another to the many dedicated biologists and ecologists at the various federal conservation agencies. CBD said the proposed changes would "crash a bulldozer through the Endangered Species Act's lifesaving protections for America's most vulnerable wildlife." Carl Hiaasen, the acerbically wonderful former columnist for the *Miami Herald*, wrote that "saving God's creations from oblivion is a worthy mission unless it means lost revenues for ExxonMobil or Koch Industries."

Slashed budgets prevent Fish and Wildlife from hiring enough biologists to determine species' status. And revenue-poor state agencies, which have primary jurisdiction over the critters, prize economic growth over the health of, say, orangenacre muckets. In 2019, the Tennessee Aquarium Conservation Institute tallied public dollars spent on species preservation across the country. While the Southeast region is home to 30 percent of the nation's T&E species, it receives less than 1 percent of all federal and state moneys spent nationwide trying to save those species.

Unlike Muir, I hunger to explore Mammoth Cave. I plan to spend the weekend camping at Mammoth upon leaving Louisville, but an ice storm bears down and forces the park's closure. I still manage to hike the Big Hollow Loop Trail, an easy jaunt with a wealth of second-generation oak, hickory, pine, and poplar that harkens Muir's time. The wind out of the southwest picks up as the sky darkens. I quicken my pace. I recall the passage in Muir's 1894 book *The Mountains of California*, where he recounts scaling a Douglas spruce during a windstorm in the Sierra Nevada "and never before did I enjoy so noble an exhilaration of motion." Me, I just want to finish the hike and ride the ferry across the Green River before the storm ices the roads and closes the park.

I return six months later, after three very nice National Park Service scientists invite me on a tour. I arrive mid-afternoon in time for another short hike and a visit to the park's museum and visitor center, where there's no mention of Muir. But I do learn that the United Nations named Mammoth Cave a World Heritage Site in 1981 and, nine years later, an International Biosphere Reserve. I stay in a one-room, paint-peeling, non-air-conditioned cabin without television built by the CCC in the early forties. It's bliss lying under the fan without electronic distraction, listening to the crickets, and conjuring the days of pre-war tourism. (Not until I return home do I realize that bed bugs come with the government room rate.)

The next morning, I meet with Tim Pinion, the park's science chief; Rick Olson, Mammoth's ecologist; and Rick Toomey, a cave specialist who runs the park's International Center for Science and Learning. Pinion, a marine biologist who used to work for Fish and Wildlife, has been at Mammoth less than a year. Olson, lanky and bespectacled with a white Vandyke, probably knows the park better than anybody. He came to Mammoth in 1973 with the Cave Research Foundation and never left. Toomey, also sporting a Vandyke and glasses, arrived in 1994. He's a paleontologist turned speleologist.

Tim and I had already hashed out where to observe the park's wondrous biodiversity. I also want to better understand how outside forces—water, pollution, sprawl, climate—impact the park and its creatures. I'm keen to focus on lesser-known species that live either underground or underwater yet whose stories speak volumes about the South's environment.

We scratch bats and their oft-told plight off our list, even though millions have succumbed to the deadly disease known as white-nose syndrome. First detected in an upstate New York cave in 2006, the pathogen quickly spread south and west. Seven years later, in Long Cave, the white-colored fungus notched its first Mammoth Cave victim. A "bat blitz" conducted in 2017 showed steep declines in the cave's northern long-eared, little brown, tri-color, and Indiana bat populations. Rick Toomey calls the carnage "devastating."

Not enough is known about where the disease came from or how it spreads. Without better science, it's difficult to ascribe environmental causes and effects to white-nose syndrome. Do cave-goers help spread the disease? Are pesticides or other contaminants responsible for the fungus? Is the pathogen air- or water-borne? Does a warming climate play a role? The uncertainty makes it difficult to draw broad-brush conclusions about Mammoth Cave's ecological health and, by extension, the region's. Which is why I decide to focus on other, more illustrative—and weirder—species.

We enter the cave through the Historic Entrance, pass the (not so) Great Bat Room, through the limestone belly of the Mammoth Dome, and into River Hall with its water-warped and escalloped ceiling and walls. Tim, the two Ricks, and I bypass the tourists, skirt behind an off-limits sign and descend even farther into what Ralph Waldo Emerson called "the great hole in the ground in Kentucky." We cross the Natural Bridge over the Dead Sea, its walkway covered in a muddy film courtesy of recent floods. It's foggy and chilly like London in winter. A nineteenth-century wooden dinghy, used long ago to ferry tourists along the Dead Sea, magically appears out of the mist.

Finally, at 360 feet below ground, we stop.

"Here," says Rick the ecologist, "is the River Styx."

Appropriate. For we have come to see the highly endangered, supremely bizarre, ghost-like Kentucky cave shrimp. Once thought extinct, the shrimp was rediscovered in the 1980s and has, supposedly, increased in population ever since. It is believed to reside in only a handful of low-lying streams and pools in and around Mammoth Cave, but nobody really knows. It is one odd creature. The Fish and Wildlife Service refers to the shrimp as a "nearly transparent decapod crustacean with only rudimentary eyestalks." But that doesn't do the shrimpy shrimp justice. An adult is about an inch long, with ten legs and two very long antennae. It molts every forty days or so, sloughing off its entire exoskeleton—antennae, mouth, legs, tail—in one whole piece which itself resembles a wholly intact cave shrimp.

But wait, there's more. The shrimp deploys its antennae to find, taste, and smell food. Because it doesn't have any eyes. It's blind. In fact, it doesn't need eyes. Because it lives in a cave where the sun never shines.

There's still more. Cave shrimp are translucent—you can see through them. Whereas I crave their ocean brethren smothered in drawn butter and cocktail sauce, my epicurean ardor will surely wane upon observing a cave shrimp floating in a muddy pool at the bottom of a cavern.

"This is shrimp habitat," insists paleontologist Rick.

Great. Show me one.

"We're not likely to find any here," he allows.

Huh?

"If we had wetsuits, I guarantee that I could show you some," ecologist Rick chimes in.

We stop at a sandy beach along the river's edge. Headlamps bounce from shallow water to water-smoothed limestone wall to the ceiling thirty feet up. I feel like I'm on the platform of a darkened, flooded subway tunnel.

The scientists find two eyeless cave beetles and a pigment-free cave crayfish. But no shrimp. They were first discovered at Mammoth Cave in 1901 by a zoologist named William Perry Hay, who promptly sent a dozen to the National Museum of Natural History in Washington where, presumably, they remain today.

If any creature is a prisoner of habitat, it's the cave shrimp. Only four species of the underground crustacean exist in the US. (One summer day, I tried, unsuccessfully, with a platoon of biologists and spelunkers, to find an Alabama cave shrimp near Huntsville, Alabama.) The Kentucky shrimp is wholly dependent on forces beyond its control for survival. The Green River, which flows above, below, and throughout Mammoth Cave, dictates whether the shrimp lives or dies. A heavy rain raises water levels, moves the shrimp around and creates the pools and slow-flowing streams where they live. The river also brings food in the form of tiny protozoans, insects, fungi, and algae. Without the sun's amazing photosynthetic qualities, the shrimp must rely on takeout food delivered via upstream (or downstream if flooding backs up the river) currents. Little rain reduces the river's flow, food sources, and places where the shrimp can live. Drought leads to death.

Though few in number, the oddball shrimp has captured the region's fancy. A decade ago the minor league Bowling Green baseball team was casting about for a new name. The Bowling Green Cave Shrimp—picture the logo of a cartoonish, sunglasses-wearing crustacean with glove on one pincer and bat in the other—was nudged out by the Bowling Green Hot Rods owing to the nearby city's love affair with fast cars.

Yet despite the blind shrimp's favorite-arthropod status, Kentucky has done just about everything imaginable the last two hundred years to kill it. As goes the Green, so goes the shrimp. Revolutionary War veterans staked claims along the river as payment for their service and initiated two centuries' worth of poor farming practices that fed sediment, poop, and pesticides into the river. Loggers felled the surrounding forests, which removed natural buffers that filtered the water flowing into the Green. The strip-mining of coal, with its acidic by-products and habitat-destroying qualities, proliferated along the river's banks. Rock quarry runoff doesn't help. Antiquated treatment plants, and a rural reliance on septic tanks, still send millions of gallons of untreated sewage into the ground and, eventually, the river.

A half-dozen dams, the first built in the 1830s, inhibit the free flow of water, impede migrating fish, trap habitat-nourishing sediments, and alter temperatures and oxygen levels, all to the detriment of the once-pristine Green. Lock and Dam Number Six, about ten miles below Mammoth Cave, kept fish and other critters from freely running the river. It also increased the amount of sediment and siltation, which clouded the water, prevented the growth of vegetation, and destroyed habitat. Fish and Wildlife once listed the dam as "responsible for the decline" of shrimp.

There were other culprits, too. Kentucky is blessed, or cursed, with an abundance of oil and natural gas. Spills once happened regularly, and the porous limestone-and-sinkhole topography offered countless entryways for the toxic fluids to reach the streams that feed the Green River. Brine, the sodium chloride by-product of drilling, was either returned underground or dumped directly into sinkholes. The feds reported in 1988 that the nearby oil and gas industry has "the potential for causing complete extirpation of the cave fauna in an entire groundwater basin." In 2014, The Nature Conservancy wrote that "this unique freshwater basin is at risk to change dramatically over the next fifty years due to compounding threats of residential, industrial, and commercial demands for water, inputs of excess nutrients, sediment, and contaminants due to ecologically incompatible land-management practices, riparian forest conversion, and potential volatile flood cycles/extended drought periods due to climate change."

The shrimp achieved endangered species status in 1983, with an estimated five hundred specimens still kicking. Five years later, between six and twelve thousand shrimp floated through Mammoth Cave. Today, maybe five thousand survive. But nobody really knows. It remains a federally endangered species.

The two Ricks, Tim, and I climb out of the cave and into the government-issued Chevy Equinox for the short downhill ride to the ferry crossing, where a team of malacologists, or mussel experts, scour the Green in search of booty. The Park Service had recently halted ferry service to allow the ramps on either side of the river to be extended. The ferry, too often, couldn't run the river due to low flows. The Endangered Species Act requires federal agencies to save as many threatened or endangered critters as possible whenever a construction project impacts their habitat. The Park Service decided to go a step further by capturing all the mussels near the ferry crossing and relocating them a half mile upstream.

A team of wetsuit-wearing divers disappear into the murky brown water only to reappear moments later with mussels in hand. It's a sun-dappled May morning with oaks and poplars along the banks wearing bright green suits, and dozens of eastern tiger swallowtails flitting by. Clayton Bey, scuba mask firmly in place and tethered to an oxygen tank floating on an inner tube, emerges from the water and muck to drop a few shells into a mesh bag.

"Look how many I've got," Clayton announces to nobody in particular. He climbs the river bank and, one by one, unloads his treasure. A pink heelsplitter. A kidneyshell. Two mapleleafs. A threeridge. It isn't a particularly remarkable haul. None of the mussels are threatened or endangered. But Clayton's work is nonetheless notable on two accounts. He and fellow divers have uncovered and replanted 2,500 mussels in just five days, a surprisingly sizable amount even for one of the most fecund stretches of the Green River. And Clayton is only five years old.

"I reckon he's the youngest malacologist around," says Clarissa Lawlis, his mother and a true mussel biologist. She says Clayton knows the names of most mussels, prefers a wetsuit to a swimsuit, and works cheap.

"I pay him in Oreos," she laughs.

Mussels won't win an endangered-species popularity contest. The World Wildlife Fund doesn't mount polychromatic fundraising campaigns devoted to saving the bizarre bivalves. Leonardo DiCaprio isn't likely to shine his star wattage on orange-footed pimplebacks as he does Sumatran elephants. Mussels, let's face it, are the eat-your-peas equivalent of species conservation, the invertebrate Everyman of the animal kingdom. Americans really only think about mollusks if they stub their toe on one while swimming, or consider their salubrious qualities before ordering a dozen (preferably with a Muscadet or Sauvignon Blanc).

If only they knew. If only they understood the critical role mussels play not only in a particular aquatic habitat, but in an entire ecosystem's interplay between water and man. Native Americans, as usual, knew the value of mussels. They'd eat the meaty mollusk and use the shell for tools, utensils, and jewelry. Mussel gatherers supplied the burgeoning button industry in the nineteenth century and, consequently, depleted Southern, Eastern, and Midwestern streams of *mollusca*. By 1912, two hundred button factories operated nationwide. The purple cat's paw, beloved for its interior deep purple hue, was nearly adored to extinction. If it weren't for plastic, the mussel kingdom might've collapsed altogether.

Mussels can live one hundred years underwater covered in sand, mud, or gravel. A hinged shell is their identifying feature; yet the variety of shapes, sizes, and colors makes instant classification difficult. They may be yellow, green, brown, black, or purple. They may be bumpy, textured, smooth, or ridged. Like trees, the shells produce annual rings that show their age.

A male mussel is a sex machine capable of impregnating downstream females while stuck in the mud. He shoots his sperm higgledy-piggledy into the water where currents carry it, magically, to a waiting female. She then packages the eggs together into a lure-like contraption on her body and goes fishing. The lures resemble insects and entice passing fish who take the bait which then attaches to their gills. The larvae hang out on the fish for a couple of weeks, fattening up on nutrients before dropping off and beginning life as juvenile mussels.

Mussels' sex life alone qualifies them for a starring role on *Animals Gone Wild*. But it's what they do to the water that's truly sexy. Mussels are filter feeders: they suck up nutrients, sediments, and contaminants before expelling the cleansed by-products back into the water. Water quality improves to the benefit of other critters as well as humans, who typically rely on expensive water-treatment plants. Some mussels filter ten gallons of water daily. And some football-field-sized riffles are home to tens of thousands of mollusks straining water like sieves do flour.

Mussels fill another critical role too. They're the early-warning system telling us that something's wrong with the water. Monte McGregor, Kentucky's state malacologist, tells me that "there is no other species that reflects what is going on in a river better than mussels." A surge in dead mussels means something—toxic chemicals, sediment runoff, temperature change—is harming water quality. If the mussels disappear, then other species are likely to disappear also. Rick the ecologist says, "Mussels are like the canaries in the coal mine." And the canaries are sucking wind.

The Green River isn't unique in its suffering. Remember the aforementioned, and seemingly abundant, Conasauga River? Sedimentation, pesticides, and runoff from chicken-processing plants plague the river once it leaves the Chattahoochee National Forest. Biologists at the Tennessee Aquarium and the University of Georgia have labeled the Conasauga the seventh most imperiled watershed in the Southeast—out of three hundred watersheds. Maybe one-fourth of its fish and mussels have died in recent years.

Remember the rare bogs of North Carolina with their mountain sweet pitcher plants? They're fast disappearing, courtesy of logging, stormwater runoff, and new home construction. Five thousand boggy acres once stippled the valley floors of the southwestern Appalachians. Today, five hundred remain.

In Muir's day, the Green River boasted fifty-eight different types of mussels. Seven species, though, have died off. And another ten species, including the fanshell, snuffbox, and pink mucket that live in Mammoth Cave National Park, are threatened or endangered. Pinion, the two Ricks, and other scientists, in a 2020 report, concluded that "habitat alteration . . . is the primary threat to fish biodiversity in the park."

It's the same story with virtually every stream Muir crossed on his trek to the Gulf.

But there is hope. The landmark Clean Water Act reduced pollutants flowing from farms, mines, and oil and gas wells into the Green River. The Clean Air Act reduced carbon dioxide from coal-fired power plants that dropped acid rain into the river. In fact, the nearby Paradise Fossil Plant shut down in 2020. More than one hundred million dollars went into the pockets of farmers upstream of Mammoth Cave to get them to quit farming along the banks of the river and plant trees and grass instead. Even the much-maligned Endangered Species Act forced nearby communities to treat their sewage instead of letting the shrimp-killing effluent reach the Green. Nothing, though, excites Pinion and the two Ricks like the demolition of Lock and Dam Number Six.

A day earlier, on my ride up from Atlanta, I stopped in Brownsville on the national park's western edge, a small town sandwiched between bends in the river with a courthouse, bank, Family Dollar store, Bertie's Ice Cream, and funeral home whose parking lot was full. I crossed the high bridge over the Green, turned left at a Mexican restaurant, and followed the two-lane blacktop to the river's edge. Yellow daisies and purple clover lined the riverbanks. Butterflies danced. A turkey vulture rode the currents high above. The river ran slow, yet steady. Fire rings and Bud Light cans indicated a favorite fishing spot. Something, though, was missing. Two years earlier, Fish and Wildlife demolished the low-head lock and dam that for more than a century had allowed barges to head upstream to asphalt and sandstone quarries. Eight miles of river, up to the Mammoth Cave ferry crossing, resumed its long-thwarted natural flow.

"In the two years since the removal of the dam we've had better development of mussel beds in the free-flowing zones," says Rick the speleologist. "As we improve the Green River, the mussels improve."

Time will tell. I checked in later with the malacologists working the ferry crossing. They plucked twenty-eight different types of live mussels from the muck. Only two were federally endangered: the fanshell and the sheepnose. Two years earlier, at a dozen sites in Mammoth Cave, a similar number of live mussels and the same two endangered species were found. And, eight years prior to that, nearly identical numbers of live and endangered mussels were found. It was hard to see much improvement.

We hop back in the Chevy and drive to the day's final stop at New Discovery Cave, which is off-limits to all but Park Service–approved scientists. No signs or trimmed pathways steer visitors to the entrance. Instead, chest-high weeds obscure a concrete blockhouse with a locked steel door. It looks like an air raid bunker and, not surprisingly, was built starting in the 1940s when the Service decided that New Discovery was too delicate for hordes of meaty-palmed, graffiti-scrawling tourists. Inside, beyond yet another steel door and down a series of steep metal steps, are passages covered in delicate gypsum "flowers" and wispy gypsum needles that sway gently as you pass. The caverns wend for miles past soaring stalactites and wall-hugging waterfalls. A flurry of fossils— sharks' teeth, horn corals, crinoids—cluster in patches along the ceiling. CCC workers left behind leather shoes, oil lamps, and sardine tins as if in a haste to escape something gnarly. The skeletons of bats, possums, and wood rats litter alcoves and complete the otherworldly, spooky tableau.

But it's a bug that brung us. The cave cricket, a brown, hunch-backed, antenna-wiggling, guano-dribbling, night-crawling insect, represents perhaps the most accurate natural barometer of Mammoth Cave and its animals' long-term health. They aren't threatened, endangered, or at risk. But they are early-warning systems, like canaries and mussels, that will determine if other critters survive.

We pass through the steel doors, the steamy sunshine giving way to cool (typically fifty-four-degree) darkness. It takes a minute for my eyes to acclimate to the dim light of a handful of headlamps. Once they do, I realize I'm completely surrounded by thousands of creepy crawlies. My helmet scrapes the cave's roof. And crickets. My shoulders brush up against moist, guano-covered walls. And crickets.

I notice two red laser beams slicing the darkness. Kurt Helf and Brenda Wells, a Park Service ecologist and biologist, respectively, are counting crickets. They position a laser projector atop a tripod and shoot the beams toward a wall. Kurt holds a Kestrel weather instrument, which gauges the temperature, humidity, and air flow, in one hand, and a camera in the other. He and Brenda count insects in ten-centimeter blocks, data they'll compare with data taken the previous four years to determine the abundance of crickets in New Discovery. They're members of the Cumberland Piedmont Inventory and Monitoring Network, studying the well-being of crickets at fifteen Mammoth cave entrances. Kurt cautions that he doesn't have enough long-term data to determine the crickets' health. After years of relative decline, though, their numbers seem to have stabilized.

"Populations seem to be increasing the last few years," says Kurt, who has monitored crickets and other bugs at Mammoth since the mid-nineties. "The last two years, there were lots and lots of cave crickets. This year seems to be a bit down. But there is definitely high site fidelity. The animals, on the whole, are mostly in the same spots all the time. That's a good thing. It enables us to track any changes in the future."

Crickets leave caves at night to forage for food. They're omnivores and scavengers able to eat twice their weight in decaying plants, fungi, and other insects in one sitting. It's what they do upon returning to their darkened lairs that's most intriguing. They poop. Their guano, smeared along cave walls and ceilings, feeds other troglophiles (animals that can live inside a cave or out) and troglobites (animals that never leave a cave). A whole host of Mammoth Cave's creatures—beetles, flies, snails, mites, millipedes, salamanders, spiders, springtails—depend upon cricket crap to survive, more so than ever with the decline of guano-producing bats. If there's no guano, the animals die. And if they die, so do the fish, crayfish, salamanders, beetles, and other critters that depend upon them. And if *they* die . . .

"Cave crickets are keystone species," Kurt says. "If cave cricket populations are doing well, you can infer that organisms that depend upon them are doing well. So it's more efficient to monitor cave crickets than other species."

Meanwhile, the two Ricks wander off to explore the cave. I catch up with paleontologist Rick who, headlamp zeroed in on a patch of wall, searches for other cave-obligates.

"Here's a *Carychium stygium*" or snail, he announces.

"Here's a *tomocerus* springtail."

"Here are some cave flies."

"I've got more cute snails."

"Ah, I have a cave millipede."

He's in his element, happy as a fly in, well, guano. I ask him why I should care about a bunch of seemingly insignificant bugs that may never see the light of day.

"You've heard the analogy of the rivets and the plane?" he says. "If you lose one rivet, it's okay, the plane can fly. But if you lose all the rivets, the plane crashes and everybody dies."

Of the crickets, Kurt has written that "there are potential threats to this keystone species that may affect the entire cave community trophic structure." Translation: Climate change may irreparably mess with the food chain. While warmer weather might allow more time to forage, a concomitant drought could wipe out food sources. So too might huge slugs of rain.

Before leaving I ask Kurt about the crickets' long-term chances for survival.

He pauses. Then looks straight at me, his headlamp rendering me temporarily blind. "We really can't say what's going to happen," Kurt says.

CHAPTER 4

A Celebration of Muir Turns Toxic

As crude a weapon as the cave man's club, the chemical barrage
has been hurled against the fabric of life.
  —Rachel Carson, *Silent Spring*

Kingston, Tennessee — I leave Mammoth Cave a bit confused and
depressed, but eager to get back on the Muir trail. My mood instantly
lifts. Route 90, which starts at Cave City and runs east to Burkesville, is
also known as . . . the John Muir Highway. Green-and-white roadside
signs attest to the very fact. Local business leaders, casting about in the
1990s for an outdoorsy marketing gambit, convinced Kentucky legislators to officially rename a thirty-five-mile stretch of blacktop in honor
of the famed naturalist, who most likely trod the same path. Dick Shore,
the Muir impersonator, told me he dressed up in character and "prosti-
tuted" himself at various schools and libraries in south-central Kentucky
to lobby for the official designation.

Not only am I traveling the supposed same, and same-name, route as
Muir, but I'm headed to the second annual Muir Fest in Kingston. That
same entrepreneurial pluck that convinced legislators to rename a rural

byway in Kentucky also rouses tourism-minded county officials over the border in Tennessee. The event is billed as an "Americana Music & Preservation Festival" with bluegrass bands, conservation-minded speakers, paddle-boarding, and handmade ice cream. And, bonus attraction: one thousand baby sturgeon will be released into the Clinch River.

It's a cloudless and warm September morning, similar to what Muir experienced. Once past bustling Glasgow, whose Scottish roots must've pleased Muir, the highway rolls through cow pastures, tobacco fields with weathered barns, and crossroads communities with churches offering varying degrees of Baptist religion. A sign reads, "You're Always Welcome Back to Barren County." Another says, "Jesus Is Coming." At the town of Summer Shade, the road climbs from creek-bottomed valley to forested knobs. In Beaumont, a charcoal briquet factory hugs the highway. The road crosses the Cumberland River in Burkesville and meanders farther east before petering out near US 127 which, each August, joins The World's Longest Yard Sale along its seven-hundred-mile route from Michigan to Alabama.

Muir was enraptured by the "deep green, bossy sea of waving, flowing hilltops." He clipped, and chronicled, mistletoe, asters, heartworts, royal ferns, azaleas, and rhododendrons. Burkesville, he wrote in *A Thousand-Mile Walk*, was "embosomed in a glorious array of verdant flowing hills. The Cumberland must be a happy stream. I think I could enjoy traveling with it in the midst of such beauty all my life."

Not all, though, was "Divine beauty" and "noble oaks." Cotton, to Muir, was "a coarse, rough, straggling, unhappy looking plant." Thorny flowers and brambles—"luxuriant tangles of brooding vines"—blocked his path and scratched his skin. "The South has plant fly-catchers," he wrote. "It also has plant man-catchers."

Nor was Muir immune to the region's postwar poverty and despair, a condition biographer James B. Hunt likened to a "context of embitterment." While Muir was ascending the Cumberland Mountains near

the Tennessee line, a man on horseback overtook him and strongly per-
suaded the naturalist to give up his satchel. After rummaging through
his belongings—comb, towel, underclothing, the New Testament—the
would-be robber returned the bag. Later, a lodger near Jamestown dismissed Muir's botanical research, insisting that "picking up blossoms
doesn't seem to be a man's work at all in any kind of times." The next
day, Muir's path was blocked by ten long-haired brigands weighing
whether it was "worth while to rob me." They let him pass, most likely
due to the flowers and plants sticking out of his plant press that gave the
impression of a poor herb doctor.

Muir's delight with the countryside faded upon entering the small
Tennessee towns. Jamestown was a "poor, rickety, thrice-dead village
. . . an incredibly dreary place." Montgomery was "a shabby village."
Philadelphia was "a very filthy village." Of Kingston, all he wrote was of
reaching the small town before dark and sending his plant collection by
post to his brother in Wisconsin.

Fort Southwest Point sits atop a steep knoll where the Clinch meets the
Tennessee River. Built in 1797 to house federal troops tasked with keeping the Cherokee in check along the frontier, the finely reconstructed
fort with palisaded walls affords a sweeping view of the river valleys,
the foothills dotted with smokestacks and wind turbines and the distant Smoky Mountains. Its parking lot is jam-packed, apparently filled
with sturgeon lovers and Muir aficionados. I'm psyched. I'm also late,
so I hustle to the fish-drop. I'm sweating by the time I reach the banks
of the Clinch, where upwards of three hundred Tennesseans, about
a third bedecked in bright orange UT shirts, ball caps, and onesies,
wait patiently to plop six-inch lake sturgeon into the drink. Muir Fest
is under way.

The sturgeon once ruled the Tennessee and other Southern and Midwestern rivers and lakes, growing to six feet and 275 pounds. They can live to be 150 years old. Their eggs, or roe, were prized by caviar lovers, which prompted their rapid demise the last century. Add dam-blocked rivers, polluted water, and sedimentation, and the sturgeon, listed as endangered by the state of Tennessee, didn't stand a chance. The state's last documented, indigenous sturgeon was recorded in Fort Loudoun Lake near Knoxville in 1960. But the Clean Water Act, and more ecologically sound dam management by the Tennessee Valley Authority, laid the groundwork for a sturgeon revival. Twenty years ago the Tennessee Aquarium, downriver in Chattanooga, began reintro-ducing sturgeon to the river. The aquarium and partners have released 200,000 sturgeon into the Tennessee and its tributaries, few with more fanfare than the 964 placed gently into the river by kids and parents during Muir Fest.

The crowd clears out quickly once the fish are dumped; the Volun-teers have a noon kickoff against the University of Texas at El Paso. (They won 24–0.) I'm left to wander through the fort and handful of exhibits with only a few dozen festival-goers. I meet Steve Scarborough, a local businessman, blogger, kayak designer, environmentalist, and fes-tival booster. He wears a straw hat and Clemson T-shirt and sips a bev-erage while waiting for the music to begin. Steve pushed for years to get Muir Fest off the ground as a way to introduce the wider world to the natural and recreational wonders of Kingston. He isn't deterred by the low turnout of the second annual Muir Fest.

"It's a new event. It hasn't really found its market," Steve says. "But what better patriarch to commemorate the outdoors can you have than John Muir? He can resurrect this town. Kingston should be on the map for a number of reasons. It's fucking beautiful."

I agree and move on. But something sticks in my craw. It isn't just the poor turnout. It isn't the swirl of ominous clouds in the east portending the arrival of a weakened Hurricane Florence. I can't quite place my unease.

I climb to the top of the hill to check out the booths set up by a handful of nonprofits. I chat with Frank Jamison of the Cumberland Trails Conference, which is cobbling together a hiking trail across the Cumberland Plateau. We talk about overdevelopment, Muir's popularity, wild and scenic rivers, invasive species, and the infamous snail darter that killed a Tennessee dam. What Frank says next stops me cold.

"You know about the coal ash spill, right?"

It finally hits me. Those towering smokestacks to the north—of course. Kingston is the site of one of the nation's worst man-made environmental disasters. So much for my feel-good story.

The first call to the 911 dispatcher comes at 12:40 a.m. on the Sunday before Christmas 2008.

"I'm over at Swan Pond and there's a heck of a mud slide or something that just came through our backyard," the caller says.

A few minutes later, another call comes in.

"The power lines are down near Swan Pond Methodist Church."

Then another: "My father lives up there and I can't contact him."

And another: "Can you tell me what's going on?"

Ten minutes, and a handful of frantic, perplexing calls later, Roane County emergency dispatcher Thomas Walden figures enough out.

"The dike has failed," he says. "That's all I can tell you at this time."

Chris Copeland, a firefighter who lives along an Emory River inlet, and his wife DeAnna are in bed, a white-noise machine humming, when a freight-train-like rumble jolts him awake. Maybe it's the wind, Chris thinks. He looks out the window. It isn't the wind. He sees trees floating up the cove. Waves, bigger than he'd ever seen before, push the trees forward. And the noise. The trees snapping in half sound like shots from an automatic rifle.

Chris walks downstairs past the Christmas tree, whose lights blink out, and outside into the cold. He can't see much. Clear as day, though, flash the lights atop the thousand-foot smokestacks of the Kingston Fossil Plant.

He calls 911.

"We live in a cove back here and it's full of mud. Everything's gone," Chris tells the dispatcher. "I don't even know where it came from."

A minute or two later, he calls back.

"I bet I know what it is," Chris says. "The dike at the TVA is collapsed. It's unbelievable."

A fifty-seven-foot retaining wall at the TVA's steam plant had crumbled, sending more than five million cubic yards of coal ash sludge into the Emory and Clinch Rivers, burying Swan Pond Creek and three hundred acres of land under as much as six feet of toxic muck. The black wave of slurry covered roads, toppled trees, caused a train wreck, and knocked out power, sewer, and gas lines. A few homes were destroyed; two dozen were damaged. Deer were buried alive; at least one dog died. Remarkably, nobody was hurt or killed.

It was the largest industrial spill in US history. The ash contained arsenic, mercury, lead, zinc, beryllium, cadmium, and chromium. The heavy metals, if eaten, drunk, or inhaled, can cause cancer and ruin the nervous system. They can also damage the heart, lungs, and kidneys, as well as lead to gastrointestinal illnesses and birth defects.

Kingston was just the most tragic example of an industrial contagion plaguing the South, the region of the country most at the mercy of penny-pinching corporations, development-hungry politicians, and job-hungry citizens. Forty percent of the South's electricity comes from coal, so, not surprisingly, the region is home to the highest concentration of coal ash dump sites in the country. The Southern Environmental Law Center reports that nearly every major Southeastern river has one or more unlined and leaking ash lagoons on its banks. Coal ash is the twenty-first-century version of DDT, a deadly chemical that nearly wiped out the bald eagle until its toxic ills were documented by Rachel Carson and Congress banned its use. Utilities, though, continue to produce millions of tons of coal ash and people continue to get sick.

Tennessee fined the TVA $11.5 million. The utility spent more than a billion dollars scooping up the muck and prettifying the area. It also encircled the coal ash landfill with a seventy-foot retaining wall. Yet little was done in the aftermath of the Kingston spill to regulate coal ash. So, sure enough, six years later, on Super Bowl Sunday, more than fifty thousand tons of coal ash and twenty-seven million gallons of tainted water leaked into the Dan River near Eden, North Carolina. Seventy miles of river bottom were coated with toxic sludge. It was the nation's third-worst coal ash spill.

The Obama administration finally mandated that all ash ponds be inspected for structural stability, and that leaking sites—utilities were legally and illegally dumping a billion pounds of chemicals and heavy metals into waterways each year—be cleaned up. Groundwater monitoring systems were also mandated. Environmental groups and the coal industry both sued, the former claiming the rules were too lenient, the latter too stringent. SELC, the Sierra Club, and others were appalled that the EPA failed to classify coal ash as hazardous, a victory for coal companies and utilities.

The TVA and its contractor shipped trainload after trainload of dried, yet still-toxic ash—enough to fill the Empire State Building two and a half times—three hundred miles south to Uniontown, Alabama, where 90 percent of townsfolk are Black and half live below the poverty line. The massive Arrowhead landfill, which surrounds the town's historic

New Hope Cemetery, received four million cubic yards of the stuff. Residents soon complained of nosebleeds, breathing troubles, nerve damage, and cancers that they attributed to the coal ash. The transfer reeked of environmental racism whereby landfills, chemical plants, and refineries crop up alongside economically depressed, minority-heavy rural communities desperate for piddling tax revenues and low-paying jobs. Uniontown residents filed a civil rights complaint with the EPA alleging that Alabama's environmental agency had unlawfully permitted the landfill. In 2018, the EPA rejected the claim.

Coal ash's toxic legacy extends beyond lagoons and landfills. More than half of the coal ash produced each year is recycled as cement, drywall, roofing shingles, agricultural additives, or snow-dissolving cinders. It's also a cheap alternative as a road-paving material. Before leaving the newspaper in 2017, I was working on an investigative piece on the widespread, yet little-known, practice of spreading recycled coal ash across miles of South Georgia roads. Rural transportation departments, with little money and miles of unpaved lanes, sought inexpensive ways to reduce their maintenance budgets. The Jacksonville Electric Authority, for example, was more than willing to sell or even just donate its treated ash, marketed as EZBase. Camden, Glynn, and Charlton Counties in southeast Georgia spread recycled ash on roads, golf course paths, parking lots, and fire stations. Complaints of headaches and breathing troubles ensued. The town of St. George bought 200,000 tons of EZBase to pave roads. Residents told me that the dried ash drifted into yards and homes, turning everything white and sickening family members. Jacksonville Electric agreed to move the remaining stockpiles of ash in St. George to a nearby landfill. I've always regretted not finishing that story.

Tommy Johnson, a self-described "country boy," camped and fished for crappie and catfish in the shadows of the Kingston Steam Plant, once the largest coal-fired plant in the world. If he wasn't fishing, he was hunting rabbits with beagles. Tommy didn't hunt deer, though he tried once.

"I had him in my sites, but he walked off," he recalls. "I couldn't shoot him."

His father pastored an AME Zion church in Rockwood, five miles down the interstate from Kingston. In high school he fell in love with a girl named Betty and took her to the prom. They went their separate ways after graduation.

"But that love never stopped for me," Tommy says.

He went to work. If there was a major construction project in eastern Tennessee, Tommy was on it. Tellico Dam. Interstate 75. Oak Ridge National Laboratory. Phipps Bend Nuclear Plant. Interstate 24. He'd drive a dozer, a loader, a scraper. In between jobs, he cut tobacco, hauled hay, worked at a nursing home. He even helped build the coal ash ponds at the Kingston plant in the early eighties.

"I worked out there building the dikes up to the very top level," Tommy remembers.

He returned to the steam plant in 2005 to build a pond to hold gypsum residue. (It leaked in 2010.) He was laid off three years later. But not before getting sick.

"I was diagnosed with a few things," says Tommy, a salt-and-pepper Vandyke framing a worn, friendly face. "Diabetes. Breathing difficulties. Headaches. Rashes. But I never paid much attention to it."

Tommy and Betty, who was divorced and raising a daughter, rekindled their love. They married in 1996, had three kids and bought the sixth house built in the Walker's Reserve subdivision in West Knoxville. They live on a corner lot with a two-car garage and two American flags on the front porch. "Welcome To Our Home," says the sign on the door.

I sat down at the kitchen table with Tommy and Betty to hear their stories of Kingston and coal ash. Family photos covered side tables, the mantle, the refrigerator. A still life of vases and pears hung over Tommy's shoulder.

When the dike broke, a call went out for men and heavy machinery.

"I knew it was going to happen," Tommy says. "I worked on top of that dike. There was rusty, slimy water running down the hill. We had told the general foreman what was happening. He came out, walked the area, and said it was just the pond relieving some pressure."

His first job was to pump diesel fuel into the front-end loaders and backhoes scooping up the muck. Up to sixteen hours a day, six days a week in the cold or the heat, surrounded by heavy machinery kicking up sixty-foot-high dust devils of toxic fly ash which, when inhaled, lodged deep into his lungs. One day, Tommy fainted. Fell down. Sat there for a moment. Shook his head. Got up. And went back to work. Another time he fell hip-deep into a mess of wet ash.

Tommy spent eight years cleaning up Kingston, eventually doing what he does best, running the dozers, backhoes, and the mighty double-barrel scrapers. His health, though, worsened. In addition to the headaches and rashes, Tommy added coughing jags and weird bumps running up and down his back. He blacked out in church. Twice.

"In our church," Tommy says, "you don't sit around."

"We praise the Lord in our church," Betty adds.

He went to doctors. Diabetes, said one. Asthma, said another. He kept working.

"When you're making thirty-four dollars an hour, with sixteen-hour days, and they're telling you it's safe enough to eat . . ."

TVA and Jacobs Engineering, the contractor hired to clean up the mess, insisted for years that coal ash wouldn't harm the nine hundred cleanup workers. In 2009, a TVA official told *60 Minutes* she would swim in the muck-filled Emory River. The top on-site safety officer repeatedly told workers they could eat a pound of fly ash daily without harm.

Jamie Satterfield, a reporter at the *Knoxville News Sentinel* who has done Pulitzer-worthy coverage of the spill and its aftermath, uncovered evidence showing that the EPA wanted workers to be protected with Tyvek suits and respirators. TVA and Jacobs pressured the agency into doing without. The workers were warned they'd be fired if they showed up on-site with protective gear; Jacobs didn't want to alarm the public. One worker testified that his doctor insisted he wear a dust mask. He was fired. EPA also directed Jacobs to provide showers and changing rooms for workers at the end of their shifts. Instead, the contractor offered pans filled with water and brushes to clean boots. Vehicles, though, were a different matter. TVA built a million-dollar car wash to ensure that trucks were cleaned—twice—before leaving the work site. And on-site air monitors were altered or destroyed, employees said. Meanwhile, trailers for Jacobs employees were equipped with air-filtration systems.

Satterfield uncovered tests conducted by the TVA as far back as 1981 showing that its coal ash contained radioactive materials and heavy metals. She also unearthed documents detailing radium levels nearly twice the EPA's maximum allowable limit during the cleanup.

Workers got sicker and sicker. The money, though, was too good to quit. It was the Great Recession, and Tommy was able pay off his house, buy a Chevy Silverado, take vacations with Betty. In 2015, the cleanup was finished. And so was Tommy.

"I would still be working if I could, but I had to retire," he says, laboring to breathe. "I was just plain out of it. I was going through a lot of pain and a lot of sleepless nights. I had coughing spells that would last fifteen minutes."

At sixty-nine, Tommy is a broken man. The list of ailments fills a notebook: diabetes; asthma; "dangerously high" potassium levels; chronically inflamed lungs; memory loss; disorientation; sleep apnea; blisters. His neuropathy is so bad "it feels like there's a zipper underneath my skin and somebody's pulling it." He's swollen to more than three hundred pounds due to excess fluids. He wears wide-fit Skechers and compression socks to prevent blood clots. He passes out any time, any place.

"I've got more doctors than I have friends, and they tell me I've got a lot going on in my body," Tommy says, ruefully. "My health is gone. I don't think I'll ever get it back."

In 2013, Tommy and dozens of cleanup workers sued Jacobs, claiming the contractor lied about the dangers of coal ash and failed to provide them with protective gear. The plaintiffs wanted Jacobs to cover their skyrocketing medical costs. A US District Court judge dismissed the suit a year later. New evidence, though, secured an appeal, and in 2018 jurors ruled that Jacobs' actions endangered workers and that coal ash likely caused their illnesses. The judge ordered mediation. Jacobs offered a reported ten thousand dollars to each of the nearly two hundred plaintiffs, who roundly rejected the settlement offer. A trial for damages was supposed to start in 2021.

Meanwhile, the *Knoxville News* tallied four dozen dead and more than four hundred sickened by the coal ash cleanup. The longer the case drags on, and the more deaths, the angrier the survivors get.

"Angry ain't the half of it, especially since TVA and Jacobs have been lying about it to us all along," Betty says. "My husband is sick and four hundred other people are, too. And Jacobs is not taking responsibility for it killing people. Coal ash is a toxic chemical and they knew it and they did not tell these people. I am angry and willing to stay on the battlefield until we get what we need."

In the South, we still build homes along coastlines, daring hurricanes and rising seas to destroy properties and lives. We still give away our precious groundwater to Big Ag, Big Industry, and Big Development, guaranteeing shortages when the droughts inevitably come. And we still allow the residue of coal-generated electricity to sit in leaky ponds and landfills, polluting our rivers and drinking water and, slowly, killing us. Study upon study has shown that coal ash is hazardous, but the federal government considers it no more harmful than household trash. In 2019, the Trump administration rolled back rules limiting the leaching of arsenic and other metals into groundwater. EPA, under the enlightened leadership of a former coal industry lobbyist, allowed power plants to continue dumping coal ash into unlined ponds for years to come. The agency also decided that cash-strapped, utility-dominated states know best how to dispose of coal ash.

How'd that turn out? Well, in North Carolina, after the disastrous Dan River spill, Duke Energy agreed to excavate eight relatively small ash ponds, yet balked at cleaning up six others. In 2020, following lawsuits by the Sierra Club, SELC, and others, as well as pressure from the state's environmental agency, the nation's largest utility agreed to dig up and transfer eighty million tons of wet ash to lined landfills or recycling facilities. The deal was touted as the largest coal ash cleanup in US history.

Duke and two other utilities had earlier agreed to rid South Carolina of all unlined coal ash dumps. Unfortunately, much of the Carolinas' ash was trucked down Interstate 85 to a North Georgia landfill. Georgia imports more solid waste—mostly coal ash—than any of its Southern brethren. The ash comes from the Carolinas, Florida, and Puerto Rico, and molders in municipal and private landfills. Impoverished rural counties eagerly accept the paltry tipping fees. When the EPA allowed states to handle their own coal ash problems, Georgia jumped at the chance. Lauren "Bubba" McDonald Jr., who chairs the state's utilities commission, said that Georgia should craft a plan suitable for Georgians and, by golly, that's what we did. Georgia Power, the state's largest utility, announced in 2016 that coal ash from sixteen ponds would be excavated. Its remaining thirteen ponds would be "closed in place," some without plastic linings to keep toxic gunk from leaching into the groundwater. Environmental groups reported two years later that water near ten of the utility's coal-fired plants was contaminated.

You'd think that if any state should get its coal ash house in order it'd be Tennessee. You'd be wrong. The state allows the TVA to investigate itself and decide if its coal ash contaminates the water and air. And then the TVA, in its best fox-guarding-the-henhouse routine, determines what should be done about it. At the time of the Kingston spill, the quasi-public utility that electrified a large swath of the rural South operated eight coal-fired plants. Today, thanks to nuclear power and an abundance of natural gas, the TVA runs four coal plants in Tennessee. All of them, though, have ash disposal problems and contaminate the Cumberland, Tennessee, and Clinch Rivers. The TVA agreed in 2019 to dig up twelve million tons of coal ash from an unlined, leaky pit at the Gallatin Fossil Plant near Nashville. The utility says it will close the Bull Run plant near Oak Ridge by 2023, but leave five million tons of coal ash sitting in an unlined pit alongside the Clinch River. (Meanwhile, the Biden administration is rolling back some of Trump's coal-ash disposal rules.)

Tommy worries that Bull Run, a few miles from his house, is another Kingston with flimsy retaining walls waiting to blow.

"I should know," he says. "I helped build them. That ash is not going to hold."

Tommy doesn't get out much these days. He might ride over to Kingston to get a haircut, but Betty worries he'll have another spell and run off the road. He faithfully tries to make it to church, Believers Voice of Deliverance, where he's a deacon, unless the swelling is too bad and he can't get his shoes on. Somebody else cuts the grass. The golf clubs sit in a corner of the garage. Vacations long dreamed of—Maine, Yosemite, Route 66, an uncle in Kansas, the Green Bay Packers at Lambeau Field—look doubtful. He's got seven grandkids who'll never learn about hunting and fishing from their grandpa.

"He promised me the world and he can't give me the world," Betty says. "But I love my husband and will stay with him. It's a blessing that we've got a good relationship and we can be understanding of each other. Jacobs took a lot from us, and our lives, but they can't take everything. We won't let them."

They've spent tens of thousands of dollars on doctors, medicines, and emergency room visits. Medicare only covers so much. Their savings are gone.

"All I want is for them to take care of my bills," Tommy says. "I know they can't give me my life back."

We've talked for three hours. Tommy's worn out. He'd lost his train of thought, mid-sentence, and stares out the window at the rain falling softly. His eyes redden. He uncrosses his arms and rubs his eyes.

"I sit and think about what we're going through, and then I look back at when we worked on the ash years ago and a whole lot of guys died," Tommy says, ticking off the names of dead co-workers. "Jacobs knew it was hazardous. They knew all about it for years."

I return to Kingston a year later and climb the steep hill to Bethel Cemetery, where Muir may have slept. Established in 1811, on land donated by a Cherokee chief named Riley, the cemetery is the final home of hardscrabble pioneers, soldiers from every American war, and riverboat captains whose tombstones are embossed with anchors and pilot's wheels. It affords a grand view of the Clinch River and Fort Southwest Point, where Muir Fest—canceled due to lack of interest—was to have been held. Upriver sits the Kingston Fossil Plant, all gussied up with seven thousand new trees, a riverside park, and fishing piers. There's no trace of the gray ash that washed over Swan Pond and swamped the Emory River. TVA, in a 2015 report, said the cleanup "is protective of human health and the environment (and) was completed to the maximum extent practicable." The utility recently announced it will shutter the plant by 2033.

Yet the plant still burns fourteen thousand tons of coal daily and stores its toxic by-product in the lined landfill next door. More than five hundred thousand cubic yards of ash remain at the bottom of the Emory and Clinch Rivers.

A large white cross with black lettering that reads "First Responders Gave All" sits on a hillside across from the coal plant. Ansol Clark built the memorial in honor of the fifty or so workers who reportedly died cleaning up the toxic mess. Ansol, who worked alongside Tommy for years, was diagnosed with a rare type of blood cancer. He died in May 2021. Tommy was devastated. I ask Betty how he's doing.

"Tommy has a few bad days," she says, "but he is holding on to God's hands."

CHAPTER 5

"The Mountains Are Calling"— and They're Not Happy

The mountains were his masters. They rimmed in life. They were the cup of reality, beyond growth, beyond struggle and death. They were his absolute unity in the midst of eternal change.
—Thomas Wolfe, *Look Homeward, Angel*

Coker Creek, Tennessee — For Muir, Kingston proved unremarkable. What lay ahead, though, would enchant the young rambler barely two weeks into his trek to the Gulf. He walked in a southeasterly direction, crossing "small parallel valleys that flute the surface of the one wide valley." The dirt paths meandered and confused Muir, frustrating his journey to the mountains. He consulted "a buxom Tennessee 'gal'" who steered him toward the Unicoi Trail, which crossed into North Carolina. He spent the night with a blunt-spoken "negro teamster" who knew the region well. Finally, Muir reached forgettable Philadelphia and, without tarrying, headed to Madisonville, which he deemed "a brisk village." The Unaka Range, or "White Mountains" in Cherokee, "entranced" Muir as he started the long ascent up the southern Appalachian chain that reaches upward of six thousand feet. The peaks, like the nearby Smokies, were draped in a white haze and afforded what he called a "most glorious billowy mountain scenery."

Muir took his time on the uphill slog, spending two nights with an elderly and loquacious mountain man who showed him the region's natural and commercial specialties. They visited gold and (maybe) copper mines, grist mills, and blacksmith shops. Muir observed "wild, unshorn, uncombed men" with bags of corn and coon-skin caps emerging from rhododendron-shrouded trails. They were headed to mills, alongside fast-falling creeks, that appeared terribly unsophisticated to the mechanically astute Muir. The mountaineer said that earlier generations of farmers had "skimmed off the cream of the soil," leaving the land worn out and unproductive, a pattern of natural-resource abuse that has plagued the region since the 1700s.

"This is the most primitive country I have seen, primitive in everything," Muir wrote in *A Thousand-Mile Walk*. "The remotest hidden parts of Wisconsin are far in advance of the mountain regions of Tennessee and North Carolina."

The farther south Muir traveled, the more the Civil War's toll appeared. Eastern Tennessee was no hotbed of Confederate support; locals had voted two-to-one against secession. Cotton and slavery weren't kings among the yeoman farmers tending small plots. In fact, thirty-one thousand Tennesseans, mostly from the east, joined the Federal army—more than from any other Southern state. Seven thousand of them died, depriving rural communities of fathers, husbands, and brothers. Farms failed. Families moved away. Local governments collapsed. Churches and schools closed. Confederate guerrillas terrorized the countryside for years after the war's end; Muir came across at least one group of highwaymen. A local historian said "bloodshed and destruction" were East Tennessee's reward for a war it didn't want.

"The seal of war is on all things," Muir wrote.

Except botany. Muir catalogued oaks, hemlocks, mosses, laurels, azaleas, asters, liatris, Joe Pye weed, and many different types of ferns, including the Christmas, interrupted, and ebony spleenwort. Finally, upon reaching the North Carolina state line on September 18, most likely near Coker Creek, Muir near-hyperventilated over the waves of Blue Ridge ranges stretching across Tennessee, North Carolina, Georgia, and Alabama.

"The scenery is far grander than any I ever before beheld," he said. "Such an ocean of wooded, waving, swelling mountain beauty and grandeur is not to be described. . . . Oh, these forest gardens of our Father! What perfection, what divinity, in their architecture! What simplicity and mysterious complexity of detail! Who shall read the teaching of these sylvan pages, the glad brotherhood of rills that sing in the valleys, and all the happy creatures that dwell in them under the tender keeping of a Father's care?"

A bit florid, perhaps, but those hills have forever seduced travelers. Including me. A three-hour drive from Atlanta brings me to a backpacker's paradise in the Chattahochee, Cherokee, Nantahala, Pisgah, or Great Smoky forests. The Appalachian Trail (AT) runs along the spine of the highest mountains. I've hiked these hills since the 1980s, when I moved to Winston-Salem. They're steep, grueling climbs oftentimes rewarded with 360-degree views from grassy balds, or hilltop meadows. I've vaulted roaring streams with tree limbs as poles. I've skittered past black bears and jumped over timber rattlers. I've surprised ginseng hunters and lovers *in flagrante delicto*. I've awakened to a foot of fresh snow outside my tent. I've gotten lost, found (in the literal, not biblical sense), frustrated, angry, and euphoric, and I keep coming back for more. It was Muir, not me, who famously said "the mountains are calling and I must go," but I wholly agree. The mountains are my playground, gym, church, happy spot, and therapist's couch.

I follow Muir's likely path from Coker Creek along a forest road to the Benton MacKaye Trail, a three-hundred-mile, lesser-traveled alternative to the AT named for the man who conceptualized the AT. The trail section above runs along the North Carolina–Tennessee border. The section below, along the Hiwassee River, is called the John Muir National Recreation Trail. Muir might've followed a trail along the river from Tennessee into North Carolina, but I'm not so sure.

I scurry up the grassy Benton MacKaye, pass underneath a power line and down to the intersection with the Unicoi Gap Trail. I've not much time. I need to get back to Atlanta. Plus, the sky is darkening. But I jump at any chance to follow in Muir's actual footsteps, since virtually all of his route today tracks highways or well-trafficked byways. And the mountains, despite centuries of hunting, logging, mining, and development, harken to an unblemished past that Muir would recognize, particularly in the federally protected parks and forests.

It's now dark. I hurry to my car and head home. I return four months later, though, keen to continue my meander through the very hills Muir embraced.

I leave Atlanta early on a Monday morning in January to beat traffic. The forecast calls for no rain and full sun by Tuesday. The weatherman is wrong.

The hilltops disappear into the clouds as I head higher into the Cherokee National Forest. The Hiwassee spills over its banks, rendering impassable the lower Muir trail. Upwards I drive through frost-wilted rhododendron groves and second-generation hardwoods. I park again at the intersection of the forest road and the Benton MacKaye Trail, shoulder my too-heavy pack, and slip under the power lines. This time, though, I stay on the BMT and continue up the ridge. Recent rains and snow ensure a slippery climb. Fog blocks the usual miles-long views. I spook a flock of wild turkeys pecking a tattered carpet of acorns. Bears or wild boars had beaten them to the spot, however. The turkeys squawk and climb awkwardly skyward, their wings sounding like the *whomp-whomp* of tiny helicopters. A hard climb gets me to the ridge and a wintry wonderland of frozen trees enshrouded in mist. Crystalline rime blankets the bushes with icicles pointing due west whence the winds come. In *The Story of My Boyhood and Youth*, Muir shares a similar wonder of a winter scene.

"The view of the woods," he wrote, "was something never to be forgotten. Every twig and branch and rugged trunk was encased in pure crystal ice, and each oak and hickory and willow became a fairy crystal palace."

I camp nine miles in at Sandy Gap in a hollow shielded from the wind. A small stream runs down the middle and provides the evening's soundtrack. I try to build a fire, but the wood is too wet. Snow and sleet chase me inside my tent. I sip some whiskey and listen to the stream and the silence, broken occasionally by airplanes high overhead.

Muir, of course, didn't have a sleeping bag or tent. If shelter wasn't available, he stretched out alongside a trail or in a copse of trees and slept on hard ground. He didn't have the relative luxury of ramen noodles, a Jetboil stove, or a Mountain Forecast app. He also didn't hike the Appalachians in winter with temperatures in the teens and frozen water bottles.

I've hiked these mountains in every season and prefer the solitude of winter. Edward Abbey, in *Desert Solitaire*, put it best: "I find that in contemplating the natural world my pleasure is greater if there are not too many others contemplating it with me, at the same time." The trails are empty, the animals unsuspecting. Firewood is abundant. And the views, through leafless trees, are marvelous.

I wake at seven as the sky lightens. My tent and fly are covered in ice. I unzip the door, sink deeper into my sleeping bag, and stare down the cove. Snow dusts the rhododendrons. A ridge line appears gray and indeterminate through the heavy mist. I listen to the wind whipping high on the ridge. Unwillingly, at eight, I creep from my bag, hurry into my clothes, answer nature's call, retrieve my food bag, and hustle back to my tent. I brew some tea, eat an apple and three granola bars, pull water from the stream, and hit the trail. The frozen tent adds considerable weight to my pack. Four arduous hours later I'm back in my Subaru. I haven't seen a soul in twenty-four hours.

The timeless beauty of the southern Appalachians is a myth, one I willingly embrace. People think the awe-inspiring trees, mountains, and vistas have always been such. Muir, in an 1897 article for *The Atlantic* entitled "The American Forests," wrote that "the forests of America, however slighted by man, must have been a great delight to God; for they were the best he ever planted." At one time that was true. Not today. Four hundred years of European influence, and destruction, laid waste to the forests, and their sylvan ideal.

The Cherokee ruled most of western Carolina, yet lived lightly on the land before the white man arrived in the 1700s. The original Americans hunted for food and pelts, cleared small plots along rivers, and periodically burned the fields and forests to scare critters into the open and rejuvenate the land. But there was no avoiding the English and Scottish traders who brought horses and guns and paid good money for beaver, bear, elk, buffalo, and deer hides. Hundreds of thousands of pelts left the mountains for the ports of Savannah and Charleston for shipment to Europe to be turned into hats, gloves, and bookbindings. Beavers were nearly wiped out by the middle of the nineteenth century; the buffalo, elk, and deer were next.

Frontiersmen and settlers followed the traders into the mountains, clearing the land along rivers and streams for crops and pastures. Their unpenned cows and pigs trampled the forest undergrowth, furthered erosion, and vacuumed up the acorns that wildlife depended on. The Cherokee, too, became farmers with cattle and swine roaming the lands.

The pioneers convinced state officials to place bounties—three dollars a scalp—on bobcats, red wolves, and Eastern cougars. The Federal Road between Nashville and Augusta (gateway to the Savannah River) ran through Cherokee country and, by the time it was completed in 1807, had supercharged the farm-to-market economy for cows, hogs, sheep, and goats.

Nothing, though, so devastated the southern Appalachians as the growing nation's insatiable appetite for wood. Mature, towering stands of red oak, eastern hemlock, pignut hickory, Fraser fir, tulip poplar, and red maple blanketed the mountainsides. Chestnut trees—maybe ten men with arms outstretched could encircle one of those ancient monsters—filled a quarter of the forests. Prior to 1800, timber cutting was limited to stands below 2,500 feet. Iron makers soon discovered the abundant southern forests crisscrossed by numerous and bountiful streams. They needed wood, and lots of it, to make charcoal hot enough to melt ore. Pigeon Forge and the Cades Cove Bloomery ran full out in the Smokies, originally known as the Great Iron Mountains. Tens of thousands of timbered acres were denuded in the region's short-lived iron age. Northern industrialists, though, were just getting started on their carpetbagging pillage of Appalachia's natural resources.

Copper mining, mostly where eastern Tennessee meets north Georgia, demanded limitless amounts of timber to fire the furnaces. The first mine opened in Ducktown, Tennessee, in 1850 and gobbled three hundred bushels of wood daily. It was "one of the most environmentally destructive industries in the Southern Appalachians during the antebellum period," wrote Donald Edward Davis in *Where There Are Mountains: An Environmental History of the Southern Appalachians*. Other mines soon followed, and within two decades nearly forty square miles of trees vanished. Making matters worse, the furnaces belched tons of sulfur dioxide into the sky, ruining forests and streams farther afield and prompting the state of Georgia to sue Tennessee for environmental damages.

It wouldn't take long for the era of "industrial logging" to reach unprecedented heights. Northern money, and the Shay steam engine, a geared locomotive that could run on any track, targeted the hardwoods above three thousand feet. Quick-buck lumber companies simply rolled up the tracks once a grove was depleted and moved them higher up the mountain. Flatbeds full of massive trees would return downhill without having to deal with fickle streams or reluctant oxen. One billion six hundred million board feet of timber was cut across the southern Appalachians in 1880, according to Jack Temple Kirby's *Mockingbird Song: Ecological Landscapes of the South*. In 1912, more than fifteen billion board feet were cut.

Profit wasn't the region's only scourge. An invasive pathogen from Japan decimated the remaining chestnuts, starting around 1920. Towering hemlocks currently succumb to another Japanese import, the woolly adelgid. Only 3 percent of old-growth forest remains across the region. From time to time I visit the old-growth Joyce Kilmer Memorial Forest, with its four-hundred-year old trees, named for the poet who wrote "Trees." A forest fire roared through in 2017 and did considerable damage.

Destruction of the forests, not surprisingly, ravaged the surrounding countryside and the variety of habitats. Streams silted over and warmed without the oaks, poplars, and canebrakes. Native trout populations dropped sharply. Carolina parakeets, the only parrot species in the East, once blackened the skies like passenger pigeons, but disappeared along with their bottomland habitat. A mighty chestnut yields ten bushels of nuts, so their demise wiped out the pantries of squirrels, turkeys, bears, and raccoons. By 1800, Chinese appetites had nearly rid the north-facing mountains of ginseng. "Forests and wildlife were brutally used," wrote Albert Cowdrey in *This Land, This South: An Environmental History*. "In the course of a generation or two, beginning in 1860, the first major regional extinctions since the last Pleistocene took place."

Without trees holding the hillsides in place, the rainfall flowed freely into the creeks and rivers of the Appalachians. A flash flood near Johnson City, Tennessee, in 1924 sent ten feet of water down a narrow valley, killing eleven people. The Mississippi Valley bore the brunt of the Great Flood of 1927, but weeks of rain swelled Appalachian streams, flooded towns and fields, and provided impetus for the creation of the Tennessee Valley Authority six years later.

Flood control, navigation, and electricity were the TVA's original goals, though a Depression-era jobs program for one of the nation's poorest regions certainly helped sell the massive public-works project. Norris Dam, north of Knoxville, opened in 1936 and created a reservoir seventy-three miles long along the Clinch River. Today, forty-nine dams control the waters that drain into the Tennessee Valley and allow barges to run from Knoxville to Paducah, Kentucky, on the Ohio River. In fact, every river in the southern Appalachians, including the Little Tennessee, Toccoa, Duck, Nolichucky, and French Broad, is controlled by a TVA dam. The environmental damage was severe. More than a million acres of land—river bottoms, swamplands, canebrakes, lowland prairies—was submerged. Thousands of miles of streams were straightened. Hundreds of mussel species vanished. Eels, gar, paddlefish, and sturgeon all but disappeared. Rainbow trout were imported from California, but the interlopers decimated native brown trout in many streams. By World War II, the TVA had become the nation's largest buyer of coal and the source of millions of tons of sulfur dioxide that rained down on Appalachian forests.

Muir and fellow environmentalists began sounding the southern ecological alarm in the late nineteenth century. In the *Atlantic* article, Muir wrote of the devastation of the eastern wilderness: "When the steel axe of the white man rang out in the startled air their doom was sealed. Every tree heard the bodeful sound, and pillars of smoke gave the sign in the sky. . . . The Atlantic coast from Maine to Georgia had been mostly cleared and scorched into melancholy ruins."

The *cri de coeur* resonated widely as a newly wealthy nation embraced tourism and the salubrious benefits of mountain air. Trains and new-fangled automobiles carried visitors deeper into the hollows and higher onto the mountains. The newcomers made it abundantly clear that they didn't like their hard-won views marred by stumpy and denuded hill-sides. Charles S. Sargent, a famous botanist and first director of Harvard University's arboretum, advocated for a forest reserve in the southern Appalachians. George Vanderbilt hired a young Gifford Pinchot to manage his Biltmore Estate in Asheville, which became the foundation of the Pisgah National Forest. Pinchot, who believed that forests can be both preserved and logged, became the nation's top forestry official in 1898. A year later, the Appalachian National Park Association was founded in North Carolina by citizens concerned that the beautiful mountains were being destroyed.

Even the logging industry got religion. Sort of. The large landown-ers endorsed the creation of forest reserves whereby the land they had already destroyed would be reforested with taxpayer money, thereby relieving them of tax burdens. The push for federal government over-sight accelerated after the devastating 1907 floods and the public's newfound understanding of the need for watershed protection. Nature lovers also rightly pointed out that the West had Yosemite, Yellowstone, and Glacier National Parks while the East had *bupkis*. Knoxville hosted the National Conservation Exposition in 1913, a two-month festival that warned of the finite nature of the Appalachians' natural resources. A million visitors, including Booker T. Washington, Helen Keller, and William Jennings Bryan, watched fireworks, motorcycle races, and "a Herd of Trained Elephants." They also took in exhibits on clean water, soil erosion, and sustainable logging. The expo fueled talk of a national park in the nearby mountains. But it was Acadia in Maine, three years later, that was designated a national monument and, eventually, the first national park east of the Mississippi.

In 1911, President William Howard Taft signed the Weeks Act, which allowed the federal government to buy "forested, cutover, or denuded lands within the watersheds of navigable streams." The landmark legislation, one of the nation's most successful conservation measures, has protected twenty million acres east of the Mississippi and led to the creation of the Pisgah, Cherokee, Chattahoochee, and (my favorite) Nantahala National Forests.

Nearly a half century after Yellowstone's creation, the nation's wilderness system was in disarray, with little funding or guidance, and overseen by a hodgepodge of federal agencies. President Woodrow Wilson established the National Park Service in 1916 with the proviso that any public parkland must be donated to the federal government. Stephen Mather, a borax millionaire and nature lover from Chicago, became the Service's first director and undertook an aggressive PR and lobbying campaign to increase the size and number of national parks. He raised money from friends, and kicked in his own, to buy land. He supported the road-building frenzy and the auto clubs whose members wanted pretty places to visit. He introduced concession stands and visitor centers to cater to an increasingly mobile society.

President Calvin Coolidge signed legislation in 1926 creating the Great Smoky Mountains National Park. The Tennessee and North Carolina legislatures ponied up two million dollars each, and John D. Rockefeller Jr. added another five million, to buy three hundred thousand acres straddling the state line. Finally, in 1934, after years spent wrangling with small farmers and large timber companies, the park was officially established by Congress.

The hard work, though, was just beginning. The Depression greatly reduced logging and mining across the southern Appalachians and gave the Civilian Conservation Corps time to plant trees, fix eroded hillsides, and restock trout streams. The white-tailed deer population exploded. Bears, beavers, and wild turkeys returned to their once-abundant lands. The CCC's dollar-a-day boys also built roads, trails, culverts, and campsites, readying the forests for the hordes of tourists to come.

"With some exceptions, the Depression years were good for the environment of the Southern Appalachians," wrote Susan Yarnell in a history of the region for the US Forest Service.

Conservation took a back seat to war readiness in the 1940s as logging and resource extraction again boomed in the mountains. The TVA built 480-foot-high Fontana Dam along the Little Tennessee River in North Carolina, which provided cheap electricity, primarily for the aluminum factory in Alcoa. The Appalachian Trail now crosses the top of the dam—the tallest east of the Rockies.

Gatlinburg, at the foot of the Smoky Mountains, is known for many things: gateway to the national park; rococo Alpine splendor; the Ripley's Believe It or Not! Odditorium; shopping for stuff you don't need; Dolly Parton; Putt-Putt Golf. I'd add Pancake Capital of the World to the list.

No fewer than six pancake restaurants dot the main drag that runs (*crawls* is more like it as I spend forty-five minutes driving from one end to the next) through the heart of town and its equally clogged side streets. It's true. I count them. There's the Little House of Pancakes. The Pancake Pantry. Atrium Pancakes. Log Cabin Pancake House. Flapjack's Pancake Cabin. Reagan's House of Pancakes. And those are just the pancake joints with the word *pancake* on their marquee. I'd proffer that virtually every other restaurant in Gatlinburg (pop. 4,100, off-season) serves them, too. So popular are pancakes that hour-long lines snake out the doors and down the streets of flapjack emporia. The customers don't seem to mind the wait. Besides, there are enough commercial distractions to bide the time of the hungriest pancake lovers.

Look left and you'll see: the Fudge Shoppe of the Smokies; Santa's Clause-et; a Margaritaville Resort; and the Honeymoon Hills Cabin Rentals (with heart-shaped Jacuzzis).

Look right and you'll find entertainment galore: the Ober Gatlinburg Ski Area & Amusement Park; museums dedicated to pinball, Hollywood cars, salt and pepper shakers, and *The Dukes of Hazzard*; and individual Ripley's for fans of miniature golf, penguins, haunted houses, mirror mazes, and exotic fish. (Dollywood is in nearby Pigeon Forge.)

Look up and you'll discover: the Space Needle; ski gondolas; a SkyBridge; zip lines; and . . . *mountains*. They're the very reason for Gatlinburg's existence and, presumably, why people come here.

Kirby, the *Mockingbird Song* author and one-time president of the Southern Historical Association, wrote that "the hamlet of Gatlinburg quickly grew into a nightmarish version of Las Vegas—nightmarish because Gatlinburg had the neon but no blowzy sex shows, much less gambling, and hardly ever the substantial architecture and confident self-mockery of Las Vegas."

I drive up from Atlanta one warm October Friday and set up my single-man tent at the Cades Cove campground. It's Columbus Day weekend and I'm lucky to get one of the last spots. I pull into the campground store to get my permit. A volunteer ranger tells a camper to avoid the picnic area because a small black bear with a white splotch is again scrounging for food. "He's a hemorrhoid," the volunteer says. "He's a pain in the butt."

I love backcountry camping; I like campgrounds. My kids, father-in-law, and I car camp a couple of times a year. The settings are usually lovely, with hiking trails nearby. Plus, you can bring chairs, bikes, blow-up mattresses, plastic pink flamingos, music, beer, and bacon. And there's always somebody friendly watching football on a big-screen TV mounted on the side of their RV.

My small tent is dwarfed by the RVs and trailers at Cade's Cove. Most campers are well into dinner or a postprandial stroll by the time I set up. A nattily dressed older gentleman in slacks, cowboy boots, and red MAGA hat happens by with his wife. Kids on bikes circle ever faster on the paved roads. Snippets of conversation waft from one side to the other.

"I caught two rats at my mother's house, put 'em in a Walmart bag, and took 'em to the Mexican restaurant," the elderly lady to my right tells her partner, who doesn't appear to be listening. I never learn why she took rats to a restaurant.

It's dark by 7:30, a three-quarter moon rising over the sweetgums and pines. Generators switch off. A dozen fire rings glow. Voices lower. S'mores get finished. Families climb into RVs awash with the telltale blue glow, or tents with Coleman lanterns turned low. An owl hoots.

Everybody warned me to hit the Smoky hotspots early in the day to avoid the crowds, but I didn't listen. After futzing about the campground in the morning I finally begin the ascent up US 441 to Clingmans Dome—"the Top of the Smokies" at more than 6,400 feet. I've hiked and driven to the dome many times; the view is spectacular, especially from the spaceship-like observation tower. The drive up follows the west prong of the Little Pigeon River, past rocky Chimney Tops and Mount Le Conte with its hike-in lodge. The glitz of Gatlinburg fades quickly into the age-old serenity of the Appalachians. Until, that is, you reach the Tennessee–North Carolina border at Newfound Gap and the side road to Clingmans Dome. I come to a complete stop a mile from the top. Cars inch forward. I make half a mile in fifteen minutes. I ditch the car and hike the last stretch to the summit.

The South's hot, dry fall persists and the trees don't wear the typi-cally brilliant oranges, reds, and yellows that attract leaf-peepers. No matter. Cars from Missouri to Florida crowd the parking lot, waiting for others to pull out. Lines to the bathrooms run forty deep. German, Chinese, Spanish, and Arabic is spoken. Bachelorettes from Tennessee take pictures with Lake Fontana far below as backdrop. A Park Ser-vice sign quotes Muir's "going to the mountains is going home" adage and, sure enough, thousands of "over-civilized people" are atop Cling-mans today. The more intrepid tourists hike, sometimes eight abreast, the paved pathway to the concrete lookout tower. En route, they see swaths of dead trees for miles into the blue-green distance. Another Park Service sign says that 70 percent of the park's firs have succumbed to the woolly adelgid that is destroying the high-country canopy. Yet another storyboard tells visitors that the park's telltale smokiness is, at times, "air pollution, sulfate particles mainly from coal-fired power plants."

The Smokies are the nation's most popular national park, with a record twelve and a half million visitors in pre-Covid 2019—more than a million more than the previous year and nearly double the amount of the second most-visited park, the Grand Canyon. Its cost (free) and day's drive from Atlanta, Washington, Nashville, and other big cities make the park a natural destination for outdoor-loving motorists.

The Smokies, though, are being loved to death. Nearly $250 million worth of roads, trails, bridges, buildings, and water-treatment facilities need fixing, according to an NPS study. The super-crowded Sugarlands Visitor Center outside Gatlinburg needs a total overhaul. Nearby, the seventy-five-year-old headquarters needs five million bucks.

I leave Clingmans Dome and drive down to Newfound Gap, where President Franklin Delano Roosevelt dedicated the park on Labor Day 1940. "We used up or destroyed much of our natural heritage just because that heritage was so bountiful," he told the crowd. "We slashed

our forests, we used our soils, we encouraged floods. We are at last definitely engaged in the task of conserving the bounties of nature."

Maybe so, but the nation's sixty-three national parks need more than
twelve billion dollars in upgrades after years of neglect, paltry appropriations, and the country's growing love of the outdoors. We're killing
the very thing we profess to love so much. Abbey, the writer and wilderness defender, rightly noted that "industrial tourism is a threat to the
national parks."

I park at an RV-only spot (all the other spots were taken) where
another sign warns that the popular Trillium Gap Trail is closed four
days a week "for trail improvements." I duck behind the memorial plaza
for a quick hike along the AT, which runs seventy of its most beautiful
miles through the Smokies. Later, I learn that the entire AT itself needs
nineteen million dollars in upgrades to trails, shelters, and access roads.
This stretch alone is eroding in spots and hikers have doubled its typical
eighteen-inch width. The trail, though, soon disappears into the familiar white-blazed woods.

In early 2014, the US Forest Service published one of my favorite government manuals of recent vintage. Granted, I'm a public-policy geek.
But the *Outlook for Appalachian-Cumberland Forests: A Subregional
Report from the Southern Forests Future Project* forecasts the future of the
natural world across the Blue Ridge mountains in 2060. It's an alarming read. The report is part of a voluminous, multiyear study by thirty
federal, state, and university researchers to gauge the future impact of
population growth, climate change, invasive species, timber prices, and
wildfire on the South's public and private forests. Nowhere is the threat
more pronounced than in the Blue Ridge Mountains.

"The Appalachian-Cumberland highland is forecasted to experience
the highest growth rate of urban land use," the report intones.

Cities and suburbs across the region currently cover four million acres; by 2060 they could comprise eleven million.

More people, naturally, translates into more visits to the Smokies and other parks and forests. Here's one of my least favorite stats from the report: today, there's about one-third of an acre of federal or state park land for every Southerner; by 2060, there'll likely be less than one-sixth of an acre.

Want to car camp? Expect as many as two-thirds more campers—and RVs, trailers, and traffic jams—at your favorite roadside sleep spot. Backcountry camping? Wilderness areas in the South's national forests could see a 72 percent increase in visitors.

Depressed, and determined to reach real wilderness before dark, I hurry down 441 to the abandoned village of Elkmont. The old timber town once bustled with a schoolhouse, a Baptist church, a post office, a baseball team, and a rail line running from Clingmans Dome to Townsend, Tennessee. The Little River Lumber Company chopped down nearly eighty thousand acres and began selling lots in 1910, first to the Appalachian Club and, two years later, to the Wonderland Club. The Appalachian was a social club founded by Knoxville swells who wanted to fish, swim, party, and get away from the summer heat. The Wonderland started as a members-only resort before allowing guests at its hotel and cabins. It closed in 1992 and, two years later, Elkmont was placed on the National Register of Historic Places.

I shoulder my pack and head up the abandoned rail line now known as the Little River Trail. The river hums, cascading around huge boulders and creating mini-waterfalls. I pass fly fisherwomen returning from a day on the exceptionally clean river, which is home to a wealth of aquatic life, including the rare eastern hellbender, the salamander fondly known as a "snot otter," "lasagna lizard," or "devil dog." The trail is also renowned for the thousands of synchronous fireflies that, in late spring, light up the forest in a surrealistic light show. (The Park Service runs a lottery to manage the legions of bug lovers.)

I soon pass the day trippers and have the forest seemingly to myself. The oaks, poplars, and sycamores cloak the river in summerlike green. After an hour I reach my permitted camp site, but continue up the trail a bit to a hidden stretch of river shrouded in rhododendrons. The drought precludes a campfire, but that's okay. Reclining on a boulder, inches above the water, bourbon in hand, I let dusk melt over the forest, and me. I'm all alone. Except, maybe, for the bears that, I hear, are as thick as two per square mile in the Smokies. I hang my food bag a good distance away before crawling into my tent.

The next morning I wake early, pack quickly, and hotfoot it down the trail to my car and, sigh, Gatlinburg. I'm on a mission, albeit an unpleasant one, and I want to get in and out of town before the crowds. Three years earlier, a wildfire fueled by eighty-seven-mile-per-hour winds escaped the Smokies and danced malevolently around downtown Gatlinburg. Fourteen people died. Twenty-five hundred buildings were destroyed. It was the deadliest wildfire in Tennessee history.

According to the National Weather Service, "exceptional" drought plagued the Southeast in 2016. The summer was the second hottest in history. I was covering the Rough Ridge fire one hundred miles to the south a week before the Smokies burned. Fifty thousand acres in Georgia and North Carolina were scorched; thankfully, the fire hit a little-populated area along the border.

I once thought Southern wildfires were rare. I was wrong. While the West loses more acres annually to fire, the Southeast tallies more wildfires than any region in the country. Most fires, including the Chimney Tops 2 Fire that started November 23, 2016, are arson. Two boys— one fifteen, the other seventeen—were hiking the well-traveled Chimney Tops Trail while playing with matches. Fire spread slowly through the desiccated underbrush but didn't unduly alarm park officials who scouted the trail that afternoon. And the terrain, dotted with big boulders and imposing cliffs, was too steep for a fire line, according to an after-action report by the Park Service. It was a holiday week, too, and most firefighters were gone. An eighth of an inch of rain fell the following day, Thanksgiving, further assuaging Park Service fears. By then, only eight acres had burned.

The fire grew slowly over the weekend, to thirty-five acres by late Sunday, and remained near the twin-peaked Chimney Tops. Park officials began to worry; the forecast predicted strong winds Monday. Helicopters made their first water drops. Ground crews, though, deemed the terrain too risky and stayed away.

Everything changed Monday. High winds from the south and west swooped through the valleys, up the drainage basins, and over the ridges. The fire jumped US 441 and the Little Pigeon River and ignited the western slope of Mount Le Conte early in the day. More than 250 acres were burning. It spotted again—hopscotching back over the highway—and scorched a fifty-acre tract. And again, just a mile and a half from Gatlinburg.

"It bounced from ridgetop to ridgetop," the incident commander told investigators. It "jumped roads, jumped trails, jumped wet drainages and wide creeks. . . . There's no way this stuff could be humanly stopped."

Just about all of the hundred firefighters, with their trucks and bulldozers, were sent to Mynatt Park on the edge of town and just a short hop to cabins, hotels, and downtown Gatlinburg. It was a last line of defense, and it was futile. The fire crossed 441 yet again and headed towards Ober Gatlinburg and its ski trails. Telephone poles snapped in the wind. Transformers exploded. Buildings all over town, mostly on the outskirts, were on fire. Downed trees blocked escape routes. Firefighters were overwhelmed, unable to respond to every blaze. Thick smoke disoriented the town's panicked residents. Some never got out.

A visitor would be hard-pressed today to find signs of the fiery apocalypse that descended upon the "Gateway to the Great Smoky Mountains" (smoky indeed). I tried, though. I read a bunch of articles and plotted a map of Gatlinburg's homes, shops, and hotels torched by the fire. Empty concrete pads on the eastern and northern hillsides overlooking the downtown offered unmistakable proof of the fire's wrath. Only the automobile bays remained at Ogle's Market and 73 Car Wash. El Soñador restaurant was gone, as was the Country Town N' Suites motel, except for a set of concrete steps leading nowhere. At the Robert E. Lee Motel, a cliffside lodge renowned for shuffleboard, wall-to-wall carpets, and rocking-chair ambiance, a worker paused to assess the charred mess.

"Everything burned," she said.

Will you rebuild?

"We'll see."

Most of Gatlinburg voiced no such hesitation. The Roaring Fork Baptist Church ("Come grow with us") rebuilt quickly with original stone and beige siding. The Alamo Steakhouse looks as it did before the fire. Builders are busy replacing the cabins that once dotted the hillsides surrounding town. In the two years since the fire, Gatlinburg issued four hundred permits to rebuild properties. In the two years before, it had issued sixty-one.

Henri Grissino-Mayer isn't surprised. But he is worried. Grissino-Mayer, a geography professor at the University of Tennessee in nearby Knoxville, and an expert on wildfires, spent the previous decade giving lectures entitled "Will Our Great Smoky Mountains One Day Go Up in Flames?" The professor describes the cabins rising one on top of the other as "fire dominoes."

Gatlinburg is an extreme, though increasingly common, example of the "wildland–urban interface" phenomenon reconfiguring the American landscape where houses encroach upon forests and grasslands. WUI (pronounced "woo-eee") has been the fastest-growing type of land use in the country in the last thirty years. Homes near forests pose two problems: more people means more chances a fire will start; and the wildfires, in turn, pose a greater risk to lives and property. Unlike rural, uninhabited areas, firefighters can't just let the fires burn themselves out.

Nationwide, one of every three homes sits in the WUI, according to the University of Wisconsin. Increasingly, Americans are answering Muir's call of the mountains: more than forty-three million new houses were added to the WUI between 1990 and 2010. And the South notched the greatest increase in WUI land in the country. Sixty percent of Sevier County, home to Gatlinburg, lies smack dab in WUI World.

"This is the greatest concentration of people in the wildland–urban interface in the nation," Grissino-Mayer told the *Knoxville News Sentinel.* "We are ground zero."

A warming climate, and droves of mountain-loving newcomers, will only make matters worse. Retiring baby boomers. Climate refugees. (A 2017 University of Georgia study predicts that rising seas will send tens of thousands of coastal residents to the southern Appalachians.) Snowbirds disdainful of Florida. Covid-fleeing urbanites. And, of course, all the service industry workers to cater to the invading hordes. With the national forests and parks off-limits to development, new homes will edge closer and closer to the wild—with deadly consequences. The Forest Service predicts a fourfold increase in the number of acres burned by wildfires by 2050.

I escape Gatlinburg and head home to Atlanta, but not before one final Smoky Mountains adventure. Alas, I'm too late. The early-morning crowds beat me to Cades Cove, the postcard-perfect valley with fields of goldenrod surrounded by fog-shrouded mountains. Cades Cove is the most-visited Smoky attraction due to the eleven-mile loop road that plugs visitors into nature without their having to leave their SUVs.

That, and the "bear jams" when traffic comes to a dead stop so visitors can snap photos of the park's iconic bruins. Sometimes people get out of their cars for a better shot. Sometimes they feed the bears. Sometimes people are dumb. Park Service signs warn self-styled bear whisperers to stay fifty yards away or else they "can be injured or killed."

It's not surprising that Cades Cove was almost destroyed. In the 1930s, a governor worried that nobody would visit the "impoverished farmland" and wanted to build a lake with a dam sixty feet high and four hundred feet wide because, after all, dam-building was all the rage at the time and the Western parks all had lakes for recreation, didn't they? Thankfully, environmentalists won the day.

I join the five-mile-per-hour procession of cars and trucks on the loop road. The fog lifts. The scenery is lovely. But no tourist-friendly bears materialize on cue. A gristmill, three churches (Primitive Baptist, Missionary Baptist, Methodist) and numerous log houses and barns have been restored. A white hearse waits outside the one-room Methodist church while funeral-goers mill about. It reminds me of the Chimney Tops fire. Charges were dropped against the boys who allegedly set the fire, with the prosecutor pointing instead at the "unprecedented, unexpected, and unforeseeable" winds. The Park Service's after-action report blames understaffing and an inability to anticipate the danger posed by the fire. It also takes the Service to task for not warning townspeople quickly enough. And it offers a warning.

"To be sure," the report says, "these same conditions are likely to align again in the future to allow for a large-scale wildfire that leaves the park and burns into the urban interface."

CHAPTER 6

More Rain, More Heat, and More Trouble

Look closely at nature. Every species is a masterpiece, exquisitely adapted to the particular environment in which it has survived. Who are we to destroy or even diminish biodiversity?
—Edward O. Wilson, *Half-Earth: Our Planet's Fight for Life*

Boone, North Carolina — It's a wonder anything survives the ice, snow, and winds that pummel the ridge, let alone the delicate-seeming yellow flowers known as spreading avens. The lovely, long-stemmed perennials are exceedingly rare, officially listed as endangered, and found only in the intemperate highlands of North Carolina and Tennessee. They sprout from shallow acidic soils underlying craggy rock faces and grassy heath balds. At times blasted with full sun, but mostly shrouded in mist, the avens are survivors, Ice Age throwbacks that refuse to die. *Geum radiatum* is only known to exist in fourteen places, including hard-to-find alpine redoubts reached via deer trail or brambly bushwhacking.

And that is where I find Chris Ulrey, the world's preeminent spreading avens expert. Granted, not a lot of botanists devote their professional lives to spreading avens. And Chris, a plant ecologist with the

National Park Service, doesn't focus solely on that particular flower, aka Appalachian avens and cliff avens. Yet I know of no other *Geum* aficionado who, over two weeks each of the last twenty summers, has scoured the highest peaks of the Blue Ridge monitoring the elusive flowers. He has also written a series of authoritative reports on the plant's status and prospects, all of which underscore that avens are heading down the extinction highway. The culprit? Climate change. Avens, after all, move higher and higher up the mountains in search of cooler climes. So what happens when there's nowhere else to go? I'd come to this off-piste mountaintop—whose name Chris requests I not mention so rare-plant hunters and rock climbers don't destroy the remaining avens—to find out.

But Chris is busy, dangling from a hundred-foot rope attached to a vertiginous cliff, rappelling between clumps of avens. At least, I'm told by a colleague that he is. I can't see Chris. He's shrouded in thick fog on the other side of a fifty-foot ravine that promises, with one slippery misstep, a most painful death. Occasionally, I can hear Chris. He chirps out the statistics of the latest avens colony—length, width, number of rosettes—either marveling at their hardiness or lamenting their fragility. The colleague duly takes notes and quickly compares them to the flower's status the previous year. A full scientific accounting will come later. Today is all about the search, and the scenery.

Chris is in his element.

"This is awesome," he yells skyward, a break in the fog allowing a glimpse of the beatific botanist, head thrown back, arms outstretched, beseeching the heavens.

Most Southerners, if they think about climate change at all, think about the weather. They know about record-breaking temperatures and increasingly nasty storms. They'll mention droughts or rising seas. They may even connect wildfires and flooding to a warming world. Yet there's a widespread perception that climate change is mainly a coastal phenomenon. Seventy percent of Americans who live within twenty-five miles of a coast say the changing climate affects their local community, according to a 2020 Pew Research Center survey. Of those who live more than three hundred miles from the coast, only fifty-seven percent say it affects them.

Perhaps the findings aren't that surprising. After all, if you witness ever-higher tides and more frequent coastal floods, you're more likely to believe that something strange is going on. The changes are more subtle, and longer range, across the mountains. But those same climatic forces—higher temperatures, more (and less) precipitation, extreme weather—that hammer the lowlands bedevil every region and ecosystem in the world. And, make no mistake, a warming world portends drastic and irreparable harm to the southern Appalachians, which Muir labeled "the most beautiful deciduous forest I ever saw."

He never made it to this corner of North Carolina, crossing the Old North State's southwestern corner instead. The same hills and vales that so entranced Muir during his post–Civil War trek kept a grip on his imagination for the rest of his life. It would take three decades, but Muir eventually returned to the verdant, botanically rich forests of the South. By then he was the nation's most famous naturalist, his name synonymous with mountains, glaciers, Yosemite, Alaska, and the Sierra Club. In an 1898 letter to Charles Sprague Sargent, the Harvard professor and the nation's top tree expert, Muir wrote: "I don't want to die without once more saluting the grand, godly, round-headed trees of the east side of America that I first learned to love and beneath which I used to weep for joy when nobody knew me."

That fall, Muir joined Sargent and William Canby, a banker and well-regarded amateur botanist, on a month-long tour of the southern Appalachians. They visited Roan Mountain, the five-mile-long *massif* of alpine grasslands that explode in a riot of red, pink, and white rhododendrons each spring. Muir, under the weather from days of heavy travel, reposed at the Cloudland Hotel, which straddled the North Carolina–Tennessee line and afforded magnificent views. "All the landscapes in every direction are made up of mountains, a billowing sea of them without bounds as far as one can look," he wrote to wife Louie, "and every mountain hill & ridge & hollow is densely forested with so many kinds of trees their mere names would fill this sheet."

Muir made no mention of the spreading avens. Other botanical luminaries did. André Michaux, the famed French botanist, visited Roan in the late eighteenth century and shipped specimens back to Paris. Asa Gray, the ensuing century's botanist extraordinaire, found avens atop Roan "in the greatest profusion."

Chris Ulrey has studied Roan's avens every July for two decades. Compared to The Unnamed Mountain (TUM) that I promised to not identify, Roan is a walk in the park. Motorists can practically drive to the top of the 6,300-foot mountain. Its accessibility, though, makes it an imperfect barometer of the plant's health. Hikers who leave the AT and other trails trample or pick the flowers. Rock climbers, acid rain, second homes, and ski resorts harm avens elsewhere. But TUM, perhaps more than any other remote mountaintop, offers a truer— and scarier—barometer of the changing climate's impact on avens and mountain ecology.

"It's pristine; nobody comes out here. There are no recreational impacts," Chris says. "It's one of the largest populations. We haven't recorded many deaths. But we rarely see any young plants, which is a concern. If it wasn't a long-lived plant, it definitely would've gone extinct long ago."

Avens, most likely, were more abundant at the end of the last Ice Age ten thousand years ago. As the glaciers retreated, and the South warmed, the plants were trapped, unable to migrate farther north. So they crept up the mountains in search of cooler, wetter locales. They settled in their alpine homes above 4,500 feet surrounded by spruces and firs and, in the case of TUM, red oaks. They thrive in humid places with annual temperatures averaging forty-five degrees. Rain and snow amounts may top one hundred inches a year. Most avens face north or northwest, avoiding direct sunlight. Fog is a constant companion. They grow in very shallow soil, as little as two centimeters deep.

Avens made the endangered species list in 1990. A Fish and Wildlife Service "recovery plan" three years later tallied eleven distinct populations of avens; five other groupings had already been extirpated. And eight of the remaining eleven had undergone moderate or significant damage during the previous decade. "Populations are declining and vanishing for reasons that are, in many cases, not clearly understood," Service biologists wrote.

Chris has a pretty good idea why. In 2016, he authored "Life at the Top: Long-Term Demography, Microclimatic Refugia, and Responses to Climate Change for a High-Elevation Southern Appalachian Endemic Plant," which appeared in the journal *Biological Conservation*. Chris wrote that "climate in the southern Appalachians is projected to rapidly change over the coming few decades [and] is likely to be particularly threatening to rare plants because of their narrow distributions, small population sizes, and specific habitat requirements."

He's blunter on top of TUM.

"At the pace we're going," he says, "they will not be able to adapt and move—they'll just blink out."

One hundred miles southwest of the unnamed ridge, outside the town of Otto, North Carolina, sits the Coweeta Hydrologic Laboratory nestled in a corner of the Nantahala National Forest. Coweeta is one of the nation's oldest ecological research stations. Its five thousand acres stretch across the same-name valley in the shadow of Albert Mountain, which the Appalachian Trail also crosses. The low-slung stone buildings,

CCC-built bridges and weirs, as well as the wealth of red maples, tulip poplars, and white pines, conjure a corporate retreat or rustic rehab facility. Peter Caldwell, though, insists that the lab is a must-see stop on any mountain climate tour.

I met Peter, a PhD research hydrologist with the US Forest Service's Southern Research Station, the year before at a sustainable-forestry confab in Atlanta. He invited me to Coweeta to learn about the ever-changing interplay of water, wood, and weather. Established during the Depression, the lab originally focused on the impact of timber harvesting on soil and water. Its portfolio has since broadened considerably into water quality, land use, erosion, streamflow, prescribed fire, acid rain, and invasive species. Coweeta is widely known for deciphering the interplay between forest and water. Streams that flow from the southern Appalachians, after all, serve as the drinking water source for ten million people. Coweeta's research is priceless in understanding the future of an ever-sprawling, drought-challenged, climate-hammered South. Which is why I visit Peter.

"This is our main climate station," he says after a short stroll under a blazing July sun to a fenced-in field. "It's done continuous measurements since 1934—through furloughs, World War II, and even pandemics."

It's an atmospheric scientist's wet dream. Or maybe a twisted gnome's playground with all manner of gauges, buckets, scales, tubs, tubes, thermometers, anemometers, and hygrothermographs. One measures relative humidity. Another gauges evapotranspiration. Yet another tracks solar insolation, or the amount of electromagnetic energy—sunlight—that reaches the Earth's surface. All of the meteorological doodads and doohickeys record the vagaries of temperature and precipitation. And they all tell stories of a changing climate.

Take the pan evaporation tub, for example. Two inches of water sit in a round metal tub, big enough to wash three babies simultaneously, along with a micrometer that measures how much water evaporates.

Temperature, rainfall, humidity, wind, and solar radiation all conspire to determine, by day's end, whether water vaporizes or consolidates. The information is critical to understanding the health of trees, plants, and soils. Until 1949, the amount of water in the pan grew an average of fifty millimeters per decade. Since 1997, the pan has lost forty-six millimeters per decade. Evaporation rates correlate unmistakably with a warming world.

Peter, like a patient high school science teacher, explains it so that even a dimwitted student like me can understand. "The mean annual air temperature has been increasing since the eighties by one half of a degree Celsius per decade," the bespectacled hydrologist in blue jeans and plaid shirt tells me. "And, since the seventies, we've seen a decline in stream flow that's partly related to the increase in air temperatures. All of this has an effect on the vegetation. And much of it is climate-driven."

Temperature. Precipitation. Drought. Flood. Climate change is most readily understood via the basics of meteorology. Southerners are weather experts. They know that an already-hot region is getting hotter with nastier storms. (As I write this, Hurricane Laura, which exploded from a Category-1 to a Category-4 cyclone while crossing the freakishly warm waters of the Gulf of Mexico, is bearing down on Louisiana. Three massive wildfires threaten to incinerate California. And the mercury just hit 130 degrees Fahrenheit in Death Valley, possibly a world record.) In the South, 2019 was the hottest year on record and 2017 and 2016 weren't far behind. Summer in Atlanta runs from June to November. Miami endured its earliest heat wave on record in April 2020: the temps hit at least ninety degrees for three straight days. People say, "Oh, it's the South. It's supposed to be hot in the summer." True, but what's different—and freaky—is how hot the nights are becoming. A century ago, the Southeast experienced seven nights a year when the temperature stayed above seventy-five degrees. Now, the temps remain above seventy-five fifteen nights per year on average. Some areas can expect an additional one hundred very warm nights by the end of the century, according to the Fourth National Climate Assessment.

In all, the temperature in the Southeast is expected to rise an average of four to eight degrees Fahrenheit by 2100. "Under the higher scenario"—which is consistent with pre-Covid levels of fossil fuel consumption—"nights above 80°F and days above 100°F, now relatively rare occurrences, become commonplace."

The consequences will be deadly. Already, the Southeast is the most dangerous region for farmers, foresters, hunters, fishers, construction workers, and garbagemen, accounting for nearly 70 percent of all heat-related deaths nationwide. By 2090, the intense heat could cost the region forty-seven billion dollars in lost productivity. Not surprisingly, the poor will suffer most. An alarming 2017 study in the journal *Science* details the economic inequality wrought by climate change. It modeled twenty-first-century weather patterns in every US county and how rising temperatures and sea levels, and other climatic impacts, will hurt the workingman and -woman. Harvests will decline. Jobs will disappear. Energy costs will soar. Wildfires will destroy homes and businesses. Heat waves will turbocharge cardiac and pulmonary diseases.

"We are really sure the South is going to get hammered," Solomon Hsiang, a professor of public policy at the University of California, Berkeley, told *The Atlantic*. "The South is really, really negatively affected by climate change, much more so than the North. That wasn't something we were expecting going in."

The heat surge won't be restricted to the Deep South. This century's first decade, for example, was North Carolina's warmest ever. The relatively cool southern Appalachians won't be exempt from the coming heat wave, either. Far western North Carolina can expect twenty or more additional "very hot" days per year by 2060, according to the state's 2020 climate report. Conversely, the region could see as many as fifty additional nights a year when the temperature fails to drop below thirty-two degrees. And it may never again drop below zero in the winter. "The cool temperatures to which these forests have adapted may no longer exist in the southern Appalachians, putting the viability of the high-elevation ecosystems at risk," the report states.

At least the blueberries will be happy. Warmer falls and winters mean longer growing seasons. Plant hardiness zones, devised by the US Department of Agriculture as a guide for farmers and gardeners, are creeping north. The moderate zone currently found in western North Carolina, for example, will migrate to West Virginia by 2040. You'll easily be able to grow a Georgia peach in the Smokies. A Georgia farmer already grows mandarin oranges near Statesboro, two hundred miles north of Florida's orange belt.

Warmer weather hits Southerners smack in the nose. Literally. A 2021 study reveals that pollen season in the United States and Canada starts twenty days earlier, and lasts ten days longer, than it did in 1990. And there's 21 percent more pollen in the air now than before. In Atlanta, green clouds of pollen fill the air in the early spring, coating cars, benches, and playgrounds. After a rain, puddles turn green. Mosquitoes, too, enjoy the warmer weather. Tennessee didn't report any West Nile cases in 2001. They've since logged more than 325, according to the Centers for Disease Control. The same bugger that spreads the West Nile virus, the *Aedes* mosquito, also transmits the Zika, yellow fever, chikungunya, and dengue viruses. Dengue outbreaks were reported in Florida and Texas in 2013. The Climate Assessment says "summer increases in dengue cases are expected across every state in the Southeast."

Humans, of course, aren't the only victims of a warming world. Robins migrate sooner. Black bears hibernate less. And eastern brook trout, the piscatory equivalent of spreading avens, swim farther upstream in search of cooler water. Highly prized by fly-fishers who now must schlep higher up the mountains of the Pisgah, Nantahala, and Smokies, the native brookies could use a break. They survived the wholesale logging of forests, rampant dam-building, and the importation of nonnative trout only to face the existential threat of global warming. Their protective canopy of majestic hemlocks—"the redwoods of the East"—succumbs to a particularly pernicious aphid-like bug imported from Japan. Nearly half of the trout's historic habitat in the cool Appalachian mountains has disappeared. But it's not just warmer water that sends the fish up a creek. Their food, including stoneflies, is also decamping for cooler climes.

In fact, the entire forest is succumbing to climate change. And folks well downstream will suffer. As Peter writes in a 2016 study, "Climate change and forest disturbances are threatening the ability of forested mountain watersheds to provide the clean, reliable, and abundant fresh water necessary to support aquatic ecosystems and a growing human population."

He and I leave the field of climate thingamajigs and walk up a gravel road to Weir No. 9. The CCC-built rock dam sits under a canopy of pines, poplars, and rhododendrons where locals (and a few scientists) love to swim. The trapezoidal weir has measured water flow every five minutes for the last eight decades. Not surprisingly, less water runs over the weir today than before. The climatic math is pretty straightforward. Temperatures at Coweeta have been rising steadily since 1980. Higher temps lead to higher evaporation rates from surrounding trees, underbrush, and soils. Consequently, the yield from Coweeta's watersheds drops more than six millimeters every year.

Peter cautions that not all of the reduced water flow is attributable to a warming climate. After all, 2018 was the wettest year on record in nearby Asheville. And the physiographic makeup of the southern Appalachian forest, for example, has undergone profound changes during the last century, beginning with the denuding of the hills and hollows for timber. Once the chestnuts, oaks, and hemlocks started disappearing, streamflows declined. They were replaced by mesophytic tree species—tulip poplar, red maple, yellow birch, Virginia pine—which drink a lot more water. Meanwhile, water-guzzling, quick-spreading rhododendron filled in the understory.

Peter estimates the new and less-improved forest accounts for nearly 20 percent of the decreased water yield. "The warming climate, though, plays a big part in the amount of water, and the quality of water, that flows from Coweeta to the sea," he says. "And with more and more severe droughts since the 1980s, the watershed is under siege."

A warming world doesn't necessarily mean a drier one. The South, historically, has been blessed with ample rain, which is why everybody from Bill Gates and Chinese investors to potato chip makers flock to well-watered sections of Georgia, Florida, and South Carolina to grow fruits and vegetables. Annual rainfall totals haven't changed much in the last century. Climate models can't predict whether they'll change much in the next century, either. What is changing, though, is *how* the rain falls. Not since 1900 in North Carolina have there been as many heavy rain events—three inches or more in a day—as there were between 2015 and 2019. By century's end, the number of extreme rainfalls could double, according to the National Climate Assessment. More frequent and more intense hurricanes have something to do with the surge in deluges. But higher temperatures are also culpable. Hotter air leads to greater evaporation from soils, plants, and lakes. Once the water vapor condenses, heavier rains, and flooding, ensue.

The South was battered by storms in October 2015. A deluge early in the month hammered the Carolinas. Mount Pleasant, on South Carolina's coast, got a whopping twenty-seven inches of rain. Sumter, in the middle of the state, got twenty-one inches. A monstrous hurricane wasn't to blame. Instead, a deep trough of moisture from the Gulf sat on South Carolina for five days. Rivers spilled over their banks. Dams breached.

One hundred and sixty thousand homes flooded. Damage topped two billion dollars. Nineteen people died in the thousand-year monsoon.

A year after the historic floods, a killer drought gripped much of the Carolinas, Georgia, and Alabama, with wildfires ravaging the Smokies and the Chattahoochee National Forest. September–October was the driest two-month period ever recorded at Coweeta. Five years earlier, Georgia suffered its second driest summer. Five years earlier than that, Alabama notched "by far the most devastating drought ever recorded," according to the US Army Corps of Engineers. And five years earlier . . .

"Drought impacts almost every aspect of southeastern forests," says Steve McNulty, a colleague of Peter's who runs the Southeast Regional Climate Hub. "Climate change increases the likelihood for severe droughts, now and into the future."

It's hard to recognize, at first, the impact of drought on a forest. Coweeta, for example, is a lush, water-blessed oasis of green where certain ridge tops receive ninety inches of rain a year. Climb the fire tower atop Albert Mountain, though, and gray and brown splotches of dead trees dot the landscape below. Some are hemlocks sucked dry of sap by woolly adelgids. Others, though, are pine trees whose inner bark is under attack from southern pine beetles. Sustained drought stresses pines, allowing the tiny beetles to readily burrow under the bark and build S-shaped tunnels in which they lay their eggs. The tunnels girdle the tree, blocking food and water passageways. The 2016 drought led to "gobs of dead pine trees," Peter says.

As our climate tour ends, he points me to Watershed No. 1. It's a short drive to the experimental corner of the forest planted in white pines in 1957. I pull off the gravel road and walk up the hill. A thicket of pines stands straight, tall and sickly, their lower branches covered in dead brown needles. Their tops, though, remain green. But not for long.

Chris Ulrey recites the safety protocols by memory in the parking lot of Elk Knob State Park, outside Boone. It's a cool and rainy July morning, more early fall than mid-summer, but the alpine forests of the southern Appalachians aren't known for seasonal conformity. I camped in the rain the night before at another state park near Asheville, with the intention of easily reaching Chris in the morning. But I miscalculated the winding mountain roads and arrived late. Chris and crew nonetheless welcome me to their spreading avens fan club. He's joined by a biology professor from nearby Appalachian State University, a state biologist, and a couple of avens-loving volunteers, including a high school sophomore who rock-climbs with the best of them.

Chris gathers us in a circle alongside his government-issued Ford F-150. He warns of hawthorn bushes that slice through jeans; of yellow jackets drawn to the same cliffs as avens; of unexpected lightning strikes on rocky peaks; and of hypothermia that can surprise on sixty-degree days.

We climb into two pickups with four-wheel drive and head north to TUM. We turn off the state highway onto a dirt road that leads to Rooster Hollow, so named by Chris for the three dozen mini-Quonset huts perched on a hillside that serve as shelters for the fighting cocks. A handful of abandoned homes and trailers, as well as salvaged cars and trucks, peek out from the kudzu and blackberry bramble. Chris recalls an earlier visit when a young boy appeared on the side of the road in a grubby T-shirt that read, "Be Glad I'm Not Your Child." Two farm gates, both locked, block our way. To the left, a pasture, stream, and cows. To the right, a smattering of hardwoods and uniformly planted pines. Chris unlocks the gate on the right and we jounce upward through tall grasses, purple-flowering raspberries, and black-eyed Susans that brush the truck like a car wash.

Our slow ascent gives me time to quiz Chris.

He grew up in Weaverville, outside Asheville, where his parents ran a nursery and landscaping business. The "artificialness" of the nursery fueled a desire for the real thing. After a stint in the army, Chris went up the road to Mars Hill College (now University) where he met a girl (his future wife) whose father taught botany. He did his graduate and PhD work in botany at North Carolina State University. "I always loved the mountains and wanted to specialize in the southern Appalachians," Chris says.

He's been at the Blue Ridge Parkway—the nearly five-hundred-mile ribbon of protected mountains and valleys that connects the Smokies to the Shenandoah—since 1999. As the park's top botanist, he focuses on the conservation of rare plants, as well as damage wrought by invasives, pests, and diseases. "I call myself a plant ecologist," says Chris, fifty-three, lanky with white beard and tortoiseshell glasses. "I want to know what makes a plant tick."

The rutted road ends, so we continue on foot. Under red oaks, yellow birch, and tulip poplars. Through thickets of rhododendron, hawthorn, and flame azalea. Around coneflowers, galax, and Turk's cap lilies. When we can, we follow the narrow trails carved by deer and bears and marked occasionally by scat. We hike below the ridge line in a northeasterly direction. It rains off and on, and fog inhibits views beyond fifty yards.

"This is the only avens population we're monitoring in the amphibolite range," Chris says over a quick lunch. "The plants here are different than those further south. They're very large, and they flower more than in other places. I'm interested to see if they respond differently here."

The amphibolites, a series of 5,000-foot peaks untouched by glaciers, run along the Appalachian spine across the northwest corner of North Carolina. Pockets of calcium-rich soil poke through the metamorphic rock and nourish rare and disjunct species, including trailing wolfsbane, purple-fringed orchids, and spreading avens. Of the fourteen avens locations that Chris monitors, ten are located on protected state or federal land. The amphibolites offer their best chance at survival.

"These are refugia for these alpine relicts, little islands of suitable habitat," Chris says. "Climate change, in the past, was more gradual, so species like the spruce and the fir were able to move uphill. But now there are no more places to go. And climate change is happening faster. Where are the avens going to go?"

Lunch over, Chris and two climbers gear up and head to the cliff. The rest of us skirt the ravine and settle on a wet and narrow ledge from which to monitor the rappelers' progress. The fog, though, keeps us from seeing anything but the wind-whipped rhododendrons on our flanks. Chris has partitioned the cliff into thirds; each climber is responsible for the avens within their transect. Individual plant sites were marked and numbered with blue aluminum tags a decade ago.

Chris descends to his first clump of flowers. He yells out the number on the tag to Sharon Bischoff, the state park biologist next to me, who records the information on a spreadsheet. He measures the length and width of the plant, as well as the number of flowers. He tallies the number of rosettes. Sharon compares this year's recording to last year's, guides Chris to the next clump, and exhorts him onward. Her laugh ricochets off the rock face. Chris, we think, drops lower down the rock face.

"This is extreme botany," says Matt Estep. He's the Appalachian State professor, a plant geneticist who specializes in the rare and relict plants of the Blue Ridge. "You're looking at the last of a species," he continues. "There's just so few of the plants left. But this is one of the best sites for 'em. So it's special."

The fog breaks. We see Chris, mid-cliff, and tenth-grader Virginia Ward, near the bottom. Marietta Shattleroe, who has interned with Chris and studied under Matt, remains invisible, tangled in rhododendrons on the far side of the cliff.

Chris continues downward, repeating in almost monotone fashion the demographics of each marked avens, and evincing little outward alarm over the avens' condition. Earlier, he told me that deaths on

TUM are few—less than 10 percent blink out from year to year—and that these avens may be decades old. But climate change is a nefarious beast. The plants themselves may not be succumbing to warmer temperatures just yet. But that doesn't mean they're not already battered by the changing climate.

Chris explains: "We don't see big changes year to year, but I'm concerned about climate change. One of my theories is that these mountains used to stay cold all winter and the avens were encased in ice. Now they're subjected to multiple freeze-thaw cycles when water gets into the rocks, freezes, and expands, causing cracks to get bigger. Eventually, the rock splits and falls apart—and the avens fall off, too. At two sites we've had major rock slides."

He reaches the bottom of the cliff. On cue, the fog dissipates, the clouds part and the valley below heaves into view. The tiny red-roofed barns, emerald-green pastures, and Christmas tree farms paint a strikingly beautiful picture, a Grandma Moses tableau from a mile in the sky. The ridge–valley pattern extends a hundred miles northward into Virginia. A red-tailed hawk rides the currents above. And, right below, on the cliff face now bathed in sunlight, dozens of long-stemmed, bright yellow spreading avens bob in the breeze.

Chris and Virginia begin their ascent. Marietta, finally disentangled, inches down her transect.

"Okay, Marietta, I'm done. I'm going back to the top to have some hot chocolate," Chris chides.

Shorn of ropes and helmets, the climbers are ecstatic. Until I start asking pointed questions.

"Nothing seems dramatically different than last year," Chris says. "We're looking for long-term trends. We'll see declines first at the lowest-elevation populations. The decline could be slow and gradual or rapid. Right now we are only seeing very small changes, usually due to stochastic events, such as rock fall or ice damage."

Change, though, is coming. Under the currently reckless pace of carbon dioxide emissions, Chris predicts, more than 80 percent of the avens' habitat could disappear by 2080. "Radical" loss of their unique ecological homes will occur by 2050, regardless of emission levels. The avens, in essence, have reached their apogee. There's nowhere else for them to go.

So why not move them? Transplant them to other Appalachian peaks farther north? So-called assisted migration is highly controversial among scientists wary of playing God. While Chris says that it's "tempting" to consider translocations, success is unlikely. The spreading avens already live in some of Appalachia's highest, coolest, moistest, and most extreme locations. Plus, there's always a fear of transferring diseases from one region to the next.

"It's just fraught with so many problems. And it feels like gardening," Chris says. "If you take a *Geum* plant to West Virginia, what are you displacing there? I'd rather use the plight of the species to educate people about climate change. We should try to bolster these populations first before we consider assisted migration."

Why? Will mankind really suffer without a near-extinct flower that most people have never heard of?

"I knew you were going to ask that—'Why should we care?'" Chris admits, laughing. "I don't know. I never feel like I have a great answer."

Eventually, though, he comes up with one.

"I feel like this an indicator of the whole ecosystem we live in," Chris says. "It's like the canary in the coal mine. If we ignore this, then what's next? In ecology, everything is connected. The more things we take out of the web of life, the more likelihood that the whole thing collapses. And philosophically, ethically, don't we have a responsibility to take care of these species?"

Virginia listens quietly to our mountaintop conversation. But the girl who first started rappelling for avens at age thirteen and was recently named a Park Service Volunteer of the Year could remain silent no longer.

"A lot of people have the opinion that they'll only fix stuff if it affects their life," Virginia says, her voice rising. "But that thinking is just horrible. How selfish. I just personally wish we could do something to save these species, especially if it's us that's killing them in the first place."

CHAPTER 7

Water Wars

Without water the dust will rise up and cover us as though we'd never existed!
—Robert Towne, *Chinatown*

Suches, Georgia — Troop 134 leaves Decatur early one Saturday morning for the North Georgia mountains and an opportunity for the Boy Scouts to boost their hiking rank. The kids need to prove their backpacking mettle to qualify for an upcoming trip along the Benton Mac-Kaye Trail, as well as weeklong treks in Tennessee and New Mexico. My son Sammy, eleven, is in Alpha Crew. I volunteer to lead the fourteen- and fifteen-year-olds in Charlie Crew so I can get in a longer hike. But I have an ulterior motive, too.

The Chapman family isn't big into Scouting. As a boy in DC, I joined so I could play basketball on Friday nights in the Catholic church basement where the troop met. I lasted about six months. Sammy and Naveed, my younger son, joined to be with buddies. We were all eager participants for about two years, earning merit badges, camping out, making silver turtles (tin-foil-wrapped dinners of potatoes and veggies), until we weren't. My boys lost interest and so did I. One less activity, in between soccer, baseball, basketball, lacrosse, sleepovers, cello lessons, camping trips, spelling bees, and birthday parties, to worry about.

The handful of boys in Charlie Crew muster in the parking lot below Brasstown Bald, the highest point in Georgia, for the blue-blazed hike up a small knob before the switchback descent to State Route 180. Springer Mountain, the terminus of the Appalachian Trail, is only thirty trail miles to the south.

It's early March, one of the most delightful times in the southern Appalachians, with sublime temperatures, roaring streams, and wildflowers aplenty. An orgy of violets, trilliums, blue phlox, bloodroot, and rue anemones line the Jacks Knob Trail. All but one of the boys zip down the trail like frisky foals. "Tom" is a bit overweight, with bad ankles. He doesn't seem to mind falling behind, and neither do I. As the crew leader, it's my job to ensure that all boys arrive safely at Unicoi Gap, nine miles and many hills to the east. Tom proves an engaging talker who will probably make Eagle Scout.

Once we're across the highway it's all up to Hiawassee Ridge, then down to Chattahoochee Gap—and my ultimate goal. Here, just below the ridge, lies the source of the Southeast's most critical, and controversial, river: the Chattahoochee.

No local stream has been so coveted, cussed, used, abused, politicked, and litigated. It is to the Southeast what the Colorado River is to the West. Mark Twain supposedly said, "Whiskey is for drinking—water is for fighting." It's little wonder that politicians and pundits (including hacks like me) label the struggles to share the Chattahoochee among Georgia, Alabama, and Florida as "the water wars." The fight is so nasty, prolonged, and expensive—Georgia and Florida have spent tens of millions of dollars on lawsuits—that it has reached the US Supreme Court not once, but twice. Each time, Georgia prevailed, including in 2021. But when it comes to the Chattahoochee, and the river's importance to Atlanta's growth, southwest Georgia's agriculture, and the Florida Panhandle's ecology and its fishing industry, it ain't ever over. That's why we hacks coined another term for the decades-long water wars: "job security."

I'm a bit giddy about finally eyeballing the source of so much Southeastern treasure and turmoil. For twenty years I traveled the length of the river, from the Poultry Capital of the World (Gainesville) to the Oyster Capital of the World (Apalachicola), where the river lets out into the Gulf of Mexico. I interviewed hundreds of farmers, oystermen, beekeepers, bankers, builders, politicians, utility executives, impassioned biologists, Peachtree Street attorneys, and more hydrologists than you can shake a dowser at along the river's 434-mile run. I wrote thousands of inches dissecting case law, riparian law, and the law of the modern jungle, which dictates that He With The Most Money (i.e., Atlanta) usually wins. But in all that time I never saw the wellspring of all that fuss. So this is my pilgrimage to Lourdes, my hydrological hajj, my Chattahoochee Crusade.

A blue sign with a white W points to the source. I leave the Scouts and bound down the trail. Two hundred steps later I gaze wondrously at . . . *a puddle*. It barely ripples. No gurgling, frothy elixir geysering from the ground. No fountain of cascading rivulets presaging its society-shaking importance. Nothing but a piddly little pool in a dimpled patch of sand surrounded by mud and rock. Upon closer inspection I notice an almost imperceptible aspiration of water coming from the earth. The spring is as cool, fresh, and clean as could be. It's also a complete letdown.

Muir offered a more starry-eyed appreciation of the Chattahoochee. He left North Carolina on September 21 and passed through "a most luxuriant forest" a few miles west of Brasstown Bald. He reached Blairsville ("a shapeless and insignificant village"), where he was kindly received by a farmer whose wife also chewed tobacco and "could spit farther & faster than any male I ever saw."

Muir quickly descended the Appalachian chain, the "hills becoming small, sparsely covered in soil. . . . Every rain robs them of fertility, while the bottoms are of course correspondingly enriched." At noon the next day, he summited the last mountain and was greeted by "a vast uniform expanse of dark pine woods, extending to the sea." Muir followed behind "three poor but merry mountaineers" bouncing along in a rickety mule-drawn wagon. They talked of love, marriage, and the days-long camp meetings, a fixture of North Georgia religious life. Through it all, the older lady clutched a bouquet of French marigolds.

Muir, as usual, was ahead of his scientific time. He presciently divined that the intersection of the high mountains and lowland knobs afforded an unusually rich, and ecologically important, gateway to the South. "These mountains are high ways on which northern plants may extend their colonies southward," Muir wrote in *A Thousand-Mile Walk*. "The plants of the North and of the South have many minor places of meeting along the way I have traveled; but it is here on the southern slope of the Alleghanies that the greatest number of hardy, enterprising representatives of the two climates are assembled."

He identified more than eighty-five species of goldenrod, as well as St. John's wort, fringed gentian, jack-in-the-pulpit, partridge pea, water oak, aster, and holly. He was particularly taken with muscadine grapes.

On the twenty-third, Muir reached "the comfortable, finely shaded little town of Gainesville" and the Chattahoochee—"the first truly southern stream I have met." He was smitten. "The Chattahoochee River is richly embanked with massive, bossy, dark green water oaks," he wrote, "and wreathed with a dense growth of muscadine grapevines, whose ornate foliage, so well adapted to bank embroidery, was enriched with other interweaving species of vines and brightly colored flowers. I was intoxicated with the beauty of these glorious river banks."

Muir stayed with the son of an Indianapolis acquaintance who owned a hundred acres near the river. They spent a couple of days walking along the banks harvesting muscadines for jellies and wine. Muir also collected plants and flowers. His host warned repeatedly of rattlesnakes.

On September 25, he set out for Athens in search of an easily fordable route across the Chattahoochee. He didn't find one. Instead, he meandered southward and got lost in the tall grass and vines along the riverbanks. Frustrated, Muir plunged in. He half-waded and half-swam, with the aid of a stout walking stick, only to get swept downstream in the deceptively strong current. Muir grabbed a rock and pulled himself from the river. He spread his limbs, plants, and money out to dry.

"Debated with myself whether to proceed down the river valley until I could buy a boat, or lumber to make one, for a sail instead of a march through Georgia," he wrote. "But I finally concluded that such a pleasure sail would be less profitable than a walk, and so sauntered on southward as soon as I was dry."

He added, "Rattlesnakes abundant."

Out of the hills of Habersham,
Down the valleys of Hall,
I hurry amain to reach the plain,
Run the rapid and leap the fall,
Split at the rock and together again,
Accept my bed, or narrow or wide,
And flee from folly on every side
With a lover's pain to attain the plain

Far from the hills of Habersham,
Far from the valleys of Hall.

Sidney Lanier, Georgia's most celebrated poet, wrote *The Song of the Chattahoochee* in 1877. The poem extols the many-splendored wonders found along its mostly north–south route—the chestnuts and oaks, the rushes and reeds—but its message is crystal clear. Further along in the poem a line reads, "The voices of Duty call." Lanier knew a century and a half ago that the river's true worth was as a moneymaker to slake the cotton fields, power the cotton mills, and uplift a defeated South. Later, the Chattahoochee would float the barges that carried the commodities, turn the turbines that electrified the factories, and fuel the sprawl that supersized Atlanta. How quaint, indeed, was Muir's Chattahoochee rapture. A decade later, Lanier understood with cold-eyed certainty that the river was but a means to a more propitious end. And for that the state's poobahs named a lake after him.

Upon leaving the hills of Habersham County, the Chattahoochee skirts Atlanta to the west and heads for Columbus. The river tumbles down the "fall line" of rocks and chutes separating the rolling Piedmont from the coastal plain. It now serves as the boundary between Georgia and Alabama. It beelines to Florida, where it joins the Flint River to form the Apalachicola River. Cotton, corn, and peanut fields give way to the swamp forests of the Florida Panhandle, wildlife-rich with Gulf sturgeon, American alligators, red-cockaded woodpeckers, frosted flatwoods salamanders, and purple bankclimber mussels. The freshwater river mixes with the salty Gulf near the port town of Apalachicola and creates a nutrient-rich cocktail that oysters and other aquatic creatures need to survive.

The steamboat *Fanny* was the first to ply the 'Hooch in 1828, beginning Columbus's transformation into a cotton hub. The shallow and rocky fall line, though, kept most vessels from points farther north.

Textile mills lined the river, turning towns like West Point into manufacturing juggernauts. Roads and rails built after World War I rendered steamboat travel obsolete. But hydroelectric power stations proliferated and introduced Reddy Kilowatt to the rural South. The US Army Corps of Engineers built four massive dams and reservoirs along the Chattahoochee, including Buford Dam and Lake Lanier, which filled up in 1957. Congress had decreed that Buford would serve three purposes: flood control, power generation, and navigation. The designation would come back to haunt Georgia a half century later.

Water wars are nastier in the arid West. No river is more contested than the Colorado, which runs through seven states and Mexico. Forty million people depend on the river's steadily dwindling supply. The states agreed in 1922 to divvy up the Colorado, yet they've pretty much been fighting over an "equitable apportionment" ever since. The Green River, which starts in Wyoming and runs through Utah before reaching the Colorado, has long been targeted by Denver and other Front Range cities. The mighty Columbia River has churned controversy and rancor among Canada, Washington, Oregon, Native American tribes, farmers, dam-builders, and salmon-lovers for centuries. And then there's Muir's beloved Tuolumne River in Yosemite, which was dammed in 1923 to satisfy the municipal needs of a booming San Francisco 160 miles away.

"These temple destroyers, devotees of ravaging commercialism, seem to have a perfect contempt for Nature, and, instead of lifting their eyes to the God of the mountains, lift them to the Almighty Dollar," Muir wrote in *The Yosemite*.

Water wars really heat up, though, when the rain and snow stop falling. And, with an ever-warming climate, the battles rage with increasing fervor, even in the comparatively wet South.

The worst drought in a century hit Atlanta in 2007. Only thirty-two inches of rain fell; forty-eight is average. Lake Lanier, the region's main water source, dropped eighteen feet. Boat ramps ended in mud. Long-submerged treetops were exposed. Then-Governor Sonny Perdue declared a state of emergency. Watering lawns was prohibited. October was declared "Take a Shorter Shower Month." Perdue even prayed publicly at the state capitol, asking "God to shower our state, our region, our nation with the blessings of water." State officials worried that Lake Lanier would run dry in four months. "If Lake Lanier or the Chattahoochee below Buford Dam dried up, then the consequences were real," wrote Chris Manganiello in *Southern Water, Southern Power.* "Modern life in the booming Sun Belt would grind to a halt."

Like its rapidly growing *confrères* in Dallas, Denver, and Phoenix, Atlanta depends on a relatively shallow stream for its watery needs. And the Army Corps has long been pilloried in how it shares the Chattahoochee with homeowners, golf courses, Coca-Cola bottlers, peanut farmers, textile mills, barge captains, fishermen, nuclear power plants, and sturgeon. It didn't help that Georgia, Florida, and Alabama did a piss-poor job of managing, let alone quantifying, how much water folks actually used. When the Buford Dam first opened its gates, Metro Atlanta tallied about a million residents. The population had quintupled by 2007. Water usage spiked 30 percent during the 1990s. Conservation was a four-letter word, a jobs-killer in a region where developers were kings and subdivisions were castles. Consider that during the height of the drought the Stone Mountain Park, in an Atlanta suburb, used millions of gallons of water to create a mountain of snow. (Public opprobrium temporarily halted the winter ritual.)

Georgia floundered around in search of more water. Desalinization projects off the coast were proposed. Sticking a very large straw into the Tennessee River, a mile above the Georgia border, gained the support of many legislators, though none in the Volunteer State, where the suggestion was ridiculed. (The mayor of Chattanooga sent a truckload of bottled water to the Georgia capitol to help slake the state's unquenchable thirst.) So Georgia found itself right back where it always is in times of watery woe.

In court.

The "water wars" began in 1990, when Alabama sued the Army Corps to keep the feds from sharing too much water from Lakes Lanier and Allatoona, another reservoir, with upstart Atlanta. Florida and Georgia joined the litigation, which was tabled so the four warring parties could work out a deal. They couldn't, so a slew of lawsuits—eight separate cases in six federal courts—challenged the Army Corps' management of the reservoirs. While Florida and Alabama targeted Atlanta's water use, in 2007 Georgia took aim at the federally endangered mussels and sturgeon in Florida that, by law, must receive an adequate amount of water, too. Governor Perdue filed an injunction demanding that the Army Corps sharply reduce the amount of water leaving Lanier because "certainly America does not believe that mussels and sturgeon . . . deserve more water than the humans, children, and babies in Atlanta."

The rains returned the following year and the drought's grip on Georgia loosened. The legal troubles, though, intensified. In 2009, a district court judge ruled that Congress never authorized Lake Lanier's water for municipal purposes, i.e., Atlanta. In the decision that the judge himself labeled "draconian," he ordered that the metropolitan region return to the water withdrawal levels of the 1970s—when Atlanta was still a Southern backwater. The judge, though, allowed an out: if the three states could agree on a water-sharing plan, he'd rescind his ruling. Georgia, and its gobsmacked business leaders, got religion real quick. A slew of water-boosting, judge-pleasing measures were enacted, including construction of new reservoirs, installation of low-flow toilets in Atlanta, and a moratorium on new wells in southwest Georgia. And then, in 2011, an appellate court overturned the judge's decision, ruling that Congress intended all along for Lake Lanier to serve Metro Atlanta.

Florida and Alabama weren't done fighting, however. The mighty oyster joined the fray.

Florida sued Georgia in 2013, claiming that the paltry amount of water flowing into the Sunshine State killed Apalachicola's oyster industry. The bay once supplied 10 percent of the nation's bivalve bounty, and I, for one, can attest to its sublimity. The case went straight to the US Supreme Court. A "special master," Ralph Lancaster Jr. from Maine, was appointed. The trial in Portland started in fall 2016. I spent a few weeks in the courtroom, tweeting by day and partaking of clam chowder and roasted halibut at night. The ancient, curmudgeonly Lancaster ruled a few months later that, while the oyster had indeed suffered from low river flows, and that Georgia had been "irresponsible" with the river's management, a cap on Georgia's water use wouldn't solve Florida's problems.

Georgia, it seemed, had again prevailed. It hadn't. The Supreme Court justices rejected Lancaster's recommendation and pointedly wondered if a cap on *Flint River* water—used primarily for agriculture—would help save the oysters. Lancaster—who turned out to be a sweet old man— had died, so another special master was chosen. Paul Kelly Jr., a New Mexico appellate court judge steeped in Western water law, determined that the oyster's demise wasn't Georgia's fault and that the Peach State's water use "is not unreasonable or inequitable." This time the Supreme Court agreed.

Case closed, right? Wrong. Florida is considering more legal action. And there's still an outstanding lawsuit filed by Alabama. Like I said, job security.

Unlike Muir, I decided to travel the length of the Chattahoochee River and catch up with some old sources whose livelihoods depend upon its muddied munificence. Each represents one of the warring factions in the never-ending water saga: an Atlanta water engineer; a southwest Georgia farmer; and an Apalachicola oysterman. I'd already visited the source of the not-so-mighty river, tucked into a hillside in the lush Chattahoochee National Forest. Now it was time to head downstream.

First, though, I had to return the Boy Scouts to their parents without anybody getting bitten by a rattlesnake.

Sandy Springs, Georgia
In 1904, the Atlanta Water and Electric Power Company built the city's first hydroelectric dam a dozen miles above town on the Chattahoochee. The then-narrower, faster-flowing river was tamed, and the bustling little city of ninety thousand residents received an electric, and economic, jolt that would help propel it to the forefront of Southern cities. Today, Morgan Falls Overlook Park sits high above the reservoir, with swinging benches and a canopy-shaded playground affording a lovely view of riverside mansions tucked into wooded hills. It's an ideal spot to catch up with Katherine Zitsch. Katherine, officially, is the managing director of the Metropolitan North Georgia Water Planning District. Unofficially, she's Atlanta's water czarina. Her job is to stitch together the water supply, treatment, and conservation efforts of one hundred disparate cities and counties. It's not an easy task, especially when neighboring states accuse you (or, more likely, Georgia's elected officials) of natural-resource profligacy of Amazonian proportions. But Katherine boasts that water withdrawals across the region have dropped 10 percent since 2001, while the population has increased by 1.3 million people. The water district's website says, pointedly, that Metro Atlanta's "per capita water use is lower than in Tallahassee, Birmingham, and Montgomery"—neighboring burgs whose states have sued Georgia to get more Chattahoochee River water for themselves.

Katherine, an engineer, started the job in 2013. Florida sued Georgia later in the year.

"The first four years," she says, deadpan, "were pretty hectic. I was hired to do happy water planning and then, suddenly, I was thrust into litigation."

She got busy. Metro Atlanta had never really tabulated its water consumption before. Katherine's data showed not only a reduction in water withdrawals, but also that the region cleaned and returned two-thirds of the water it used back into the Chattahoochee. Georgia's lawyers hammered home the water-saving measures in reams of pre-trial filings and in the Maine courtroom. It worked. Judge Kelly lauded Metro Atlanta's toilet-rebate, conservation-pricing, and leak-detection programs for slicing water usage.

The Supreme Court's ruling notwithstanding, Katherine knows that Florida and Alabama aren't going away. Southern governors, after all, get great political mileage beating up on rich, sprawling, liberal Atlanta.

"I feel like we're the Hatfields and the McCoys, and we don't really know what we're fighting over," Katherine says. "For Florida, it's less about the economy—the big-picture economy—and more about a way of life. It's about the oystermen who are certainly hurting. For Alabama, it's more complicated. Alabama has a lot of water. For them, it seems, the water wars are about the economy and competition with Georgia."

The water planning district is comprised of civil engineers, elected officials, chamber of commerce executives, and other civic-minded, pro-growth business types. They know in their bones that, without easy access to the Chattahoochee, the region withers and dies. So when Georgia, the day before Katherine and I talked, signed a deal guaranteeing unfettered access to drinking water from Lake Lanier in perpetuity, the hosannas flowed like wine. "A landmark victory," claimed one official. "A milestone," said another. Katherine was more blasé, expecting the deal to prompt more legal challenges. Indeed, in three days she would file an affidavit in Metro Atlanta's water war against Alabama. Job security.

With the legal dominoes falling in line, Georgia clearly has the upper hand. Katherine looks forward to spending more time on non-litigious endeavors like protecting the Chattahoochee watershed and readying communities for climate change. Insulating the region against drought is of paramount importance. Katherine, the daughter of a civil engineer and an English teacher, has studied precipitation records dating back nine hundred years to glean climate trends perhaps useful for an ever-warming future.

"In that time, we had numerous seven-year droughts and one twenty-year drought," she says. "It's easy for us to think we know all the answers, but we don't have any clue what happens in one hundred years. We have to make sure we're ready for longer, deeper droughts than ever seen to date."

She likes some of the ideas floating around. Another reservoir or two. Fill old rock quarries with water. Sewer lines instead of septic tanks. Raise the water level at Lake Lanier by two feet. Aquifer storage and recovery.

I ask Katherine what the Chattahoochee means to her. She looks down at the river.

"It's amazing how far we've come since the 1970s and the Clean Water Act, and the Chattahoochee Riverkeeper filing a lawsuit to clean it up, and all the infrastructure we've put in place up and down the river since," she says. "It's such a beautiful resource. It's amazing how many people are connected to the river. My kids paddleboard right below us here."

She pauses, swaying slightly on her bench.

"We're really sitting in a good place."

Hopeful, Georgia

The soybeans are just now yellowing, so it'll be at least a month until harvest. The sweet corn, tall and tassled, will come in sooner. The peanuts, plumped to perfection by the South Georgia sun and the steady drip-drip of irrigation, are ready to go. But they'll have to wait.

"Everyone around here is behind on peanuts because it rained so much in September," says Casey Cox. "But it's that time of year."

The best time—when all the hard work, luck, and prayer come together in a crop. Casey speaks in near-reverential terms about her farm, Longleaf Ridge, and the bounty it brings. She's the sixth-generation Cox to farm this corner of southwest Georgia. Twenty-four-hundred acres of field and forest. Three miles of Flint River frontage. A house deep in the woods surrounded by longleaf and wire grass. And an Australian shepherd named Sabal who rides shotgun in Casey's F-150.

"This is one of our favorite spots," she says as we pull up to the river, Sabal relegated to the back seat in my honor.

The Flint's running high; a sandbar favored by an eight-foot alligator nicknamed Grendel is all but submerged in the torrents of water. Low-hanging oaks, sycamores, and cypresses line the river. A fish jumps.

"The river is really important to us," Casey continues. "It's so deeply connected to our history and heritage that it feels like a member of the family. It's a really incredible place to go and recharge—there's such a sense of peace. One of the things my dad always says is that the river is part of his soul, and he's instilled that deep spiritual connection to the river in me."

The Flint, though, attracts no such reverence downstream. The crux of Florida's last lawsuit targeted the Flint and the farmers who sucked dry the river and its tributaries, including the underground Floridan aquifer, during the 2012 drought. There wasn't much water left by the time the Flint reached the Florida line. Georgia's farmers, Florida contended, were "consuming exponentially more irrigation water from the Flint River Basin."

Georgia, seeking to mollify the judge, slapped a moratorium on new wells dipping into the Floridan, an underground sea that stretches from Charleston to Miami. Some farmers, ever resourceful, extended their wells down into other, deeper aquifers. Georgia agricultural officials apparently didn't get the message either: they ended up approving another 240 well permits.

At the time, Atlanta officials told me, off the record, they were furious at the profligate ways of their rural Georgia brethren. They were more than willing to throw farmers like the Coxes under the tractor if it meant keeping the urban spigots flowing.

"Agriculture is very complex and risky, and people don't understand the context of the decisions we make—where we get our water, why we irrigate, how we use water," Casey explains while trundling along the riverside trace in her pickup, ponytail bobbing beneath a baseball cap. "There's a big misperception about what we do. Our industry is so critical to the state's economy. If we did not have access to water, we wouldn't be number one in peanut production or number two in cotton. We couldn't grow a crop. Irrigation is the single most effective risk-management tool for farmers."

Casey isn't your typical farmer. For one, she's a woman and there's not another full-time farm boss like her in all of Mitchell County. For another, she's deeply involved in her industry's future, serving at one time or another on the National Peanut Board, the Flint River Soil and Water Conservation District, and a stakeholders group of citizens and scientists trying to resolve the water wars. She's also a diehard environmentalist planting longleaf pines, protecting endangered species, and conserving the ever-precious commodity that grows her crops.

Casey irrigates a thousand acres with a center-pivot system that draws water from the aquifer and dribbles it, in a circular fashion, over the land. Her daddy, Glenn, retrofitted the pivots a decade ago with evaporation-reducing nozzles. Her iPhone receives up-to-the-minute data from moisture sensors buried in the ground. She then programs the pivot where, and how much, to spray. Casey says she's reduced water usage by 20 percent. "In the future," she says, "we'll come up with even more innovative ways to manage water."

She'll have to. The changing climate dictates whether the corn tassels, the peanuts shrivel, or the soybeans drown. Southwest Georgia receives a bountiful fifty-two inches of rain each year, on average—enough precipitation to make a High Plains farmer jealous. But the rain doesn't always fall at just the right time. A warming world makes droughts longer and harsher. Hotter temperatures—South Georgia, by mid-century, can expect temperatures hotter than 105 degrees Fahrenheit for three months of the year—pressure farmers to tap the three underlying aquifers more frequently. And, increasingly, the rain comes in buckets, deluging the crop and then rolling uselessly off the land. Hurricane Michael dumped a half foot of rain on Longleaf Ridge. It hit with hundred-mile-an-hour winds and destroyed Casey's sweet corn, farm office, grain bin, and 15 percent of her timber.

"But we were very blessed compared to some folks who lost so much more," Casey says while passing the rebuilt office. "It was extremely traumatic for the community. Hurricane Michael was a wake-up call for all of us. Conditions in the future will only get worse with climate change. More severe weather, and temperatures, will drastically impact our farm."

We cross the blacktop that runs through her property and pull up alongside a hundred-acre peanut field. Peanut wagons sit off to the side, ready to carry the crop to the buying point in Camilla. A cattle egret rises from a distant pond. Casey jumps from the truck and walks between rows, oblivious to the gnats swarming around her head. She kneels down, rips a plant from the ground, and shakes dirt from the pods.

"They look good," she says. "Want to try one?"

I crack a few shells and put the rest in my pocket. Raw peanuts, like boiled peanuts, aren't my thing. Give me some peanuts and Cracker

Jacks. Or a PB&J and milk. Casey feeds a handful to Sabal, who slurps them down.

We get back in the truck, cross the road, and head for the river. We pass the soybeans and the corn and a fallow field of goldenrod rimmed with black-eyed Susans. Nothing, though, is as beautiful as the well-tended longleaf pine forest. The Coxes are faithful stewards of the iconic trees, which once stretched from Virginia to Texas. The pines are well spaced, towering over a healthy understory of wire grass and saw palmetto. They burn their longleaf forest every couple of years to maintain the unique ecosystem prized by gopher tortoises, red-cockaded woodpeckers, eastern indigo snakes, and other rare species. (Muir, also a longleaf aficionado, "sauntered in delightful freedom" through a stand outside Savannah.)

No sooner do we leave the forest than we're enshrouded in dark swamp. Brambly bushes claw at the truck. The mud reaches axle high. We get stuck. We get out and wedge sticks and rocks in front of, and behind, the tires. Casey tries to rock the Ford free. No luck. She calls her dad to come and pull us out. It gives us more time to talk. I ask about the Supreme Court ruling.

"This will not be the end," she says. "We're just closing one chapter before the next one starts. We need to work together with the other states and the other stakeholders, including the oystermen, to come to a resolution. People try to pit us against the oystermen, but it's much more complicated than that. Our whole life revolves around the natural environment, and so does theirs. We have so much common ground."

Glenn arrives, hooks up the chains, and tries to pull the pickup out of the mud. No luck. He gets stuck, too. He calls the farm manager, who comes with his truck. Finally, we're free. But I can't help but ask Casey if getting bogged down in the mud is a metaphor for the never-ending water wars.

"It feels more like an endless slog," she says.

Eastpoint, Florida

Shannon Hartsfield got his first oyster boat when he was sixteen, a flat-bottomed twenty-one-footer with a Johnson outboard. He'd tong the eastern edge of Apalachicola Bay, the more abundant side, using a wood-handled wire basket to rake across the shallow estuary with its just-right mix of fresh and salt water. It was the mid-eighties and he'd harvest seventy, eighty bushels a day.

"There was 180 oyster boats here then," Shannon says from the back deck of an old oyster house turned restaurant and raw bar. "You used to be able to walk from boat deck to boat deck without stepping on water. Apalach had fourteen, fifteen shucking houses. Eastpoint had fifty-eight. And now we're down to one."

I called Shannon upon leaving Casey's farm and asked where to meet. Lynn's Quality Oysters, he says, and I immediately agreed. We drink cold beer and eat mahi-mahi fish dip with Saltines. St. George and Dog Islands shimmer across the bay in the afternoon sun. Lynn's used to wholesale shucked oysters and truck them daily to Atlanta and other cities. Now, though, they sell mostly seafood and beer. Their oysters come from Texas. My family vacations each summer on St. George, and we always stop by Lynn's on our way home.

Shannon says that only a few guys bother oystering the bay. The state limits a fisherman to two bushels per day. At fifty bucks a bag, it isn't worth the time. (The state closed the bay to oystering a few weeks later.) Apalachicola without oysters is like Baltimore without crabs or Maine without lobsters. It's a workingman's town that, even after discovery by vacationing Northerners, retains its laid-back, end-of-the-road vibe. It has little of the touristy dreck associated with Seaside, Destin, or Panama City Beach.

Shannon is president of the Franklin County Seafood Workers Association and the go-to spokesman whenever a governor, judge, or biologist does the oystermen wrong. He's now helping Florida State University restore the bay's health. "My goal is to see this bay back to where it's productive so at least a couple hundred families can make a living off it," says Shannon, who put down his tongs eight years ago.

The historic 2007 drought that curdled Atlanta and southwest Georgia wreaked havoc on Apalachicola. The Army Corps slashed the amount of water flowing over the Georgia–Florida line. The bay's delicate ecology was thrown out of whack. Saltwater sat around too long without the downriver surges of freshwater that flush the bay. High salinity levels allowed parasites and other marine predators free rein to attack the oysters, with devastating consequences.

"Stuff started showing up in the bay we'd never seen before," Shannon recalls. "We started seeing sea urchins and scallops and conch. We saw oyster drills [predatory snails] that drilled into the oyster shells. That's when our bay really started struggling."

The rains returned and the oystering did, too. But then an oil spill 250 miles away put the fear of God (as well as the greed of mere mortals) into the oystermen. The *Deepwater Horizon* oil rig exploded on April 20, 2010, killing eleven, and releasing more than three million barrels of oil into the Gulf. The oil slick threatened Apalachicola, though it never reached the bay. Fishermen from all across the Gulf descended in droves upon one of the few oyster grounds to remain open. Florida officials upped the amount of oystering time from five to seven days a week. Areas set aside for winter harvests were also opened up. Within a year, the number of commercial oyster boats doubled to four hundred.

"The bay looked like a city because there were so many oystermen on it," Shannon told me in an interview at the time. "We freaked out. We thought the oil was coming. We put a lot of stress on our bay. We overworked it."

And about killed it. Another drought seared southwest Georgia and northwest Florida in 2011 and 2012. Only about a third of the usual amount of water flowed from Georgia into the Apalachicola River—the lowest ever recorded. Oyster hauls dwindled to almost nothing. The Obama administration declared a fishery disaster in August 2013. The next day, Governor Rick Scott announced that Florida was suing Georgia for using too much water.

"But what does that accomplish?" Shannon wonders, another beer in hand. "We've been suing forever. Georgia can't give what ain't there."

Commercial fishermen are a resilient bunch. Nobody just oysters. Shannon has taken a number of "land jobs" whenever the river dwindles and the bay turns salty. Construction. Work in a fastener factory. Deadhead logging for longleaf pine. He fished, too. Mullet. Pompano. Red snapper. He worked an oyster dredge off Louisiana. He always came back, though, to the East Bay. In 2009, after a car wreck, Shannon became president of the fishermen's association—"the voice of the seafood industry"—lobbying in Tallahassee and beyond for a dying industry. He says there's more than enough blame to go around.

"Georgia's a rural state and Atlanta's a really rich city. It can look at another source of fresh water, like the Tennessee River," Shannon says, all tanned and chill in T-shirt and flip flops. "I don't know if you can hold the farmers responsible because they had the opportunity to tap all those wells. But when we have low flows, they create problems by drawing up the aquifer. Georgia is growing. We know that. But there ought to be a moratorium on what they can withdraw, especially during a drought."

Shannon says the Supreme Court's decision was "a big loss for us." He sees Congress as the last, best chance to force the Army Corps to keep a steady flow of water coming down the Apalachicola. Enough water, and rebuilt oyster beds, could save an industry, and a lifestyle.

"But another drought will devastate the bay completely," Shannon admits.

And a warmer climate will mean more droughts.

Shannon isn't so sure. "I see the weather change," he says, "but who's to say it won't change the other way? I have faith in Mother Nature."

CHAPTER 8

The Deeper the River, the Greater the Pain

> He who hears the rippling of rivers in these degenerate days will not utterly despair.
> —Henry David Thoreau, *A Week on the Concord and Merrimack Rivers*

Augusta, Georgia — John Muir dried himself off, pocketed his money, and returned the leaves and flowers to the plant press before heading east from the Chattahoochee River. The low-slung hills and well-trodden paths of the Piedmont whisked the intrepid explorer toward Athens. The cotton harvest was newly under way and the "picking is now going on merrily," Muir wrote.

He reached "remarkably beautiful and aristocratic" Athens the following afternoon and was smitten by the college town's outward grace and civility. It reminded him of Madison, Wisconsin. "This is the most beautiful town I have seen on the journey so far, and the only one in the South that I would like to revisit," he said.

Yet Muir ignored, or failed to realize, the sinister undercurrents coursing through Athens and the Deep South. Athens, a hotbed of

Confederate support, had been occupied by Federal troops until early 1866. Only then did Georgia's flagship university, which lost one hundred students and alumni to the War of Northern Aggression, reopen. Klansmen were numerous and prominent and they burned the home of an African American legislator who was set to testify against them to Congress.

Muir ascribed to the usual racist rhetoric. In Athens, he noted that "the negroes here have been well trained and are extremely polite." Why, they even removed their hats if a White man approached within fifty yards! "Robber negroes," ex-slaves looking for work or long-lost families, were to be avoided. In *A Thousand-Mile Walk*, Muir wrote that "one energetic white man, working with a will, would easily pick as much cotton as half a dozen Sambos and Sallies."

Pretty harsh, and inane, commentary for such an otherwise enlightened young man. His more forgiving critics chalk up the racist talk to his Midwestern upbringing and the ignorant groupthink pervasive across the lily-white region. Whatever. He should've stuck to his knitting.

Yet there's a sense that Muir *was* changing, that the heretofore happy chronicler of God's great outdoors was divining something wicked and dangerous about humanity. He was no dummy. He'd seen the abandoned homes, stoved-in barns, and overgrown fields of Kentucky, Tennessee, and North Carolina. He'd broken bread with the rail-thin mothers and corn-likkered fathers who looked twice their age. He'd experienced the desperation of the highwayman and the bitterness of the landowner brought low by the Civil War. And he survived it all with characteristic pep and unbridled optimism.

Until he reached Georgia.

Georgia was hot, humid, tropical, and full of mysterious species that Muir had never before seen.

"Strange plants are crowding about me now," he wrote. "Scarce a familiar face appears among all the flowers of the day's walk."

His money was running out and he was often hungry, tired, and lonely. "The winds are full of strange sounds, making one feel far from the people and plants and fruitful fields of home," Muir said. "Night is coming on and I am filled with indescribable loneliness."

The cypress swamps were "impenetrable" and unwelcoming, their waters murky and filled with fearsome alligators.

"Increasingly, Muir felt that he was in a strange and unfamiliar world—a theme he repeated several times in his journal in southern Georgia and Florida," wrote James B. Hunt in *Restless Fires*. "In Georgia, Muir felt an undefined threat from the tropical character of nature."

The rivers with lyrical Indian names—Chattooga, Keowee, Tallulah, Tugaloo—flow from the southern Appalachians into what eventually becomes the Savannah River. The Savannah is born in northeast Georgia and, over the next three hundred miles, serves as the boundary between the Peach State and the Palmetto State. It passes through reservoirs and dams, Augusta and North Augusta, cotton fields and pine plantations, before slowing and spreading amoeba-like across the swampy coastal plain and into the Atlantic Ocean. A gauge above Savannah puts the river's average flow at twelve thousand cubic feet per second, one of the greatest freshwater discharges in the Southeast. The river's force carries nutrient-rich sediments downstream to mix with the fresh, salt, and brackish waters near the coast. The mash of food, minerals, and liquids makes the Savannah River the most biologically rich in native fish species (108) of any Atlantic-draining river, according to The Nature Conservancy. Three-fourths of the fish are at risk, threatened, or endangered, including the prehistoric-looking shortnose sturgeon. Other rare species abound: wild cocoa trees, rocky shoals spider lilies, and false rue anemones; flatwoods salamanders, striped newts, and Carolina heel splitters (clams). Charles Seabrook, in *The World of the Salt Marsh*, writes that the "rich bottomland hardwood forests (offer) haunting beauty and amazing wildlife diversity." The river also cuts through the Savannah National Wildlife Refuge—"one of the last great sanctuaries of tidal freshwater marshes in the eastern United States," Seabrook says—with its old rice plantation levees and dikes welcoming millions of migratory birds each spring and fall.

Like virtually every major American river, though, the Savannah's beauty can't hide its industrialized decay. The postwar South offered Northern industrialists cheap land, labor, and river-generated electricity. In descending order, the Lake Hartwell, Richard B. Russell, and J. Strom Thurmond dams emasculated the Savannah, all in the name of economic development, flood control, and recreation. The huge dams and miles-long reservoirs altered the river's natural flow, harming the fish, salamanders, and mollusks that depend upon seasonal bursts of water. The maximum peak flows near Augusta are less than one-third what they were before the dams were built, according to the University of Georgia. Lower flows move less sediment, scour less of the river bottom, and deliver less water to the floodplain. Even the US Army Corps of Engineers, which built the dams, acknowledges that its "operation of dams on the Savannah for the last fifty years has caused notable degradation of ecosystem integrity."

Below Augusta, the Savannah takes on all the municipal and industrial characteristics of the Ohio and other heavily polluted rivers—with some unique twists. While it provides the drinking water for Augusta and Savannah, as well as for Beaufort, Hilton Head, and Hardeeville, the river also accepts their treated sewage. "Chemical Alley" runs along the river just below Augusta, its fertilizer, resin, and paper factories spewing a witch's brew of treated wastes into the water (and air). So nasty was the water that Augusta placed its water-intake pipe ten miles upstream to avoid the concentrated stew of chemicals on its doorstep. The sprawling

Savannah River Site, famed for its past production of plutonium and tritium for nuclear bombs, sits a short boat ride downriver on the South Carolina side. Massive amounts of river water are still required to decontaminate the radioactive debris left behind from the Cold War. So, too, does Plant Vogtle, the nuclear power plant conveniently located across the river from SRS, with its four whitewashed cooling towers looming over the countryside. It sucks up millions of gallons of water daily and returns it, considerably warmer, to the Savannah—to the detriment of cooler-water-loving animals.

The Nature Conservancy labeled the Savannah "among the most highly stressed Southeastern rivers." Environment Georgia, another nonprofit, once called the river the nation's third-most toxic, with more than five million pounds of chemicals discharged into it annually.

A lively barge trade used to ply the river from Augusta to Savannah, hauling cotton, timber, chemicals, and kaolin to the port of Savannah. As the sediment piled up, dredges could no longer ensure deep enough passage. So the Army Corps, in the 1950s, slashed a navigation channel nine feet deep and ninety feet wide. As a bonus, the engineers decided the trip would go even faster by cutting right through forty bends in the river, thereby shortening the Savannah by twenty-six miles. Not long after the Army Corps completed its hydrological wizardry, barge traffic all but stopped, as did dredging between the two cities.

In the summer of 1970, the river below Augusta was closed to fishing due to the Olin Mathieson Company's discharge of methyl mercury. Blue crabs, in the estuary 180 miles below the chemical factory, were also declared unfit for human consumption.

Just then, Nader's Raiders descended upon the still-sleepy, terribly polluted city of Savannah. A dozen college students, recent grads, and a lawyer set about to expose "the environmental tragedy that has encompassed the city and its friendly people for decades." They worked for crusading consumer advocate and four-time presidential candidate

Ralph Nader and his Center for Study of Responsive Law. Nader sicced the Center and a bunch of smart, idealistic twenty-somethings on a variety of powerful, unresponsive agencies and corporations—the Federal Trade Commission, the Food and Drug Administration, segregated nursing homes, air and water polluters—to unmask unethical and oft-times illegal practices. In Savannah, the target was the Union Camp paper bag factory and fellow environmental malefactors who turned the river into their industrial trashcan, all the while promising Progress and pocketing tax breaks.

"The pale flow of Savannah River water is not adequate or suitable for human use because of what Union Camp and its corporate brethren have done to pollute those waters," James Fallows and his fellow Raiders wrote in *The Water Lords*. "These Savannah-based companies are outlaws."

The river served as the city's direct-pipe sewer during its first two hundred years of municipal existence. The Union Camp mill was notoriously foul, dumping lignin, fungicides, and chlorinated resin acids into the river. But the real problem with the coffee-colored effluent was eutrophication, or the overloading of the river with nutrients, which led to excessive amounts of algae and oxygen depletion. It didn't help that an awful, sulfuric, rotten-egg stench from the mill's smokestacks wafted for miles, depending on which way the wind was blowing.

Union Camp, known affectionately as "the Bag," opened in 1935 in the depths of the Great Depression. It was touted as the world's largest paper mill and considered an economic godsend. Within a year, though, a local civic committee labeled the mill "a potential menace." The river in front of the gold-domed city hall "literally boils as pockets of hydrogen sulfide and methane gas rise from the wastes on the river bed," Fallows wrote, adding that a sugar refinery, the port, and other industrial polluters shared the blame.

But the Bag wasn't too worried about water quality or its reputation. Glenn Kimble, evidently in charge of the mill's air- and water-pollution control efforts, decried the enviro crowd's "hysterical 'Doom's Day' predictions." "People get extremely emotional about losing a species," Kimble said, "but animals have been dying out every year clear back to the dinosaur, and in most cases man had nothing to do with it. For that matter, it probably won't hurt mankind a whole hell of a lot in the long run if the whooping crane doesn't quite make it."

To reach Carol Claxton, and her unique view of the world, I ride a two-man elevator into the sky before clambering onto a steel catwalk for the heart-thumping, open-air dash to the cramped cockpit where Carol works. She's a ship-to-shore crane operator, spending eight hours each day in yellow hardhat and leather chair ten stories above the Savannah river, fiddling two joysticks that magically load and unload steel shipping boxes off massive container ships far, far below. It's a daunting, critical, adrenalin-inducing job where winds sway the crane, clouds envelop the cockpit, and bathroom breaks are adventures. Carol, though, handles the high-wire job with aplomb, deftly maneuvering a forty-foot container from a ship's deck onto the chassis of a flat-bed truck. Container after container, truck after truck, one every two minutes, hundreds each day.

Her job comes with one of the industry's best perks: a corner office to die for. Carol, in between toggles, can see the cobblestoned streets of Savannah, the beaches of Tybee, Daufuskie, and Hilton Head, and the indiscriminate horizon of the Atlantic Ocean. She also gets the full sweep of the port of Savannah, a two-mile-long whirl of trains, trucks, warehouses, and massive cargo ships whose decks are stacked ten high with steel boxes. I've twice ridden upriver on the bridge of a container ship and never tired of looking down on the ant-sized pedestrians on River Street. Savannah is the nation's fourth-busiest container port—second only to New York–New Jersey on the East Coast—handling five million containers each year.

Carol, though, has little time to play tourist. Not with fifteen tons of steel dangling at her fingertips. Her eyes rarely wander beyond the busy world below her cabin in the sky. One morning, after loading the CMA CGM *Matisse* bound for New York and Rotterdam, Carol watches as the freighter eases away from the dock and into the middle of the river. A cloud of brown mud billows in the *Matisse*'s wake.

"You can tell that the river's not deep enough there," she says.

Which is why the port, the Army Corps, and taxpayers are in the midst of a billion-dollar deepening of the river from the Garden City Terminal into the open Atlantic forty miles away. Dredges the world over dig deeper and deeper channels to handle the ever-larger ships with ever-heavier loads. Ports in nearby Charleston, Jacksonville, and Norfolk are all going deeper in a maritime arms race without end. Savannah, for example, is dredging its river from forty-two to forty-seven feet, which will still require friendly tides to allow the most heavily laden ships to reach its terminals. Even that won't be enough: the Georgia Ports Authority, along with its archrival in South Carolina, is planning to build yet another major port terminal downriver in the future.

Politicians glom onto pork—I mean *port*—projects like piglets on a teat. And the Army Corps has never met a construction project it didn't like. Theirs is a marriage made in Hell if you're a manatee, a sturgeon, or a crustacean. The port, and its deepening, represents the final environmental indignity suffered by the Savannah River on its long, tortured path to the ocean. Scouring the river bottom disrupts entire ecosystems, home to fish, crabs, mussels, clams, and plankton. The animals either flee or die. Dredging also increases a river's turbidity, which reduces

the amount of light that aquatic plants need to grow. The floating particles of clay, silt, and algae absorb heat and increase water temperatures. Dredging also kicks up all sorts of nasty contaminants that were
once locked into place on the river's bottom. Lead, mercury, chlorinated
acids, and other toxic chemicals get disturbed and flow farther downriver where they harm other habitats. Or they get dredged and deposited
on riverbanks to await birds. A lawsuit was filed against the Savannah
River's deepening, claiming toxic cadmium would be dumped on the
South Carolina side of the river.

The health hazards increase every time a scow drops a shovel into
the Savannah. Each scoop allows salt water to move farther upriver. A
US Geological Service study shows "salinity intrusion" at high tide near
Hardeeville, South Carolina—fifty miles from the ocean.

It's not just the salinity that's worrying. Salt water contains chlorides
that, by themselves, aren't necessarily dangerous to health. But chlorides
corrode lead and copper pipes, which, upon leaching, is indeed dangerous to kidneys and brains. Savannah's main drinking water intake sits
a few miles below Hardeeville on the river. The Army Corps, as part
of the ongoing deepening project, built a hundred-million-gallon raw
water reservoir to supplement the city's intake when chloride levels get
too high.

If she crooks her neck, Carol can see the forty-four-million-dollar reservoir. She doesn't have to twitch a muscle, though, to eyeball the damage done by the inexorable upstream surge of salty water. The Savannah
wildlife refuge, across the river from the port, is one of the East Coast's
most critical wildlife preserves and a key stop along the Atlantic Fly-
way. Twelve thousand acres of nourishing tidal freshwater marsh lined
the river before the repeated deepenings. Today, three thousand acres
remain, all in the refuge.

The preserve was cobbled together from old rice plantations whose
latticed freshwater impoundments attract hundreds of thousands of

ducks, gallinules, coots, and mergansers each fall. Warblers, tanagers, vireos, and other neotropical songbirds pass through in the winter en route to Mexico and points south. Great blue herons, snowy egrets, and bald eagles live year-round in the marsh amidst the cattails, pickerelweed, and wild rice. Salt water, though, kills the life-sustaining vegetation and messes with the marsh's ecological balance. The Audubon Society said the saline intrusion was "representative of a habitat in serious decline." The US Fish and Wildlife Service, which manages the refuge, said that deepening the river could wipe out 40 percent of the remaining freshwater marsh. The conservation agency pushed, unsuccessfully, for a depth no greater than forty-five feet.

Salt water poses yet another danger to the river's denizens. The saltier the water, the less oxygen it contains. If oxygen levels drop too low, fish die. Just ask the striped bass, if you can find one. Before 1977, the Savannah River supported Georgia's most important striper population. After repeated deepenings, the number of striper eggs dropped 95 percent. Sturgeon face a similar fate. Shortnose sturgeon are smaller than their lake brethren, topping out at sixty pounds and five feet in length. But their roe was equally prized by caviar lovers, who almost destroyed the species in the late nineteenth century. The next century's dams, pollution, and dredging didn't help. The bewhiskered shortnose attained endangered status in 1967. Nobody knows how many sturgeon run the Savannah between the estuary and the spawning grounds near Augusta. An estimated three thousand of the armored, big-mouthed fish prowled the river's depths at the turn of the most recent century. It seems that only the annual stocking of shortnose into the river keeps the fish from disappearing. Fish and Wildlife predicted the deepening will reduce the sturgeon's habitat as much as 20 percent.

"Low oxygen was not supposed to be a problem in the Southeast's estuaries, especially those of Georgia and South Carolina," Seabrook wrote. "Scientists assumed that the region's vigorous twice-a-day tides efficiently churned the water, mixing in enough oxygen from the atmo-sphere to supply marine life—from aerobic bacteria to fish—with all they needed."

Ah, but the Army Corps has just the technology to save the now-beleaguered sturgeon—"bubblers." The engineers are spending one hundred million dollars on sketchy machines that pump oxygen into the Savannah to mitigate the impact of saltwater intrusion. The so-called Speece cones look like rocket ships. They suck in river water, mix it with oxygen, and inject the concoction back into the river. The Savannah, in essence, will be on mechanical life support in perpetuity.

Even the Army Corps admitted that the cones "could have lethal impacts to fish species."

The Southern Environmental Law Center sued the Corps in 2012, claiming the depletion of dissolved oxygen, and the dredging of toxic cadmium, pollute the river and kill sturgeon, striped bass, and Ameri-can shad.

The SELC eventually settled the suit after millions in additional mit-igation dollars were added to restore the river's health. In all, half the cost of the billion-dollar deepening project goes to fix environmental problems caused by the deepening.

"The exorbitant cost of the mitigation suggests that you think twice about doing this project in this location," Chris DeScherer, a law center attorney, told me.

Tonya Bonitatibus grew up on the river, learning to swim before she could walk. Her mom was a lifeguard, and the backyard pond in South Augusta doubled as a swimming pool. Tonya lives in the same house today. It's no surprise, then, that her kids also took to swimming before walking. Water, and the Savannah River, dictate the rhythms of Tonya's life. She is, after all, the Savannah's riverkeeper, the waterway's official protector and advocate, as well as executive director of the Savannah Riverkeeper organization. I needed to hear her take on the river's health and prospects. Plus, another controversy was brewing. Tonya invited me to join her for a boat ride up the river. I jumped at the chance.

The coronavirus had me holed up at home with my family, working remotely during the day and writing at night. I escaped to a neighbor's backyard to plant a huge garden of tomatoes, cucumbers, eggplant, squash, potatoes, carrots, snap peas, and pollinator bushes. I played baseball with Naveed, took bike rides with Sammy. Bita and I binge-watched *Tiger King*, *The Great*, and *The Plot Against America*. I singlehandedly kept our neighborhood book store, liquor store, and *gelateria* in business. But I, like virtually everybody else in America fortunate enough to have a job and to work from home, was bored. Besides, I'd run out of stuff to write. I needed to get back on the road. Traveling, though, seemed weird, like I was doing something illicit, a guilty pleasure in a deadly serious time. Not that most Georgians felt that way. Georgia was just about the last state to acknowledge the pandemic's first-wave nastiness and was one of the first to open back up after the early lockdowns. Prematurely, as it turned out, as the case numbers again rose.

I meet Tonya on a blue-sky June morning at the New Savannah Bluff Lock and Dam. She's backing the *Tidal Boar*, her thirty-foot patrol boat, into the river when a camo-capped angler, fishing for metal with magnets, tells her, "I really appreciate what you do."

Tonya monitors the river's water quality, badgers polluters, harangues elected officials, educates school kids, advocates for ecosystems, organizes cleanups, raises money, and manages a staff of six. Social justice and economic opportunity, to her, aren't incompatible with environmental action. She runs Veterans for Clean Water, a volunteer water-quality operation conducted by ex-servicemen and -women. Fishermen love her. Not everybody else does, though.

"I'm the Antichrist to many people," Tonya says as we head upriver towards Augusta.

She makes a lot of enemies. Polluters, politicians, and editorial writers mostly—anybody who wants something antithetical to the river's overall health. She gets death threats. Streams of invective flow her way. A local rag wrote that Tonya "has a special brand of aggressive self-serving cluelessness." The *Augusta Chronicle*, in a 2020 editorial, said: "She's a menace. She's a rock-weir-sized millstone around the city's neck."

Tonya is tough. She was six months pregnant the day we went on the river. Two weeks later, she rafted the Chattooga River in northeast Georgia, whose Class IV rapids were made famous in *Deliverance*.

Most of the animus spewed Tonya's way these days revolves around the decrepit lock and dam built in 1937 that the Army Corps, the Riverkeeper, and most environmentalists want torn down. Deep cracks line the spillway. The concrete crumbles in spots. All navigation through the locks was halted in 2014; Tonya was on the last boat through.

The dam's fate is linked to the harbor deepening. And the sturgeon. The federally endangered fish historically traveled nearly two hundred miles upriver from saltwater estuaries to spawn in the freshwater riffles above Augusta. The lock and dam blocks them from traditional breeding grounds, furthering their slide toward extinction. The Army Corps realized that scooping another five feet of river muck from the Savannah wouldn't help the sturgeon's long-term prospects, with or without the bubblers. So they came up with a plan: spend sixty-three million dollars tearing down the dam; lay a massive weir across the river to hold back some water; and build a fish ladder so the sturgeon can reach the egg-laying shoals above Augusta. Tonya, mostly, supports the plan. South Carolina, and the cities of Augusta and North Augusta, do not. They sued the Army Corps to halt the demolition, claiming that a rock weir would unduly lower the river and possibly impact water supply, recreational opportunities, and waterfront development.

(Riverside landowners were particularly incensed that a lower river might mean more mud and rocks and less resale value.) They want the Army Corps instead to fix the lock and dam and construct a "modest fish ladder." Their congressional representatives even consider stripping endangered-species status from the sturgeon.

"People blame me for the fish passage and the dam's removal, which is pretty fundamentally false," Tonya says as she eases the *Tidal Boar* to a stop under a blackjack oak on the South Carolina side of the river. I scan the moss-covered limbs for water moccasins. Tonya looks for hornets.

"But the dam doesn't serve its purpose anymore," she continues, "and these people don't care about the sturgeon. With something like this, you're never going to get everybody to agree. But my job is to tell them that people in Elberton, Georgia [upriver], and Hilton Head, South Carolina [downriver], are all in the same boat. It's a big river. We have to manage it as a cohesive unit."

While Tonya is, ostensibly, responsible for the entire three-hundred-mile river's health, she's pragmatic. The upper Savannah's ecological fate was sealed long ago when the three dams turned one hundred miles of once-quick river into a series of boring reservoirs. And, though she won't admit it, the lower Savannah is so environmentally compromised by decades of deepening, dredging, and shipping that it's beyond natural redemption.

"When you're standing on River Street in Savannah you're, basically, standing by the ocean," Tonya says. "When the SELC settled the [2013] lawsuit with the Corps, we realized that, 'Okay, you've destroyed that area,' so our best bet was to protect the river upstream all the way up to the lock and dam."

She focuses on "middle earth," the riverine stretch between Augusta and Savannah. There have been some notable successes since the 1970s, when the mercury flowed freely, the porpoises hightailed it, and Nader's Raiders wrote that "a house has a garbage can; Savannah has a river."

Water quality has improved and straight-piping sewage and chemicals has all but ceased. Dolphins occasionally frolic north of Interstate 95.

Despite the massive damage wrought by the deepening, the mitigation money will help restore and preserve large swaths of the river. The Savannah refuge, for example, received two thousand acres of hardwood forest in exchange for the freshwater marsh lost to saltwater intrusion. On a recent visit to the Abercorn Island tract, I saw an elegant white ibis skirting the shoreline and a committee of black vultures drying their wings in the sun. Nearby, a largely intact Native American midden exposed layer upon layer of shells.

The Army Corps, expiating its previous ecological sins, will spend more than twelve million dollars "re-bending" the serpentine Savannah. Wildcat Cut, Spanish Cut, Devil's Elbow, Saucy Boy Point, and more than two dozen other meanders will be restored to their pre-1959 glory.

"The river is in much better condition than in the past," Tonya says as an anhinga darts downstream. "But the river's best chance is to be put all back together again so that it functions normally. You need to return to a slower river with all the swamps and oxbows that serve as kidneys and livers to clean up all the junk that's put into it."

Her message resonates in some unlikely corners of the Savannah watershed. Upon leaving Tonya, I visit an old cotton plantation near Estill, South Carolina, owned by descendants of John Winthrop, founder of the Massachusetts Bay Colony. It's a beautiful, well-tended piece of property befitting the scions of American royalty, who enjoy hunting quail, deer, turkeys, and hogs. The upland savannah of longleaf pine and wire grass mixes with fields of sorghum and soybean before ambling downhill to the cypress-kneed swamp and oak-filled bends in the river. Bald eagles, red-cockaded woodpeckers, painted buntings, blue herons, and ospreys abound. Groton Plantation's owners signed a conservation easement—the largest private easement in South Carolina history—ensuring that twenty thousand acres would never be developed and the streams flowing off the property and into the Savannah would remain pristine. What was truly impressive about the deal was who helped pay for it—a water utility fifty miles downstream. The Beaufort-Jasper Water & Sewer Authority, keen to lower water-treatment costs, chipped in more than a half-million dollars to defray the easement's cost. Walmart, International Paper (which now owns the Bag), and other corporations put up hundreds of thousands of dollars more.

"Whatever you can preserve upstream is going to have beneficial impacts downstream," Joe Mantua, general manager of the water authority, tells me. "Usually, utilities are focused on spending money on technology and processes that are implemented at the intake. But there's so much value in protecting the source of the water and what eventually comes to the plant."

Few utilities act as foresightedly as Beaufort's to finance the preservation of land that filters pollutants *before* they reach a stream. New York City invested one and a half billion dollars in a watershed protection plan in the Catskills. Here, in the heavily forested lower Savannah basin, five water utilities have joined together with the goal of protecting nearly two million river-buffering acres.

"One thing that makes the South unique is the way we approach management of a river and our ability to pull people together to solve problems," Tonya says while pulling away from the riverbank. "You can't be all about water quality and the fishes. You have to manage the river so that people can also make a living. In Oregon, you've got a bunch of lefties that pretty much decide what's going to happen to a dam. Here, if you're only working with Democrats, you're going to fail. You have to incorporate everybody's interests if you want to succeed."

I ask her what she's learned after a decade as the riverkeeper.

"Working on this river has made me a lot more practical because there's no way to solve every issue at once," she says. "It's crazy. And it's definitely entertaining. But you have to choose your battles."

We dock and I return to my car to retrace Muir's route to Savannah. I checked back with Tonya a few months later. The lock and dam's future was still up in the air. Her enemies weren't letting up. But she didn't care. She was the proud mother of a baby girl named Charlotte Elizabeth River.

CHAPTER 9

A Coastal Playground
Is Disappearing

"You don't like it, do you, Rocco—the storm? Show it your gun,
why don't you? If it doesn't stop, shoot it."
—Humphrey Bogart, *Key Largo*

Tybee Island, Georgia — Paul Wolff leans over the railing and yells
down at me.

"Chapman," he bellows. "*What* are you driving?"

"A Subaru," I say, sheepishly.

"You should be driving a Prius or a Leaf or some other alternative.
Not an SUV," he scoffs.

I mumble something about my kids and good gas mileage and it not
really being an SUV. No good. Not even my Grateful Dead bumper
sticker mollifies Paul, the Apostle of Climate Weirding, who preaches
the gospel of a warming world.

I pass the jumble of old bikes, kayaks, and other beachy paraphernalia crammed into his open-air garage and climb to the third-floor aerie
amid the treetops. A placard in the side yard certifies the property as
wildlife habitat. I let myself in. The smell of four cats hits me before I

see Paul's smiling face. He offers me a beer. I decline. I want to take a bike ride.

Paul is one of the Georgia coast's leading environmentalists, a former Tybee Island city councilman who dragged the hippie-redneck outpost into the vanguard of climate-change activism. I've interviewed him many times over the last fifteen years and learned boatloads. On an island full of characters, known affectionately one time or another as the "Truck Stop by the Sea" or "Mayberry on LSD," Paul stands out. Everybody knows him, and not solely because of the shoulder-length, electric-white hair with matching beard that lends itself to prophetic comparisons. That long-legged dude cruising the island on a low-ride Dyno Roadster beach bike? That's Paul.

He wheels the Roadster out to the street. I get the less sexy Dyno Glide with the broken seat that keeps me swiveling like a bobblehead as we begin Tybee Climate Tour 2020.

First stop: The island's back side dredged from Venetian Inlet muck in the 1930s so sharpie real estate types could sell swampy lots to sun-seeking Savannahians. Hundreds of cottages were laid out in a checkerboard pattern of streets (east-to-west) and avenues (north-to-south). Today, the modest homes of administrators, artisans, and Atlanta retirees underscores Tybee's Everyman charm. The allure, though, fades as higher tides, heavier rains, and more-frequent hurricanes lash the lower-lying half of Tybee—elevation seven feet on a good day. Lying along a very vulnerable Georgia coast, Tybee's back side is one of the spots most vulnerable to the vagaries of a warming world and the realities of sea-level rise. So-called sunny-day flooding is a problem, too. And when the hurricanes and big storms hit, the folks living along Tybee's southeastern edge bear the brunt of Mother Nature's fury.

We dismount on Chatham Avenue. Kayakers skim the river. Little Tybee Island, barren and recently scorched by wildfire, fills the distance.

"This is the land that wasn't there," Paul says of big Tybee's back side. "It's all reclaimed mud and floods like crazy. It's impermeable, with the worst drainage on the island, because it's not sand. It's going to be the land that isn't there in the future, too."

Next stop: Nineteenth Street and the island's southernmost point, which stands naked to the Atlantic Ocean. The beach is near full just days after the governor (prematurely) loosened coronavirus rules on public gatherings. Container ships line the Tybee Roads, the offshore anchorage, waiting for a chance to steam up the Savannah River to the port. Big houses loom over the beach, taunting tropical disturbances to come ashore, something they've done with alarming frequency in recent years. Hurricane Irma was downgraded to a tropical storm by the time it hit Tybee in September 2017. But the storm surge reached nearly five feet—the second-highest ever recorded—and flattened sand dunes, flooded living rooms, and tossed sailboats onto streets.

"The surge was really bad here," Paul recalls while standing at the end of the boardwalk. "It's the most quickly eroding end of the island."

Last stop: North Beach. We mount our Dyno steeds and cruise Butler Avenue, the main drag, past the pier, city hall, Fort Screven, and the lighthouse. Daufuskie Island, where Paul owns a cabin and runs a golf cart rental business, reflects the late-afternoon sun across Calibogue Sound. Fifty-foot dunes once towered over the beach, but when the War Department gave Fort Screven to the City, the dunes were leveled and spread along nearby streets. Little dunes now, bravely, stand sentinel.

"I hope they'll protect us from the consequences of sea-level rise," Paul says, wishfully.

Paul's tour bummed me out, but I was still enjoying the freedom from my self-imposed Covid exile. After leaving the riverkeeper, I re-created Muir's route from Augusta to Savannah as best I could. Muir, too, was eager to quit Augusta after spending one dollar for a comfy night at the Planter's Hotel downtown. He got up early the next day, wolfed down "a cheap breakfast," and set off along the river road. James Hunt wrote that Muir "dove into his botany" and that "his temperament improved." He chronicled different grasses, apricot vines, liatris, goldenrods, saw palmettos, and pomegranates.

"Toward evening I came to the county of one of the most striking of southern plants, the so-called 'Long Moss' or Spanish Moss," Muir wrote. "The trees hereabouts have all their branches draped with it, producing a remarkable effect."

He lodged one evening with a Mr. Cameron, a wealthy planter who was scouring rust off the cotton gin saws he'd hidden in a farm pond to avoid destruction by General Sherman's troops. Mr. Cameron waxed eloquent about the future of "e-lec-tricity" and how one day it would run trains, steamships, and the world. The hydroelectric dams on the Savannah River would prove Mr. Cameron prescient.

I'm keen to find the planter's antebellum home along the old Central Georgia Railroad outside the town of Sylvania. Cameron Station, though, no longer exists. But Indian Branch Creek supposedly runs along his property, so I aim for it.

I pass Chemical Alley and, within an hour, the Vogtle nuclear power plant's hulking cooling towers. Row upon row of RVs and campers fill nearby farm fields, providing temporary housing for thousands of construction workers building the nuke plant's last two units. I reach US 301, the old north–south highway that sun lovers took to reach Florida before the interstates. The Dreamland, Skylark, Pine View, and Syl-Va-Lane motels, some covered in kudzu with caved-in roofs, beckon motorists outside town. A frayed "Join the SCV" sign attached to a fence post invites Southerners to rekindle their Lost Cause ardor. At the futuristic-looking welcome center at the river, opened in 1962, ice-cold Cokes and salty peanuts await travelers who prefer the slow lane. The "hostesses" who worked there in the sixties once regaled me with hilarious tales of Northern motorists inching up to the counter to determine whether the young women wore shoes.

I can't find Mr. Cameron's plantation. I get lost and end up on the other side of Sylvania. Suddenly, the two-lane blacktop turns into a narrow dirt road. The GPS stops working. The oak trees creep closer, shrouding the road in leaves and moss. Deep potholes reduce the speed limit to fifteen. Small farms with long-exhausted cotton fields and fat cows are bordered by dark-water cypress swamps. It's a tableau eerily similar to Muir's time. I picture him loping down this country road looking for a spot to sleep, fearing the serpents of the swamp, and hoping a farmhouse magically appears. Rare today are the locations along Muir's route that resemble life in 1867. I even see a man with a walking stick crossing a field.

But then, just as quickly, I return to the twenty-first century of paved roads, jacked-up pickups, and center-pivot farms. Muir most likely followed the Old River Road, an Indian trail transformed, according to a roadside historical marker, into "the longest white man's way in Georgia." He probably passed through the settlement of New Ebenezer with its red-brick, green-shuttered Jerusalem Lutheran Church, circa 1769. But he didn't mention it. Nor did he mention Mulberry Grove Plantation outside Savannah, where Eli Whitney supposedly invented the cotton gin that remade the South. This was also the likely route of William Bartram, the South's other preeminent botanical explorer, who trekked between Savannah and Augusta on a couple of occasions in the 1770s.

I hurry, as Muir did, the last miles into Savannah. The port's sprawl has turned US 21 into a mash of warehouses, truck-repair depots, skanky motels, rundown churches, and public housing. The Bag still emits the smell of rotten eggs.

Muir arrived on October 8 and headed straight to the Adams Express office in search of a package from his brother. It hadn't arrived. "Feel dreadfully lonesome and poor," Muir wrote. "Went to the meanest looking lodging-house I could find, on account of its cheapness."

The next day he took the Thunderbolt Road south of town for his fateful stay in Bonaventure Cemetery.

I pass Bonaventure the following morning after a pleasant evening camping alongside a salt marsh at a state park below Savannah. I cross the Wilmington River and descend onto Skidaway Island, home of the University of Georgia's Skidaway Institute of Oceanography, whose director, Clark Alexander, has also educated me about climate science over the years. Clark, wearing a blue face mask, welcomes me to his near-empty office building. We exchange socially distant fist-bumps. He's hunkered over a computer, trying to figure out how to cut 10 percent of the Institute's budget in light of the state's projected pandemic-depleted tax receipts. Virtually all research has been shut down. Clark is a marine geologist who has studied the impact of sedimentation on river systems, tidal flats, and continental shelves in China, Brazil, Russia, South Korea, and California. In Georgia, he's now focused on the tidal and climactic forces that move shorelines. When he's not balancing budgets.

"After Hurricane Irma [in 2017] I have given more talks on storm surge, coastal hazards, and the implications of sea-level rise on the coast than I did over the last twenty years," says Clark, whose office affords a lovely view of expansive lawns and moss-covered oaks leading to the Skidaway River. "It's on people's radar now. They're paying attention."

They'd better. Clark tells me how the oceans absorb a third of all carbon dioxide emissions and act as the planet's largest carbon sink. That's a good thing. Imagine how hot it'd be if the oceans didn't act as one big heat-sucking sponge. But all that heat is making the oceans warmer, too—a lot warmer. That's a bad thing. The world's oceans have warmed one and a half degrees Fahrenheit since 1900, according to the Intergovernmental Panel on Climate Change. More recent studies, though, show that the United Nations may have woefully underestimated the warming by 40 percent. Scientists in the United States and Canada reported in 2020 that the Atlantic Ocean is the hottest it has been in nearly three thousand years. All that hot water leads to a host of climate ills: melting glaciers; sea-level rise; coral bleaching; animal migrations; nasty weather.

The Skidaway Institute sends underwater gliders packed with sensors in front of hurricanes to measure temperatures and salinity levels in order to help predict the storm's intensity. Variations in temperatures at different depths are believed to impact a hurricane's force. The torpedo-shaped crafts surface occasionally to transmit the data via satellite to hurricane modelers who determine whether a storm is weakening or strengthening before reaching land. Hurricane Laura was a Category-1 storm upon leaving Cuba for the open waters of the Gulf of Mexico in August 2020. It was a Cat-4 eighteen hours later when it hit Cameron, Louisiana—one of the strongest storms to ever hit Louisiana—and killed thirty people.

"We don't know if there are more storms, but we do know that they're more intense," Clark says. "The warmer water is just more fuel for hurricanes."

Tropical storms and hurricanes vacuum up moisture from the Atlantic and the Gulf, adding to the already substantial amount of rainwater embedded in the storms. Researchers from the National Oceanic and Atmospheric Administration (NOAA) and the University of Wisconsin reported in 2020 that the odds of tropical storms turning into Category-3, -4, or -5 hurricanes are increasing due to global warming. In fact, six of the worst hurricanes over the last fifty years have occurred since 2016. Hurricanes are coming earlier and staying later. And 2021 was the seventh year in a row that a tropical depression formed prior to official hurricane season.

A warmer Atlantic wreaks havoc underwater, too. Marine heat waves kill coral reefs by killing the food source—algae—they need to survive. Maybe half of Florida's reef, which runs from West Palm Beach to the Lower Keys, is dead. Nitrogen from fertilizer and septic-tank sewage also harms reefs. Nevertheless, scientists consider the warming water Enemy Number One, particularly for the hundreds of species that live among, and depend upon, the reefs as breeding grounds and food pantries. Turtles. Crabs. Lobsters. Jellyfish. Grouper. Snapper. Lobster. Shrimp. They're all in trouble.

Georgia shrimpers first observed black gill disease in the 1990s, but the energy-sapping, livelihood-killing parasitic fungus that causes the disease has spread widely in recent years. Skidaway biologists discovered that smaller harvests occur after particularly warm-water winters. In one study, they deduced that raising water temps by two degrees Fahrenheit increased mortality rates for infected shrimp as much as 70 percent. The shrimp, like many warm-water fish, keep moving north.

As do lionfish, an invasive predator discovered off Fort Lauderdale in 1985. These red-white-and-black killers, with venomous, pointy fins, corral their prey into coral corners before attacking. They can eat fish more than half their size. They're rather indiscriminate gourmands, too, devouring more than seventy different types of fish and invertebrates, including snappers, groupers, parrotfish, and shrimp. Once a lionfish moves in, the neighborhood empties out. Florida officials implore fishermen to kill them on sight. Restaurants, though, prize their moist and buttery flesh.

"They're quite tasty," says Clark, who has partaken of lionfish at local restaurants.

A warming ocean expands lionfish habitat. They're now wreaking havoc off the coast of Georgia. Mangrove forests are also on the doorstep, threatening to outmuscle *Spartina alterniflora*, the iconic cordgrass that frames the state's saltwater marshes. Mangroves provide many of the same ecological benefits as salt marshes, like erosion control and carbon sequestration, but they also displace indigenous plants, animals, and wading birds. The sinewy, stilt-like plants typically only grow at tropical or subtropical latitudes because they hate the cold. Clark says mangroves "change the food web. They change the ecosystem. The big woody plants drop their leaves, which are more refractory than *spartina* and harder to break down, which makes it harder for organisms to get good nutrition from the plants."

He adds, "Species will continue to migrate in response to climate change. You see it in fish. You see it in plants. You see it all around us. That's not going to stop. With increasing temperatures we'll see new diseases from warmer climates that we've never seen before."

After thirty years in the business, I left newspapering in 2016. But I wanted one last hurrah: Hurricane Matthew.

I've covered so many hurricanes that I've lost count. My first was Hugo in Charleston in 1989, a Category-4 monster that killed more than eighty-five people and dropped a tree on my rental house in Winston-Salem, more than two hundred miles away. (I didn't learn about it until I returned a week later.) I'd spent the night of the hurricane in Wilmington, North Carolina—the projected landfall—in my car in the parking lot of a motel where TV reporters with coiffed, yet tousled, hair did their stand-ups before returning to the bar. The next morning I hightailed it down US 17 to Charleston. The devastation was jaw-dropping. Homes obliterated. Fishing boats tossed across highways. Every tree at Francis Marion National Forest sheared in half. In Charleston the National Guard patrolled with M-16s, and lines for water stretched for blocks.

Matthew, in 2016, raked Haiti before riding up the East Coast and swiping Tybee Island. I'd driven down from Atlanta two days before it hit, talked my way past a cop enforcing (sort of) the mandatory evacuation of the island, and quickly accepted Paul's offer of his girl-friend's sturdy house on the island's north end. For company I had Mary's mama cat and four babies, who mewled all night as the storm worsened, the water rose, and the winds topped one hundred miles per hour. Roof tiles peeled from neighboring homes. The garage flooded and seawater climbed halfway up the first-floor steps. The beach, on a good day, was two hundred yards away. When the power went out, and I could no longer file updates for the newspaper, I hung out with the cats. We enjoyed each other's company. I spent the brunt of the storm in a well-fortified bathroom.

It was the worst hurricane to hit Georgia in more than a century, though the winds weren't terribly destructive. Eighteen inches of rain fell. The tidal gauge at nearby Fort Pulaski hit twelve and a half feet—a record. Flooding typically starts at ten feet. The ocean's surge deposited a ten-foot sand dune on Nineteenth Street. My rental car was flooded with ocean dreck covering the engine and floorboards. Friends asked me to check on their houses.

Melissa Turner lives on Lewis Avenue, which runs between two branches of Horse Pen Creek. The Palm Terrace subdivision was built in the fifties and retains its Florida bungalow charm. As the storm approached, Melissa, a former *Atlanta Journal-Constitution* reporter and editor, husband Thomas, and two cats evacuated to Savannah. A state of emergency kept them from returning to Tybee. So I clambered over downed trees, around electric wires, and through lake-sized puddles to reach her home. I peered inside windows and doors and found nothing amiss, the furniture seemingly in place in the darkened home. I texted Melissa the good news and left.

"We finally got to come back on the island three or four days later and I walked up to the front door, opened it—and it was just devas-tating," Melissa tells me after my bike tour with Paul. "Everything had been sitting and moldering in mud for four days. There was salt water on the table tops. But Dan Chapman had said everything was *fine*."

Oops.

They ripped out the walls, tile floor, and kitchen cabinets and placed them on the curb alongside furniture and appliances. They put in new furniture, appliances, and "a really fantastic floor" because, really, what were the chances of another hurricane hitting Tybee? It had been 119 years since the last one. They moved back in May 2017. Four months later Tropical Storm Irma inundated Tybee, pushing the second-highest tide on record across the island.

"It hit at exactly the *right* wrong moment—high tide," Melissa recalls. "The creeks were full. We were sitting in the living room and saw water coming across the street. Then we saw water coming from the back, filling up the pool and meeting the water from the street. We still didn't think we had anything to worry about. But then the water just kept coming and coming and coming. It started coming under the doors, then under the walls. We put the cats on top of the bed. We were sitting on the bar stools in the kitchen and the water came up under our seats."

Two uncharacteristically wicked storms in two years. Something ain't right on Tybee Island. The Fort Pulaski tidal gauge, a couple of miles from Melissa's house on the Savannah River, tells why. It sits in a squat, windowless brick building at the end of a dock used by the Savannah River pilots who guide the big ships upriver to the port. This is where NOAA scientists monitor the Atlantic's steadily encroaching waters. The sea off Georgia rises more than three millimeters per year. It has risen ten inches since 1935—three inches since 1990 alone.

The surge "is projected to accelerate in the future due to continuing temperature increases and additional melting of land ice," says the Fourth National Climate Assessment. How much so? Possibly another forty inches by 2110. Researchers at Georgia Tech predict that 30 percent of Chatham, Liberty, and McIntosh Counties will be underwater by then. The barrier islands will be swamped. Coastal towns will experience billions of dollars of damage to roads, water and sewer facilities, and private property. Two-thirds of Georgia's saltwater marshes might disappear. And poor Tybee Island could lose one-third of its commercial property and half of its residential neighborhoods. Bye-bye, Lewis Avenue.

"I feel sorry for the next generation, including my own kids," says Melissa. "I know that at some future point Tybee will not be Tybee anymore."

Higher temperatures, as any armchair hydrologist knows, makes water expand, further filling the world's oceans. An already-full bathtub exacerbates the storm-surge damage done by hurricanes by pushing water farther inland and blocking rivers from flowing easily to the ocean. The watery double whammy, according to the National Climate Assessment, will cost the Southeast as much as one hundred billion dollars *annually* by 2090.

Hurricanes are nasty beasts, but the inexorable thrum of rising tides may prove more dangerous in the long run. High tides, of course, are products of wind, weather, and lunar cycles. Add an ocean that's ten inches higher than before, though, and the tides more easily reach dunes, homes, and roads. Our favorite Fort Pulaski gauge recorded two high-tide, or "sunny day," floods in 2000. In 2019, a record thirteen high-tide floods swamped nearby Tybee. By 2050, there could be anywhere from forty to ninety-five sunny-day floods.

And let's not forget the king tides that coincide with full or new moons and are infinitely more frightening than the now-common nuisance tides. When the Earth, moon, and sun are perfectly aligned, usually in the spring, the Atlantic rises higher and higher and inundates places usually deemed safe. Who can forget the startling photo of the ghostly octopus splayed in a Miami Beach parking lot in 2016 during a king tide? US 80, the only road on and off Tybee, now shuts down a few times a year due to king tides. Paul was tooling back from Savannah one fine spring evening when he crossed the Bull River bridge and ran smack-dab into a couple feet of water that wasn't supposed to be there. (He was driving a Chevy Metro, 46 mpg on the highway.)

"The water was coming right over the marsh. It was scary," Paul recalls, as was the repair bill for the Chevy's undercarriage.

For years islanders have pushed the state to raise US 80. The cost: minimum one hundred million dollars. Tybee's low-lying precariousness, and the recent spate of bad storms, furrows many an islander's brow. There's this dread, this gnawing suspicion each hurricane season, that living on an Atlantic barrier island is frivolous, foolhardy, dangerous.

"We had the come-to-Jesus discussion—'Do, uh, we really want to go through this *again*?'" says Melissa, remembering the fraught conversations with Thomas and neighbors after the house was flooded a second time. "We never contemplated leaving Tybee. But we had to figure out how to live comfortably on Tybee without every hurricane season being stress-inducing. So we decided to raise the house up."

After Irma they again dragged everything to the curb, hired a contractor to replace the sheetrock, and another to lift the fourteen-hundred-square-foot house ten feet off the ground. It took nine months and $300,000.

I ask why Melissa she stayed.

"Look at this," she commands, her arm sweeping wide to take in the view beyond the pool, lawn, and mandevilla to Horse Pen Creek. "You're looking at nature! I grew up on a coast and wanted to retire on a coast. We're not on the ocean. We're not even on the Back River here. But every morning I look out on that big, open marsh and see egrets and herons and listen to the waves—it's the most peaceful existence."

Melissa retired recently from running the Tybee Post Theater, popular with fans of rock tribute bands and old movies including *Jaws*, which runs every Fourth of July weekend. She no longer organizes the island's

Polar Bear Plunge, the famed New Year's Day spectacle where hundreds of locals and visitors (including me) dip into the chilly Atlantic to sober up and raise money for the theater's restoration. Melissa savors her "very funky little beach town" and backyard sanctuary free, for now, of the zoonotic and climatic events sweeping the globe.

"I am certainly not a climate-change denier. I know sea level rises every single year," she says as a grackle, perched on the hot tub, listens to our conversation. "It sounds terrible, but it's not going to put me out of my house for the next twenty years. This is my little slice of paradise and I plan to enjoy it."

Paul didn't want his Tybee Climate Tour 2020 to be a complete bummer. So he made a point during our bike trip of showcasing the good work of local officials, university researchers, nonprofit experts, and dedicated volunteers in the fight against an aggrieved Mother Nature. Each Dyno-propelled stop highlighted a climate-mitigation project that promises to quell the rambunctiousness of high tides and killer storms. With two-thirds of Tybee possibly underwater by century's end, the odds against success are long. But the commitment to try and save Tybee is undeniably strong.

As far back as 2011, City officials began discussions with Clark Alexander and others on the damages wrought by sea-level rise. This was the Deep South, and deeply red Georgia, remember, where most folks either dismissed climate change as a hoax or disputed its manmade origins. Governors routinely dodged my questions on climate. Then-US Senator David Perdue, who lives on an another highly threatened barrier island sixty miles below Tybee, told me "the scientific community is not in total agreement about whether mankind has been a contributing factor."

In 2015, though, a remarkable report by Georgia's natural resource agency declared climate change "a threat (that) presents unprecedented challenges." A year later, the Tybee city council, with Paul leading the charge, unanimously approved a Sea Level Rise Adaptation Plan with all sorts of short- and long-term fixes. Tybee was the first Georgia community to officially acknowledge climate change.

"We hope we'll have time to adapt," Paul told me at the time. "If we don't want to be treading water or having our grandchildren growing gills, we definitely need to spend this money now instead of putting it off. The longer we procrastinate, the more expensive it will be."

Paul is a Tennessee boy, an Army brat, and Vanderbilt grad. Armed with degrees in English and sociology, Paul "hobo'ed for a couple years" out West, settling in Boulder, where he managed a Kentucky Fried Chicken. He returned to Wartrace, Tennessee, the home of the Tennessee Walking Horse National Museum, and took a day job as a buyer for a construction company. He raised organic cattle on the side, an unheard-of, yet far-sighted, undertaking in the mid-seventies South. He lived on $5,000 a year so he could retire young.

A friend told him about Tybee.

"He said, 'Paul, you got to check out this Tybee Island. There's people like you down there.'"

Paul and a girlfriend visited one weekend in 1994. She left. He stayed. Paid cash for his house. Married, and divorced, again.

"Tybee's a beach community that still feels like a small town," Paul says. "It's got height limits and no room for a golf course. People are very down-to-earth. I've never met anybody from Tybee who's not a character."

He turned part of his house into Tybee Moons bed-and-breakfast and entered local politics. "Protect our island paradise!" was his rallying cry, a campaign slogan good enough for twelve years on the city council. He pushed curbside recycling, green building, water conservation, carbon-free transportation (i.e., bicycles), and made "Tybee" synonymous with "sustainable." He tried to ban plastic bags and offshore drilling. He was the 2015 "Solar Advocate of the Year" in Georgia for helping to persuade dozens of local homeowners to put panels on roofs. He pushed offshore wind energy, to the consternation of some view-conscious constituents. He uses steel straws. His home is cluttered with newspapers, magazines, and bottles with no place to go, since the current council abolished his recycling program. (A sore point.)

On our Dynos we pass Melissa's jacked-up house, the Back River, and "the land that wasn't there." En route, we pass a tidal gate installed by the City to keep rising seawater from clogging storm drains and flooding the island's reclaimed-mud neighborhoods. During very high tides—even on sunny days—stormwater can't escape to the river so it flows backwards onto streets, yards, and crawl spaces.

At Chatham Avenue, with Little Tybee in the distance, Paul extols the wonders of an all-natural "living shoreline" made of earthen berms and oyster reefs.

We follow the designated bike route to the Nineteenth Street boardwalk and the island's "hot spot" where Hurricane Irma and sundry storm surges destroyed the low dunes. The City built acres of artificial dunes six feet tall and planted sea oats—resembling hair plugs on a bald man's pate—to hold it all together.

"Theoretically, it's going to work," Paul says, "but we haven't had a hurricane yet."

Finally, at North Beach, we dismount to marvel at the thirteen-million-dollar "re-nourishment" project that widened and thickened Tybee's main beach in 2020. Offshore dredges scooped up more than one million cubic yards of sand and deposited it between Fort Screven and the pier, two miles away. The town and the state paid for a series of herringbone-patterned dunes with fencing to keep the sand from migrating. Paul pounded wooden posts into the dunes. Sand is already piling up around the eight-foot poles, an encouraging sign.

"Hopefully, within five years, those fences will be invisible," Paul says, admiring his handiwork. "That's the goal. Build a fence and watch it disappear. It should help protect us against the consequences of sea-level rise."

The Tybee-saving projects and others—raising US 80, low-lying homes, and water pumps—are all part of the island's sea-level adaptation plan. The trick, basically, is to surround the island with barriers and put stuff on stilts. "Defend, adapt, and retreat" is the mantra of the climate-change-fighting crowd, though nobody dares suggest retreat in this tourist mecca. It's really a finger-in-the-dike strategy to wring as much living, and money, out of Tybee as they can before the inevitable tides and storms make residence on the barrier island impossible.

"Tybee is endangered from several perspectives," Clark, the marine geologist, tells me. "A lot of the fixed infrastructure and hard structures will eventually fail. Even if you put up a sea wall to protect the front side of the island, the back side of the island is still exposed to the standard rate of sea-level rise. And a wall on the back side of the island is exorbitantly expensive and not feasible. Tybee is going to have to significantly change unless they get some really rich benefactor who wants to put a wall around the entire island."

Just about every town up and down the Atlantic grapples with the changing climate. The US Army Corps of Engineers proposes encircling downtown Charleston with a two-billion-dollar, eight-mile-long sea wall with floodgates and pumping stations. Not to be outdone, Army Corps' engineers in Florida say that nearly five billion dollars is needed to wall off six miles of Miami coastline, elevate thousands of properties, and plant mangroves.

Paul believes that Tybee, one day, will need a wall, too. We park the Dynos at Huc-a-Poo's Bites and Booze, a typically Tybee laid-back establishment, and order a to-go pizza with extra anchovies for Paul's cats. The place is packed and maskless. We grab a couple of beers and hustle to a distant picnic table. We aren't in a celebratory mood. Paul motions to the revelers and returns to the other existential threat facing our planet.

"Their kids won't know the natural beauty we have," he says, more sad than bitter. "Climate change is inevitable. We're on the front lines of sea-level rise. We need to set an example for everybody else. We are doing irreversible damage to the planet and we're almost at the point where we can no longer minimize the damage."

The bartender brings the pizza to us. We pedal to Paul's house and eat dinner. The cats dig the anchovies.

CHAPTER 10

Where Hogs Rule and Turtles Tremble

Why do people always have to take something extraordinary and make it ordinary? Human thinking and planning really doesn't have a very good track record and human awareness is proven to be limited. Unknown things are hopeful—it's the known that I dread.

—Elizabeth Pool and Eleanor West, *The God of the Hinge*

Ossabaw Island, Georgia — Codey Elrod twists a silencer onto the barrel of the AR-15, grabs an extra clip, and disappears into the live oak and saw palmetto forest. A light rain falls. Thunder thumps in the distance. Codey, eyes scanning the ground for telltale signs, espies a deer's antler.

"That's good luck," he says.

Codey leaves the maritime forest and enters the marsh of mud flats, cordgrass, and black needlerush. The surf whispers in the distance. Two wood ducks, spooked, fly off. Codey speed-walks the animal trails following the pawprints of hogs, deer, raccoons, and rabbits.

"There she is," Codey whispers, stopping and shouldering his rifle. A fifty-pound sow, full of milk, roots through the muck thirty yards away. Codey fires three, quick, muffled shots. The black-haired mama pig squeals.

"She won't do that no more," Codey says.

He drags her body deeper into the marsh before returning to the trail. Five minutes later Codey tops a grassy knoll and, in the time it takes to turn a page, he fires again. And again. And again, the silenced shots nonetheless ricocheting around the tree-lined marsh. In all, eight shots fired. Five more dead hogs.

"It turned out to be a pretty good afternoon, didn't it?"

Hunting doesn't bother me. There's enough game in the South's woods and wetlands without jeopardizing any species' survival, unlike a century ago when hunters blasted Bambi into near-extinction. And one billion dollars a year in excise taxes on the sale of ammo, guns, and gear goes for land and animal conservation. What Codey hunts, too, shouldn't unduly bother the most ardent PETA supporter. He kills feral hogs, the alien, invasive, and insatiable wild boars introduced to the Americas in the 1500s by Spanish explorers. Not only do the pigs Hoover up nuts, roots, flowers, snails, snakes, fruit, and vegetable crops—costing billions of dollars in lost revenue annually—but they also eat eggs. On Ossabaw that means the eggs of federally endangered loggerhead sea turtles that come ashore between May and September and dig nests on the state-protected island's thirteen miles of pristine beach. Codey, in fact, is the South's only full-time, state-paid hog hunter. He is, officially, a "hog control technician" for the Georgia Department of Natural Resources.

"My job," Codey says, "is to kill hogs."

Something he does with deadly consistency. He has killed ten thousand hogs on Ossabaw. And yet they never disappear. Sows can have two litters a year, with maybe a dozen piglets at a time. Codey plays a real-life version of whack-a-mole every day. He's Bill Murray in *Groundhog Day*, but with a gun.

"Taking a life is not a small matter to me," he says, mossy oaks silhouetted against a darkening sky. "But they're not native to this habitat. And they're outcompeting other wildlife."

In the pantheon of nasty Southern invasives, feral hogs rank near the top. But the dais is crowded. Every forest, waterway, and farmer's field has its alien nemesis. In 2016, President Obama signed an executive order defining an invasive species as "a nonnative organism whose introduction causes or is likely to cause economic or environmental harm, or harm to human, animal, or plant health." They come from other countries or other regions of this country. Some estimates peg the number of invasive species at fifty thousand. Others say they're the second biggest threat to endangered species after habitat loss. Climate change pushes the foreign plants, animals, and pathogens farther north as once-unwelcoming climes become more hospitable. Daniel Simberloff, a conservation biologist at the University of Tennessee, says, "This is a huge problem that's getting worse."

Nowhere more so than in the South, a veritable hothouse of alien awfulness. Virtually every step along Muir's route today is home to some unwelcome import. Kentucky's nickname is the Bluegrass State, but there's nothing indigenous about its famed turf. It's native to Europe, northern Asia, and the mountains of Algeria and Morocco. (And it's not blue, either.) Carp from Asia were brought to waste-treatment plants and commercial catfish ponds in Arkansas and Mississippi in the 1970s to clean up parasites, weeds, and algae. Floods set them free and they've since traveled up the Mississippi (to Chicago), the Ohio, and the Tennessee Rivers and their tributaries. I recently spent a few cold days along the Tennessee talking to biologists, fishermen, river guides, and elected officials. Everybody was freaked out by the speed and rapacity with which silver and black carp had moved upriver, and beyond a handful of TVA dams. Black carp, with human-like molars, eat mussels and snails. Silver carp slurp up the plankton that all native mussels and fish depend on. Also known as "flying carp," silvers can jump ten feet out of the water, leaving boaters and water-skiers with broken bones and insane Instagram memories.

"They're going to keep migrating upriver, I don't care what you do," a marina manager at Lake Pickwick told me.

The mountains have also been ravaged by Asian imports. Four billion American chestnuts, the woody workhorse of the Appalachian forest prized by furniture makers and nut lovers, were destroyed by a pathogenic fungus from Japan in the early twentieth century. Now it's the Fraser fir's turn to disappear, courtesy of the woolly adelgid bug that hitched a ride from Japan to Virginia in the 1950s.

Armies of armadillos and caravans of coyotes roll across Georgia following the ever-warmer weather north. (Let's not even mention kudzu.) Northern snakeheads—the slimy, big-toothed fish that crawl like snakes, breathe on land, and eat other fish as well as frogs and lizards—were found in a pond outside Atlanta in 2019.

The nearby port of Savannah is a convenient jumping-off point for all manner of invasives that hitch rides in ballast water or burrow into wood pallets. Redbay ambrosia beetles jumped ship in 2002 and quickly introduced a wilt-causing fungus to laurel trees around Savannah before spreading across the Atlantic coastal plain. Hundreds of millions of redbay trees from Texas to North Carolina have succumbed to the disease that's now targeting sassafras and avocado trees, according to the National Invasive Species Information Center.

And then there's Florida, the poster child for Nature Run Amok, where the same conditions that welcome nine hundred humans daily—warm weather, sprawling cities, early-bird buffets—attract foreign interlopers, too. The US Fish and Wildlife Service says the Sunshine State harbors more nonnative plants and animals—skunk vines, walking catfish, vervet monkeys, Muscovy ducks, bloodsucking worms, dog-sized

Brazilian rodents—than any other state. One-fourth of the wildlife in Florida, and one-third of the flora, ain't from around there. It doesn't help that three-fourths of the nation's imported plants come through Florida. Nor that the world's reptile trade is headquartered in and around Miami. *Time* magazine called Florida "America's soft underbelly when it comes to invasives." The state spends a half-billion dollars a year fighting 'em. It even sponsors an Exotic Pet Amnesty Day where owners can turn in their "alien" animals, no questions asked.

Atop anybody's list of the most Frankensteinian of Florida's alien creatures is the Burmese python. Up to twenty feet long and wide as a telephone pole, the python wreaks havoc on the state's ecology by swallowing any mammal that dares to cross its path. Natives of Southeast Asian jungles, the reptiles were brought to Florida as exotic pets. When they got too big—upwards of two-hundred pounds—owners dumped them in the canals and lakes west of Miami. In 1992, Hurricane Andrew destroyed reptile farms near the Everglades, allowing countless constrictors to escape. Females can lay one hundred eggs at a time. No animal is safe from the Burmese python's maw. The US Geological Survey reports that 99 percent of Everglades raccoons and opossums have disappeared. Gone too are marsh rabbits, cottontail rabbits, and foxes. Pictures of pythons wrestling alligators or having deer-shaped bulges in their bellies underscore their power and dominance.

What's more frightening, though, is their relentless territorial expansion and the futility of trying to stop them. They've been observed at both ends of the Florida Keys, a wellspring of biodiversity. The adorably cute Key deer, the almost-as-cuddly Key Largo cotton mouse, and the Lower Keys marsh rabbit—or *Sylvilagus palustris hefneri*, named after the *Playboy* founder who donated money for bunny field research— are all federally endangered and could be next on the python's plate. Apparently not satisfied with destroying South Florida's wildlife, the pythons spread parasitic worms that kill pygmy rattlesnakes in North Florida.

Pythons, though, have competition for the title of Florida's grossest invasive. Cane toads, native to South and Central America, were brought to the Sunshine State in the 1930s and '40s to eat sugarcane pests. When bitten, the toads secrete a toxic poison that can kill a dog. They usually hang out in South and Central Florida, but have recently been found near Gainesville.

And then there are the lizards. Green iguanas literally fall out of trees when it gets cold. I ran over one on US 1 in the Keys, felt horrible, and confessed my sin to a biologist who laughed and said he swerves *towards* the lizards. They're pernicious buggers, burrowing beneath foundations, devouring eggs and snails, and pooping everywhere. Spiny and medieval-looking, the iguanas grow more than five feet long. They're also strong swimmers that can hold their breath for a long time, which allows them to work their way into . . . toilets. A Roto-Rooter plumber got the surprise of his life a few years back when he pulled an iguana from a Fort Lauderdale toilet. The Florida Fish and Wildlife Conservation Commission encourages homeowners to shoot them on sight. Their reptilian brethren, South American tegus, will also eat small alligators and young gopher tortoises. In 2019, they were discovered in southeast Georgia. A year later they were in South Carolina.

Miami, of course, is home to one of the state's more bizarre interlopers. Giant African land snails, once eradicated, were smuggled from East Africa a decade ago for use in religious rituals. The snail's mucus allegedly heals certain ailments. The shelled gastropod, one of the world's largest terrestrial mollusks, also has an insatiable appetite for any and all plants. Or stucco. Or car paint. Anything with calcium. They're hermaphroditic love machines, with both male and female bits, capable of reproducing with anybody. Their shells can puncture tires. Oh, and they can kill you. Snail slime serves as a warm, comfy home for parasitic rat lungworm, which causes meningitis.

Another chapter could be written on alien and invasive plants, but I won't bore you. Safe to say, the same forces that attract some of the world's weirdest mammals lure nonnative plants to Florida, too. Fourteen hundred invasive plants call the Sunshine State home, according to the University of Florida's Institute of Food and Agricultural Sciences. Two—the Old World climbing fern and the melaleuca tree—march in deadly synchronicity across the Everglades, smothering the island-like hammocks and marshes and the flora that sustain a host of threatened and endangered species, including wood storks and snail kites. And they're both riding the Climate-Change Express for destinations north.

What a difference a bellyful of gingerbread makes. John Muir, after five or six days hungry, alone, and afraid in Bonaventure Cemetery, stumbled—"staggery and giddy"—into Savannah for yet another visit to the express office in hopes that his brother had wired the money. He had. Within minutes Muir had purchased "a jubilee of bread" and, a bit later, a full-fledged breakfast. His spirits soared; his mind, though, still seemed addled by his Bonaventure experience.

"Of the people of the states that I have now passed, I best like the Georgians," Muir wrote, "even the negroes."

The naturalist took stock of all the wonderful plants, flowers, and trees he had encountered along the way, including magnolias, tupelos, live oaks, Kentucky oaks, Spanish moss, long-leafed pines, palmettos, mimosas, bamboo, and lilies. "Yet I still press eagerly on to Florida as the special home of the tropical plants I am looking for, and I feel sure I shall not be disappointed," he wrote.

It's a mystery why he sailed, instead of hiked, to Florida. The hundred-mile stretch from Savannah to St. Marys, where a ferry would've readily carried him across the same-name river to Florida, is rich in flora with wide, plodding rivers feeding estuarine marshes. Perhaps he was scared of the jungle-like stretches of swamp and seclusion. Maybe he was tired of walking and wanted to get on with his life. Possibly he was feverish and shell-shocked from his Bonaventure stay. Muir never explains why he didn't walk to Florida, and neither do his biographers. But what he missed—the maritime forests, the saltwater marshes, the barrier islands—has mesmerized nature lovers for centuries.

William Bartram, the Philadelphia botanist who introduced Southern biodiversity to the world, traveled not once but twice between Savannah and Florida in the 1770s, which he chronicled in *Travels of William Bartram*.

"It was drawing towards the close of day," he wrote while strolling a greensward near St. Marys, "the skies serene and calm, the air temperately cool, and gentle zephyrs breathing through the fragrant pines; the prospect around enchantingly varied and beautiful; endless green savannas, chequered with coppices of fragrant shrubs, filled the air with the richest perfume. The gaily attired plants which enameled the green had begun to imbibe the pearly dew of evening; nature seemed silent, and nothing appeared to ruffle the happy moments of evening contemplation."

The salt marsh is an otherworldly kaleidoscope of above- and below-water fecundity, which enraptured poet Sydney Lanier in *The Marshes of Glynn*.

Oh, what is abroad in the marsh and the terminal sea?
Somehow my soul seems suddenly free
From the weighing of fate and the sad discussion of sin,
By the length and the breadth and the sweep of the marshes of Glynn.

Ye marshes, how candid and simple and nothing-withholding
and free
Ye publish yourselves to the sky and offer yourselves to the sea!

Rachel Carson, my Fish and Wildlife soulmate, wrote an ecologically
and spiritually rich account of the coastal world in *Under the Sea-Wind*,
her first book, published in 1941:

> To stand at the edge of the sea, to sense the ebb and flow of the tides,
> to feel the breath of a mist moving over a great salt marsh, to watch
> the flight of shore birds that have swept up and down the surf lines
> of the continents for untold thousands of years, to see the running
> of the old eels and the young shad to the sea, is to have knowledge
> of things that are as nearly eternal as any earthly life can be.

Muir, though, would experience little of these coastal riches. He
sailed that afternoon for Fernandina on the *Sylvan Shore*, a steamer that
carried him down the Savannah River to the Atlantic, and past Tybee,
St. Catherines, Sapelo, St. Simons, and Cumberland Islands. Muir,
from a comfortable distance, observed the forests of live oak, yellow
pine, cabbage palm, and magnolia, as well as the jungled understory of
yaupon, wax myrtle, sparkleberry, and saw palmetto. He could've filled
another plant press with cordgrass, yucca, glassworts, resurrection ferns,
and beach-tea croton. It was peak birding season, so Muir missed the
wealth of great blue herons, rufa red knots, piping plovers, American
oystercatchers, and short-billed dowitchers idling along the untrammeled beaches. Instead, he seemed quite relieved to sail "past a very
sickly, entangled, overflowed, and unwalkable piece of forest."

I drive to Savannah early one February morn. Codey picks me up at the
state dock a couple of miles below Bonaventure Cemetery. It's a blue-sky

day with a wisp of wind, ideal for hunting hogs and side-stepping snakes and alligators slowed, I hoped, by the cool weather. It takes twenty minutes to motor across the Little Ogeechee and Ogeechee Rivers to reach Torrey Landing. I'd visited Ossabaw before as a newspaperman to write a lengthy profile of Sandy West, the island matriarch whose father bought the island in 1924, joining a slew of Northern grandees named Carnegie, Morgan, and Vanderbilt who gobbled up Georgia's barrier islands for winter retreats. Sandy, then 103 years old, was broke, infirm, and destined to leave the island she loved like nothing else. My story, disguised as a "life-well-lived" paean to a selfless philanthropist and environmentalist, with testimonials from Jimmy Carter, Annie Dillard, and Greg Allman, was really a fundraising plea to help Sandy remain on Ossabaw. It didn't work.

Codey eases the scruffy, state-issued Chevy pickup down the Main Road, past Sandy's pink stucco mansion, and over to Half Moon Road. He's chewing a plug of Grizzly tobacco with a rifle across his lap, his head on a swivel. Anything moves, Codey sees it. He aims to hunt alongside the Bradley River, which serpentines through tidal marsh, cypress swamp, and maritime forest. I ask how he got one of the most coveted jobs any Southern boy could dream of. Codey tells me his story.

He grew up in Taylorsville, an hour northwest of Atlanta. His father was a welder; his mom worked at a bank. He started hunting and fishing with his great-grandfather, Papa J, when he was four years old. Codey earned an associate's degree in wildlife management at a small South Georgia agricultural college. He first came to Ossabaw as an hourly hog hunter in 2010. A year later he was hired full-time and told to kill as many wild boars as possible. "I never would've imagined that this would be my job," Codey says. "But I sure do enjoy doing it."

He spends three hundred days a year on Ossabaw, usually alone, in a cabin. He had a girlfriend in Savannah, but is now "happily single." He saves vacation days for the spring to go—what else?—turkey hunting.

Codey, twenty-nine years old, uses every hunting trick in the book to kill pigs: dried corn bait; thermal-imaging scopes; dogs Bobo (a pit bull) and Rudy (a black mouth cur); and traps. Trapping garners the highest yield, but takes a lot of time. He won't hunt the dogs in hot weather; cool-down ponds also attract alligators. Codey prefers shooting hogs one at a time with non-lead bullets that won't harm bald eagles and other scavengers. Danger abounds: alligators; rattlesnakes; ticks; and, of course, hogs. Once, in South Carolina, Codey was hunting with dogs when he came in for the kill with a pocketknife. Momentarily distracted, the hog gored him with his tusks. Fourteen stitches in the arm, another twelve on the wrist.

"I've had some dreams about hogs, more like nightmares of being attacked by hogs," says the sandy-haired, bearded hunter. "It's like being in your house when a burglar breaks in and all you've got is a pillow to hit him in the head with."

Codey has been hunting Ossabaw since 2012. He kills, on average, 1,117 hogs a year. In 2016, he killed 1,561 hogs—an Ossabaw record.

"That's always the goal—kill all the hogs you can," Codey says, classic rock playing low on the truck radio. "But I might work myself right out of a job. Maybe not. There's a problem with hogs pretty much everywhere in Georgia now."

Not everybody considers hogs a nuisance. Christopher Columbus brought eight pigs to Cuba in 1493. Spanish conquistadores and missionaries later introduced them to Florida, Georgia, and the Carolinas. The hogs are a renewable and nutritious resource. Tasty, too. Restaurateurs in Charleston and elsewhere swear by the taste of Ossabaw pigs due to their genetically pure makeup, fat quotient, and acorn-heavy diet.

Sandy West considered them pets. She had run through her family's plate-glass fortune by the 1970s, spending millions on world-renowned artists' and writers' colonies (Ralph Ellison, Margaret Atwood, Annie Dillard), an environmental retreat for college kids, and the preservation of the forty-square-mile island's natural splendor. Developers salivated at the prospect of building a bridge and high-end golf course community a few miles below Savannah. Aristotle Onassis and wife Jackie Kennedy offered to buy it sight unseen.

Sandy sold Ossabaw Island to the state in 1978 for eight million dollars and a so-far solid promise that it forever remain wild and undeveloped. (The deal let her live in the Spanish revival mansion until her death.) Ossabaw became Georgia's first Heritage Preserve. To cut down on expenses and damage, the state ordered all the cows and horses off the island, angering the animal-loving Sandy. When wildlife experts said the pigs rooting up the island needed to be heavily culled, Sandy, who considered two pigs named Lucky and Mrs. Musgrove as dear friends, exploded.

"I am not going to be pushed around," she told the *Atlanta Journal-Constitution* in 2000. "I'm not going to let them destroy every bit of the power and magic we had. It would be so easy to do, the minute you put the hand of man here."

John Muir would've loved Sandy. Codey likes her a lot, even though Miss Sandy can't abide his profession. For a while, they were the only full-time residents of Ossabaw: the eccentric naturalist (she also had a diesel-sniffing Sicilian donkey named Mary Helen who'd barge into the pink mansion unannounced); and the hog killer.

"She's a real special person," Codey says. "If you can't respect her decision not to sell out, I don't know what to tell you. That says a lot about her character."

It's near dark and Codey cruises South End Beach Road with a half dozen kills on the day. A never-logged cypress marsh hugs one side of the road, the forest the other.

"Look at that!" Codey shouts.

I see nothing.

He shifts into park and opens the door in one motion. Out he jumps, rifle on the rise. He aims. One shot. That's all it takes. In the middle of the marsh, seventy-five yards away, a two-hundred-pound hog with a bright pink spot on its chest thrashes before falling silent.

"He thought he was hid good enough, didn't he?" Codey says, adrenaline flowing. "He was dead in the water. I usually get 'em."

The 2020 International Wild Pig Conference was set for Jacksonville, Florida, in early April and I was raring to go. It was on my way, after all, even though Muir skirted the town en route to the Gulf. Sponsored by the National Wild Pig Task Force, the annual gathering of hog hunters, farmers, foresters, biologists, nonprofit conservationists, and state and federal officials promised the latest insights into pig diseases, trapping techniques, and poisoning practices. Wild boar have "arguably become one of the greatest wildlife management challenges facing natural resource professionals and landowners," the task force website says. I needed to hear these guys. Plus, a pig pickin' would kick things off.

Alas, the conference got corona-canceled. So I contacted the conference organizers to get some information on the feral swine menace. Anywhere from two to six million hogs, I was told, wreak havoc across forty states and four Canadian provinces. Texas appears to be the most overrun. They thrive almost anywhere: farms, fields, swamps, mountains, barrier islands, suburban golf courses. Hogs are "opportunistic omnivores" who'll eat anything. They can root down three feet below ground. They devour fields of corn, sorghum, soybeans, rice, wheat, melons, hay. Wild pigs dig up the soil surrounding streams, causing erosion, sedimentation, and fish kills. Invasive plants fill the holes left behind by their inhalation of grasses and forbs. They'll even eat snakes, quail, deer, lambs, and calves. The US Department of Agriculture admits that its one-and-a-half-billion-dollar tally of annual damages caused by hogs is low. Texas alone estimates four hundred million dollars in hog damage.

And that's the death and destruction wrought by just *one* invasive species. What about all the damage done by other alien intruders? For that I need David Pimentel, a Cornell University professor of agricultural sciences. In 2005, he penned what's still considered the most comprehensive assessment of the damage done by invasive species. Unfortunately, Pimentel died in 2019, at ninety-four, after a long, illustrious, and prolific—forty books—career advocating on behalf of the natural environment. It was Professor Pimentel and colleagues who calculated that fifty thousand foreign species have been introduced to the United States. Some, like corn, wheat, rice, and cattle, have proven beneficial. Other (mostly) welcome species include dogs, cats, and insects that control biological pests. Most plant and vertebrate invasives have been intentionally introduced, Pimentel said, while most invertebrates and microbes have not.

"In the past forty years, the rate and risk associated with biotic invaders have increased enormously because of human population growth, rapid movement of people, and alteration of the environment," he wrote. "In addition, more goods and materials are being traded among nations than ever before, thereby creating opportunities for unintentional introductions."

Pimentel pegged the damage done annually by all alien species at a staggering $120 billion. And that was fifteen years ago. Imported invasives, for example, account for nearly three-fourths of all types of weeds, and they reduce crop yields by 12 percent, or thirty-three billion dollars, a year. Nearly four hundred alien bugs cost the forest-products industry more than two billion dollars a year.

But it's the colossal, yet incalculable, damage that invasives do to the biodiversity of the natural environment that threatens to sunder the South. The professor determined that 42 percent of all the threatened and endangered (T&E) species are "declining because of invasive species."

But is the invasive invasion *really* such a bad thing? Alien species have been around ever since Gronk tottered out of the Great Rift Valley. We've grown accustomed to them, if we even notice them. Feral hogs, after all, were introduced to the Southeast five hundred years ago, and hunters and chefs love them. Sweet-smelling honeysuckle strangles native plants, yet studies show that the flowering ornamental boosts the abundance and diversity of birds. Domestic cats aren't native to the United States, and kill up to four billion birds a year, but try telling your mother that cuddly Coco must go.

Mark Davis, a Macalester College ecologist, roiled the academic world in 2011 with an essay in the journal *Nature* entitled "Don't Judge Species on Their Origins." Davis and associates acknowledged that certain alien species are harmful, yet most are benign or even beneficial to their respective ecosystems. He likened discrimination against invasives to nativist wrongheadedness and a foolhardy desire to return to some naturally pure state, like the crazy notion of "wilderness."

"The natural systems of the past are changing forever thanks to drivers such as climate change, nitrogen eutrophication, increased urbanization, and other land-use changes," Davis wrote. "It is time for scientists, land managers, and policy-makers to ditch this preoccupation with the native–alien dichotomy."

Codey rises before the sun to hunt Ossabaw's south end. It's cool and windy, with last night's rain lingering and the tide running high. The weather, again, is ideal, unless you're a pig. The wind swooshes everything around, discombobulating animals' sense of smell and direction. Rain muffles footsteps. High water drives hogs up onto dunes and hammocks.

Codey puts on the night vision goggles at the edge of the Buckhead

Field and scans the old cotton patch. Nothing moves. He gets back into his truck and drives farther south as the sky lightens. A rabbit bounds across the road. A cormorant takes wing as Codey parks along Mule Run Road. He crosses a tidal creek, skirts a pile of hurricane debris, and heads south along a sandy ridge. An alligator lolls in a pond.

"All right, Mr. Hog, where you at?" Codey asks. "Probably laid up in some palmetto somewhere."

He crosses more sloughs and hammocks. Three hours in and nary a hog to be found.

Suddenly, the forest crashes. A family of four hogs tries to escape into the swamp between palmettos. Codey gets two of them, the mama and a baby.

"Well, we didn't come up empty-handed," Codey says, smiling. "Let's find us another and save some turtles."

Codey makes a big difference on Ossabaw, particularly during the May-to-September turtle nesting season when he concentrates on the beach. In the five years before Georgia hired a marksman, 31 percent of loggerhead turtle nests were attacked by hogs or other predators. In the last five years, only 10 percent were.

I have a boat to catch, so Codey steers the pickup north on Willows Road. Two unsuspecting baby pigs race across the road and into the swamp. Codey doesn't bother giving chase. He knows he's got them on the run.

CHAPTER 11

Take My Water, Please

It seems to me that the earth may be borrowed but not bought.
It may be used but not owned. . . . We are tenants, not posses-
sors, lovers and not masters.
    —Marjorie Kinnan Rawlings, *Cross Creek*

High Springs, Florida — The *Sylvan Shore* docked at the "rickety wharf"
in the "rickety town" of Fernandina, and Muir headed straight for the
woods. He seemed ready for the journey to end. All that remained was a
quick hike through the flatland forests to the port of Cedar Key, where
a fast ship to more exotic locales surely awaited. A straight shot to the
Gulf of Mexico. A week tops. Easy.

Yet here were the subtropics—"the flowery Canaan"—the land of
the majestic palmetto and the mysterious alligator that Muir had long
dreamed of. His scientific, and childlike, curiosity would not be denied.

The steamship dropped Muir at the little port along the Amelia River.
A rail line pointed westward into the "shady, gloomy groves" bordered
by salt marsh. Muir bought some bread and, following the tracks, disappeared into the wild.

"Everything in earth and sky had an impression of strangeness; not a mark of friendly recognition, not a breath, not a spirit whisper of sympathy came from anything about me, and of course I was lonely," Muir wrote upon finding a dry spot to eat breakfast.

The tracks had been laid by David Levy Yulee—the "Father of Florida Railroads"—who connected the Atlantic Ocean to the Gulf of Mexico, thereby allowing ships to avoid the lengthy route around the Florida peninsula. Yulee was quite a character. Born into a wealthy Moroccan-Jewish family on the Caribbean island of Saint Thomas, he emigrated to Florida as a teen. A lawyer, sugarcane plantation owner, and railroad builder, Yulee was the first Jew to serve in the US Senate. His pro-slavery and pro-secession bona fides earned him another, more colorful moniker: "Florida Fire Eater." The Civil War, though, brought him low. Union troops destroyed his Margarita plantation. He was arrested and charged with treason, and spent nine months in a federal prison. Pardoned in 1866, Yulee returned to Florida and the railroad business. He died in 1886. The community of Yulee, and the county of Levy, are named for him.

Muir passed through Yulee. He hugged the tracks; the surrounding jungle of swamp, vine, and pine proved near-impenetrable. He heard a rustling in the rushes. Alligator!

"I fancied I could feel the stroke of his long notched tail, and could see his big jaws and rows of teeth, closing with a springy snap on me, as I had seen in pictures," Muir wrote in *A Thousand-Mile Walk to the Gulf.*

It was just a white crane. Muir blamed his jumpiness on "Bonaventure anxiety and hunger." He started to relax. He'd occasionally leave the tracks and venture into "the hot gardens of the sun" to add grasses and lilies to his collection.

"But the grandest discovery of this great wild day was the palmetto," Muir reported. "This palm was indescribably impressive and told me grander things than I ever got from human priest."

He trudged on. He sought dry spots to sleep "safely hidden from wild, runaway negroes." He finished his bread and drank brown, tannin-infused water from streams. The next morning, starving and edgy, he came across a shanty where loggers were eating.

"They were the wildest of all the white savages I have met," he wrote. "The long-haired ex-guerrillas of the mountains of Tennessee and North Carolina are uncivilized fellows; but for downright barbarism these Florida loggers excel."

Nonetheless, they fed him pork and hominy.

Muir crossed the Santa Fe River before reaching Gainesville ("rather attractive—an oasis in the desert"). None of Florida's streams impressed Muir. They didn't flow rapidly through steep-banked valleys or provide the sibilant sounds of water rushing over rock. They were slow-moving and meandering, and "in deep places . . . black as ink, perfectly opaque, and glossy on the surface as if varnished."

"The flowers here are strangers to me, but not more so than the rivers and lakes," Muir continued. "Most streams appear to travel through a country with thoughts and plans for something beyond. But those of Florida are at home, do not appear to be traveling at all, and seem to know nothing of the sea."

He was wrong, of course. The Santa Fe is a wily and purposeful river that flows from east to west and disappears underground only to re-emerge three miles later amid natural springs before reaching the famed Suwannee River. Muir, in his defense, was a young plant lover who had yet to embrace the watery wonders of the Colorado and Tuolumne Rivers, or of the Alaskan glaciers. But he clearly missed the boat on the importance, and mystique, of Florida's streams and springs.

I drove to Fernandina Beach on an already-hot summer morning, keen to follow Muir's path as faithfully as possible. I'd camped the night before across from the Okefenokee National Wildlife Refuge, enjoying the sweet-rotten stank of the swamp and a blanket of stars until the mosquitoes chased me inside my tent. Like many small Southern ports, Fernandina is a mash of shrimpers, millworkers, tourists, and retirees. Its quaint downtown of ice creameries and women's clothiers is sandwiched between two paper mills, one making cardboard, the other pulp. A bronzed David Yulee sits on a bench with pocket watch at the ready. Trawlers and sailboats run the Amelia River north to the St. Marys River and out to sea.

I take the road closest to the river, past mountains of wood pulp. Logging trucks share the road with pickups and Mercedes as I pass the usual assortment of fast-food restaurants and used-car lots. I pick up speed to leave behind the suburban dross when, all of a sudden, I see a sign next to a small parking lot. I could've sworn I'd read the word *Muir*. I pull a U-ey. And there it is: The John Muir Ecological Park.

What a treat. What karma. What . . . *is* this place? A wooden boardwalk leads a quarter mile into the viny swamps and thick woods. Gazebos and benches, with initials and expletives carved into the soft wood, afford respite from the heat. Trash cans are chained to the railings. Cicadas replace the thrum of traffic. Two signs, one detailing Muir's life, the other Yulee's railroad, welcome me at trail's end. The forest of palmetto and pine, of fetterbush and yaupon holly, seems impassable until I make out the remains of an old railroad berm.

This is where Muir trod. This is what he saw and, more crucially, what he conquered en route to the Gulf. I was in awe. In the dark and the quiet, I genuflected to Muir's perseverance and passion. But not for long. The mosquitoes hurried me away, back into the sunlight and the four-lane traffic. Eventually, I learned that, thirty years ago, a gastroenterologist came up with the idea for the park to honor Muir. It wasn't until environmental fines were levied against the county two decades later, though, that the park was built. Talk about karma.

Buoyed, I continue my westward trek past a development with room for twenty-four thousand homes, the nothing-burg of Yulee, and Interstate 95. Traces of old Florida occasionally crop up, like the boiled peanut stand in Callahan or the state prison outside Starke. Endless miles of pine plantations run to the horizon. The towns of Lawtey and Hampton were once nationally renowned speed traps preying on beach-bound Northerners. US 301, today, with its divided highway running past dozens of "Land For Sale" signs, foretells nothing as much as the outer edge of Jacksonville sprawl.

I turn off the highway and take back roads to High Springs and the Howard T. Odum Florida Springs Institute, near the spot where the Santa Fe River comes out of the ground. Odum's father, also named Howard, was a famous Southern sociologist. His older brother, Eugene, was credited with turning ecology into a respected science. Howard junior was no scientific slouch either. He pioneered much of the science surrounding the ecology of ecosystems. At the nearby University of Florida, in Gainesville, the younger Odum studied the role that wetlands play in purifying surface water. He focused on the natural springs, the water that flows from underground aquifers to the surface. Odum's groundbreaking work at Silver Springs, near Ocala, where glass-bottom boats have introduced millions of tourists to the underwater world since the 1870s, revolved around the productivity and energy generated by springs.

Bob Knight is an "Odumite," an environmental scientist whose dissertation on the ecology of Silver Springs was shepherded by Odum in the late 1970s. Bob went on to build wastewater-treatment wetlands across the South. His systems returned clean water to the underlying aquifer, where it regenerated the springs and became, once again, available for human consumption. Bob founded the Springs Institute in

2010. And that's where I found him, behind a long white table at the storefront nonprofit that sits across from the New Century Woman's Club in quaint downtown High Springs. The institute monitors the health of Florida's thousand springs—Weeki Wachee, Ginnie, Wakulla, Ichetucknee—and raises the alarm whenever a spring is threatened by sewage, ag runoff, phosphate mines, municipalities, or businesses with supersized straws.

"Somebody's got to speak up for the springs—it's just so necessary," says Bob, a trim septuagenarian with white goatee and wire-rimmed glasses. "We've made enormous inroads into the understanding of springs. They're the best-kept secrets of North Florida."

And they're mesmerizing, blue-green "bowls of liquid light," according to Marjory Stoneman Douglas, author of *The Everglades: River of Grass*, a classic of environmental literature. Yet the natural springs are more than boat-ride attractions and cool swimming holes (always around 70 degrees Fahrenheit). They're portals to underground oceans—the aquifers that civilizations are built upon. The Floridan Aquifer, from whence these local springs *spring*, contains trillions of gallons of water and sustains communities in South Carolina, Georgia, Alabama, Mississippi, and Florida. More than ten million people, including the denizens of Gainesville, Orlando, Tampa and Savannah, depend upon the Floridan for drinking water. It's one of the most productive aquifers in the world, a one-hundred-thousand-square-mile reservoir filled with highly filtered rainwater. Rain, though, only refills a smidgen of the underground limestone caverns. Most disappears via evaporation or transpiration, or it just runs off into the ocean. What's left gushes up through the springs. Or gets sucked up by wells.

"The bubbling spring would rise forever from the earth, the thin current was endless," wrote Marjorie Kinnan Rawlings in *The Yearling*, her 1938 Pulitzer Prize–winning novel about a boy, a deer, and familial angst set in the nearby Ocala National Forest.

Marjorie, though, was wrong.

Water withdrawals in Florida and Georgia, the two biggest Floridan drinkers, shot up more than 400 percent between 1950 and 2010, according to the US Geological Survey. Water flowing from the springs themselves has declined by a third during that period, the Springs Institute says. At Bob's beloved Silver Springs, the flow has dropped from five hundred million gallons to two hundred million gallons daily.

Where's all that water going? Funny you should ask.

Florida is the nation's third-most populous state, home to twenty-two million snowbirds and flume-ride operators. Nearly a thousand people a day move to the Sunshine State. They've got to drink. And flush the toilet. And most of the state's water comes from the Floridan. But it's not just Florida Man sticking straws into the aquifer. Irrigation—orange groves, hayfields, golf courses—consumes nearly half of the aquifer's yield. Cities and towns take more than a third.

"Concern persists that the widespread use of the Floridan aquifer system for multiple and sometimes competing uses will result in unforeseen hydrologic consequences," says USGS.

It's not a particularly startling prediction, especially with rising populations, temperatures, and sea levels. In 2015, NASA and the University of California, Irvine, reported that twenty-one of the world's largest aquifers had passed their "tipping points" whereby more water was taken out of the aquifers than put back in.

"The water table is dropping all over the world," said a NASA water scientist in the report. "There's not an infinite supply of water."

Certainly not in north Florida.

"The aquifer and surface water are intimately connected in Florida—more so, obviously, because of our springs," Bob tells me as the outer bands of Hurricane Sally reach High Springs. "But we're killing our springs, permit by permit. My new book is titled *Death by a Thousand Cuts*. There are roughly twenty-nine thousand larger permits in the springs region of Florida. So if everybody pumped to the maximum amount, we would lose half of all the springs flow in Florida. And all the lesser springs would stop flowing."

Until 1887, the Floridan was largely untouched. Savannah, though, had so polluted its surface water that it began tapping the aquifer. By 1898, more than two hundred wells had been dug across coastal Georgia. Fernandina, Jacksonville, Tampa, and Fort Myers soon joined the drilling frenzy. But it little mattered, because the "huge limestone sponge" held so much water that it naturally bubbled to the surface. White Sulfur Springs, "way down upon the Suwannee River," became Florida's first tourist attraction, with hotels and a four-story bathhouse, thanks to the supposed healing powers of its mineral-rich waters. The Sunshine State's real estate boom—built largely on dredged wetlands and the P. T. Barnum-esque allure of endless sun, sand, and water—would soon test the Floridan's seemingly limitless capacity. And then came the pulp and paper mills along the coast of Georgia and North Florida, none bigger or thirstier than Union Bag in Savannah.

Groundwater "is one of our most important and underappreciated resources," writes William Boyd, a law school professor at UCLA. "Because it is not visible . . . we tend to take it for granted. Its invisibility leads to neglect, misuse, and waste. The groundwater crisis in coastal Georgia, as in so many other places around the world, can be viewed as a failure of regulation, a failure of governance, and a failure to value the resource in a manner that will sustain it. Underneath all these failures, however, is a failure of politics—a failure to recognize collectively that the Floridan aquifer is a shared resource that will surely be ruined if subjected to a relentless industrial logic of extraction for too long."

In March 1968, when the International Paper mill in Riceboro, Georgia, switched on its massive underground pumps, the outdoor fountains on Sapelo Island, twenty miles away, went dry. Eugene P. Odum labeled the silence "deafening." Mills had sprung up in Brunswick, St. Marys, and Jesup, too, and by the 1990s they sucked up 60 percent of all permitted daily withdrawals along the Georgia coast. Wells had to be dug 150 feet deep just to reach the aquifer.

Huge "cones of depression" formed below the mills as the water receded. Less water meant less water pressure, too. Where the aquifer once surged into the Atlantic Ocean in some places, the salty Atlantic Ocean now surges into the aquifer—with potentially ruinous consequences. Beaufort and Parris Island, South Carolina, for example, had to abandon their too-salty wells. The Bag's cone of depression caused saltwater intrusion under Hilton Head, sullying its drinking water. South Carolina threatened repeatedly to sue Georgia. A moratorium on new well permits, and lower withdrawals, has so far mollified the Palmetto State.

But nobody expects the watery truce to hold, not with climate-induced droughts becoming more frequent, in turn prompting farmers, factories, developers, and lawn-lovers to suck up more and more of the aquifer. California, for example, taps aquifers for 60 percent of its water during droughts as rivers and reservoirs dry up. It usually relies upon aquifers for only 40 percent of its water supply.

"We also have major droughts in the Southeast, periodically, every ten years, and really big ones every twenty years," says Bob, who first scuba-dived into the world-renowned underwater caves at Ginnie Springs fifty years ago. "May 2012 was the lowest level of spring flows I've ever seen. The Santa Fe river stopped flowing completely. It turned into a cesspool. It was an algal bowl. There were dead fish everywhere. That had never happened before. And some springs, like Poe, Rum Island, Worthington, and Hornsby, stopped flowing. Some of them never came back."

Disappearing flows, though, are only half the battle. The springs, increasingly, are polluted. Thirty percent of Florida's homes rely on septic tanks to dispose of waste. The nitrate-rich poop and pee seep into the soil, then the groundwater, through the porous limestone, and into the aquifer before rising back up to the springs and into the wells. Toxic nitrates, which can cause blue baby syndrome, are the most prevalent class of chemical found in the Floridan. Eighty percent of the springs tested by the Institute contained nitrates at levels that exceeded the state's water-quality standard. At Wakulla Springs near Tallahassee, where *The Creature from the Black Lagoon* was filmed, half of the nitrates come courtesy of septic tanks, according to the state's so-called Department of Environmental Protection. That's *really* scary.

Fertilized fields, and manure from cows and chickens, all produce nitrates that reach ground and surface waters. So, too, do dairies, wastewater-treatment plants and always-green lawns and golf courses. Untreated stormwater flows directly into the Floridan from dozens of drainage wells in the Orlando area. Several towns no longer depend solely on the upper Floridan aquifer for drinking water; they've had to dig deeper to reach the lower Floridan.

And then there are the phosphate mines, the sprawling, land-scouring, aquifer-sucking, water-fouling industrial operations that turn deeply buried rocks into—wait for it—fertilizer to grow crops, lawns, and gardens. The same fertilizer that, once it trickles through the soil or runs off into the nearest stream, pollutes the whole groundwater/aquifer/springs system. The irony doesn't amuse ecologists. Florida is the nation's leading producer of phosphate, with twenty-seven mines covering nearly five hundred thousand acres of central Florida. Mining, though, isn't limited to the so-called Bone Valley region. Four North Florida families want to strip-mine eleven thousand acres straddling the New River, which feeds into the Santa Fe. The Santa Fe is already under siege from nitrates. A river gage at the State Road 47 bridge shows a tenfold increase in nitrate load in just fifty years.

Not even Gill-Man of Black Lagoon fame would want to hang out in that toxic mess. The fertilizing properties of nitrates and phosphorus create massive algal blooms, especially during low flows. Hydrilla—one of the nation's most invasive aquatic plants—gets supercharged, too. Combined, the twin biological terrors decrease dissolved oxygen levels (which harms fish), displace native plants (which fish eat), and block sunlight, which turns once-crystal springs into turbid lagoons. The glass-bottom boats at Wakulla Springs rarely run these days due to the murky water. "Whole river systems are dying in Florida," Bob says. "The springs are just the most visible canary in the coal mine."

He can quote chapter, verse, and nutrient-load levels for just about every spring in Florida. So he takes it personally when a spring dries up, algae bloom, fish die, or once-pellucid waters, where divers could spot underwater turtles three hundred feet away, turn brown and opaque. He created a report card for Florida's major springs. Mama would not be pleased with the grades. In 2018, the Springs Institute rated thirty-two "sentinel" springs on water flow, salinity, and nitrate pollution. None received an A. Half got a D+ or lower. Silver Springs—Howard T. Odum's baby, which he assiduously researched in the early 1950s—got an F.

Silver was once Florida's largest, most abundant spring, discharging an average of 530 million gallons of water daily. Steamboats began ferrying tourists up the Ocklawaha and Silver Rivers to the springs in the 1850s. Hotels sprang up and glass-bottomed boats plied the azure waters of the state's top tourist destination. Six Tarzan movies were shot there. Environmental pressures were few. Its springshed, after all, was only 3 percent urbanized.

But nature, of course, abhors a vacuum, so developers and horse lovers filled Central Florida. The Rodman Dam and reservoir along the Ocklawaha opened in 1968 as part of the cross-state barge canal which, thankfully, was killed by Richard Nixon three years later. The dam remains, however, and it keeps fish and manatees from running the St. Johns River to Silver Springs. By 2005, Ocala's sprawl had covered 37 percent of the Silver River's springshed. Water flow has dropped by more than a third. Nitrate concentrations are twenty-eight times higher than the natural background. And slimy gizzard shad have replaced mullet and catfish as the dominant fish species, thanks to Rodman Dam. Bob's report card laments the "overall degradation of the former crown jewel spring in Florida."

"Silver is characteristic of the whole system; the problems are ubiquitous statewide," he says, arms and legs crossed, staring beyond me to the busy street. "The springs, when Dr. Odum studied them, were finely tuned machines. They were productive, healthy ecosystems. Now you can't find a healthy spring in Florida."

We've talked for two hours. Bob is driving the next day to his mountain home in North Carolina for some nontropical R&R. Time to go. But first he asks where I'm staying the night.

Ginnie Springs.

He laughs. Ginnie, I will learn, is famous.

He tells me to take a swim first thing in the morning to experience the crystalline magic of a Florida spring.

I promise him I will.

"It's just a glorious sight," Bob says.

I take the county road that parallels the Santa Fe River west out of town. I pass a modern, nondescript factory set back from the road and follow the signs to Ginnie Springs Outdoors, the privately owned campground and dive center along the river. "A slice of pure Florida," its website proclaims. A gatekeeper issues a parking pass and directs me to the check-in-center-cum-general-store-cum-dive-shop-cum-T-shirt-emporium with wall-sized coolers and all manner of tubes, rafts, and kayaks for sale. The ten cash registers give an idea of the crowds that typically descend upon Ginnie Springs. This gloomy Monday evening, though, only a couple young women run the registers. I ask for the most secluded campsite.

It's a lovely spot on the river surrounded by mossy oaks and knee-capped cypresses in pocket swamps. (Cypresses eventually break off at knee level.) Folks riding inner tubes languorously float by in the intermittent rain. I set up my tent in the gloaming and take a walk. I follow the river. And the music. Reggaeton blasts as I pass by Dogwood Spring. Phish comes next. Bro-country predominates as I reach the Ginnie Spring. Everybody's drinking beer or wine coolers; wafts of fine herb freshen the air. Even off-season, on a school night, Ginnie lives up to her reputation as Saturnalia-by-the-Spring. It's one of the few springs that allows drinking, while it turns a blind eye to the booze, bong, and booty bacchanal. In the summer, it's a two-hundred-acre frat party with live music, impromptu wet T-shirt contests, and revelers floating the river stopping for the occasional volleyball, corn hole, or hacky sack experience. On busy days it can take an hour just to enter the park. One unhappy camper posted that Ginnie Springs is "a cross between Woodstock and Mardi Gras with the 'Thong Song' as the theme song."

Which all sounds perfect to me, or at least the twenty-year-old me. But I'm well past my dissolute days and now lean more towards the natural beauty and quiet of an uncrowded stay along a lovely river. Which I mostly experience at Ginnie Springs, named for a "Virginia" who supposedly did her laundry in the clear blue waters. Jacques Cousteau dove here in 1974 and marveled at what he called "visibility forever." Three of the park's springs—Little Devil, Devil's Eye, and Devil's Ear—attract divers the world over with their connected underwater caves and limestone passageways. The Ginnie Spring offers a leisurely descent into a multi-hued, amphitheater-sized Ballroom. But an iron grate at the back of the chamber keeps divers from entering the deadly, maze-like cave system that claimed twenty-two lives prior to 1984.

I retrace my steps to my campsite. A committee of vultures swarms the field alongside Ginnie Spring—an omen, perhaps. The Springs

Institute, after all, gives Ginnie a D+. The music fades along with the light. I pop a beer, eat fried chicken and Gouda cheese, and scan the river. A doe steps cautiously on the opposite bank. Frogs start pitching woo. An egret flies low upriver. I go to bed early, the occasional drunken yelp or guitar twang hardly interrupting my sleep. But I'm jolted awake at 5:45 a.m. by four owls *who-whoo*-ing loudly, one directly over my tent. Muir got it just right when he wrote that "hollow-voiced owls were calling without intermission [and] pronounced their gloomy speeches with profound emphasis."

I get up an hour later as the sky turns brilliant orange. I fulfill my promise to Bob and jump into Twin Spring. Seventy-two degrees and clear as a bell. It is glorious.

My visit to Ginnie Springs wasn't solely restorative. I was actually on a secret mission behind enemy lines. The owners of the campground are involved in one of the most lucrative, and contentious, water grabs in Florida history. That factory I passed on the way to the campground? It's a Nestlé water-bottling plant—the water coming from a well at Ginnie Springs Outdoors that taps into the imperiled Floridan aquifer. For twenty years, Nestlé and its bottler forefathers in High Springs were content to draw four hundred thousand gallons of water from the aquifer daily. Now they want three times as much. Locals are up in arms, furious that the world's largest food company, with annual sales nearing one hundred billion dollars, is sucking up *their* water and putting it in polluting plastic bottles while insisting that it's all "environmentally sustainable." And how much does the permit cost to pump all that water? One hundred and fifteen dollars—a pittance for water owned by Floridians and then bottled and sold to Floridians, all the while depleting the Santa Fe River cherished by Floridians.

Merrillee Malwitz-Jipson leads the anti-Nestlé charge. I find her at Rum 138, the canoe and kayak rental shop that she and husband Doug own downriver from Ginnie Springs. Rum Island Spring is a quick bus ride from the store, which also sells springs-themed art, burgers, booze (including rum), kayaks, jewelry, and tie-dyed T-shirts. Jam bands take the stage out back. It's hard to miss the bright yellow building with turquoise shutters off County Road 138. There's no ignoring Merrillee, either, a whirl of entrepreneurial savvy and political moxie who cofounded the not-for-profit Our Santa Fe River, Inc.

"One hundred and fifteen dollars? That's completely moronic," Merrillee says while maneuvering through her riverkeeper war room strewn with reports, brochures, CDs, and posters. "The Santa Fe is already depleted and it's got serious water-quality issues. The people, overwhelmingly, do not want this international water grab of a natural resource that comes from an already delicate planet."

Her group has collected nineteen thousand comments from folks opposed to the permit extension. When staff of the local water district surprisingly recommended against the extension in 2020, the permit's owners petitioned the state to overturn the decision. Merrillee's group then raised fifty thousand bucks for attorneys to continue the fight.

Her activism comes naturally. A child of divorce, with a hippie mom and a Republican dad, Merrillee moved at age ten from Milwaukee to the master-planned, springs-free town of Coral Springs, where she could bike to the Everglades. Her father owned a graphic design firm, kindling an interest in art. Merrillee studied at the Ringling College of Art and Design in Sarasota, where she "learned that artists create culture." She bopped around Miami, Everglades City, and Tampa, creating colorful and abstract paintings and murals and styling hair to pay the bills. Merrillee and new husband Doug left St. Pete in a Greyhound-sized bus bound for North Florida and a Walden-esque upbringing for their future children. They'd camped at Ginnie Springs and loved the once-chill vibe of the place. In 2002, they bought a house at the end of a road with a quarter-mile of Santa Fe riverfront. A decade later, they bought the old convenience store "with bats in the belfry and crap in the toilet" and turned it into a canoe livery, hair salon, restaurant, and gallery.

Merrillee's environmental activism began within six months of landing in Columbia County. Workers were spraying pesticides along the river to kill hydrilla. She complained to state officials. A few years later she learned that four water-bottling plants were planned across the Santa Fe watershed. The river-protection organization was formed in 2007 "to educate people about bottled water," its website says. Merrillee ("I didn't know hardly anything about water") attended county, state, and legislative meetings on water flows, quality, permits, and pollution. At times she was the only citizen showing up. She learned of similar water battles across the country and began sharing information and tactics with Food & Water Watch, the Polaris Institute, and other activist groups. She became a paid organizer for the Sierra Club, fighting an interstate gas pipeline and fertilizer-fueled red tides. Her river group stopped the four bottling plants. But thirty others in Florida swill copious amounts of the Floridan aquifer.

"All of the springs and rivers are connected, so if you take out water at one spot, you draw down everything else," Merrillee says, raising her voice to be heard over Hurricane Sally's latest deluge. "Florida shares this river with Georgia. The Santa Fe is a tributary of the Suwannee River, which comes out of the Okefenokee. We're not separate. The state line is just a political line that divides us. Nature does not divide us."

The river, according to the Springs Institute, has lost 30 percent of its historic flow.

"When I moved here I had cypress swamps on my property and there was much more vegetation in the river," Merrillee adds. "It should be flooded now, with all the rain we've had. But now I have cypress knees. The forest is telling us this is not normal."

Nestlé and the Wray family, which owns Ginnie Springs Outdoors and, consequently, the water-withdrawal permit, are getting hammered in the court of public opinion as greedy enviro-killers sucking dry a beloved river. But they're fighting back hard. The Wrays rightly note that the existing permit already allows them to pump three times more water daily—1.2 million gallons—so why shouldn't the next permit? Nestlé, which sold its US and Canadian bottling operations in 2021, says the full amount represents less than one half of 1 percent of the river's average flow. Risa Wray, who doesn't disclose how much Nestlé pays for the water, adds that her family has protected the land along the river for forty-five years and "for people to insinuate that we would allow it to be harmed is reprehensible."

Unspoken, mostly, is the reality that agriculture, municipalities, and septic systems do more harm to the Santa Fe and the aquifer than Nestlé. Farmers, after all, withdraw 40 percent of the river's daily allotment. So I put the question to Bob Knight.

"Nestlé is totally small potatoes," he admits. "But they're also an international company, profiting from a local product, and they're not paying for what the water's worth. They're against putting a price on water. They mark it up one thousand times the amount they extract it for."

Merrillee, too, acknowledges that agriculture is a bigger environmental culprit.

"There's no doubt farmers should use less water and fertilizer," she says. "But at least they're growing food, and all Nestlé is doing is giving you tap water and more pollution with plastic bottles. It's an international money grab for our natural resources."

It's also a familiar fight everywhere "natural" water is bottled. Nestlé pulled three million gallons daily from Florida springs near Zephyrhills, Vernon, Lee, and Bristol. In Michigan, the Swiss beverage giant recently won approval to withdraw hundreds of thousands of gallons more daily from two trout streams. The annual permit costs two hundred dollars. In water-starved California, Nestlé paid two thousand dollars a year to pump millions of gallons from the San Bernardino National Forest.

Merrillee's busy. The board president stops in to talk legal tactics. A landowner seeks advice on a potential landfill. A census taker wants to know who lives in a house on Rum Island Terrace. And there's a business to run.

She offers a final thought.

"We are all completely frivolous and consumption-oriented people and not thinking of our footprint on the planet," Merrillee says. "We are all connected, and water is what runs through us all, in our bodies and on our planet. It is the most basic thing we need to exist. It's the most simple thing. And yet . . ."

CHAPTER 12

The End of the Road

Oystermen, cotton planters, millionaire quail hunters, moonshine-makers, vocal conservatives, doctrinaire liberals, scientists, game wardens, fortune tellers, and hermits inhabit a land that is above all things deceptive because it looks as if it offered hardly any variety at all.

—Gloria Jahoda, *The Other Florida*

Cedar Key, Florida — "To-day I reached the sea."

It was October 23, 1867. John Muir was ecstatic. His journey was near its end. The sea breeze conjured memories of the Scottish coast "and my whole childhood, that seemed to have utterly vanished in the New World." He'd been on the road fifty-three days. He'd walked nine hundred miles, and sailed another hundred, across the Cumberland plateau, Appalachian highlands, Piedmont forests, and coastal marshlands. Hunger and loneliness were constant companions. Confederate brigands and "robber negroes" threatened throughout (or so he feared). Poisonous snakes and man-eating alligators awaited around every corner (ditto). He'd had his fill of filth, fear, and poverty. He was weary, feverish, and in need of rest.

Finally, where the railroad tracks ended at the blue-green waters of the Gulf of Mexico, Muir could glory in a hike well done. He could dip his boot-mangled toes into warm water, sketch the "tasteful bouquet" of barrier islands, plan his Amazon adventure, and quaff a mai tai or two. Muir sorely needed a vacation. Why, just a few days earlier he'd been talking to trees.

"This palm was indescribably impressive and told me grander things than I ever got from human priest," he wrote.

A respite, though, wasn't to be. Muir got malaria, probably from Bonaventure Cemetery. He was laid up for three months. He wouldn't visit the Amazon for forty-four years. In that time Muir would become the nation's preeminent environmentalist, father of the national parks, and defender of wild things and wild places. His near-death experience and lengthy convalescence, though, gave him time to crystallize his thoughts on nature, man, God, and the tortured relationship among the three. Muir lamented that sheep were put on earth solely to provide food and clothing; that whales were best used as oil for lamps; and that hemp was meant for "hanging the wicked." Lord Man's arrogance, and the presumption that God intended the Earth's bounty for human enjoyment alone, irritated Muir.

"The world, we are told, was made especially for man—a presumption not supported by all the facts," Muir wrote in *A Thousand-Mile Walk*. "A numerous class of men are painfully astonished whenever they find anything, living or dead, in all God's universe, which they cannot eat or render in some way what they call useful to themselves."

Even malaria, which nearly killed Muir, served a purpose: man "was never intended for such deadly climates."

A lesson he learned a little too late.

En route to Cedar Key, Muir spent the night at a tavern in Gainesville, a clean, prosperous college town in thrall to the munificence of nearby cotton plantations. Up early the next day, he continued along the railroad track marveling at the "dignified simplicity" of the magnolia tree and the "fine sunny areas of the long-leafed and Cuban pines." The pastoral idyll, though, proved short-lived. At noon, he inquired as to dinner from an exceedingly poor, dirty, and malarial couple, and there ensued an irksome disquisition on the difference between dirty Northerners and dirty Southerners. Muir huddled that night against a log, cold and, by morning, drenched in dew. He didn't dare make a fire for fear of robbers. He drank water from "slimy pools," afraid that an alligator would jump out at any moment.

Muir's travails were rewarded the following evening upon arriving at the home of a Captain Simmons, a former Confederate soldier and "one of the very few scholarly, intelligent men that I have met in Florida." The captain wanted to talk about slavery. Muir steered the fireside chat to birds, flowers, and the weather. Simmons took a liking to Muir and invited the Northern longhair to spend a few days hunting. Muir said he'd first prefer to see the local flora and fauna, including "some large alligators." The captain introduced him the next morning to a seven-mile-long palmetto grove.

To reach the palm prairie, with its "dazzling sun-children," Muir followed a sketchy trail through the swamp, where fallen trees, pools of muck, and a briar patch with sharp thorns awaited. He made it to the grove largely unscathed and duly impressed.

"I walked enchanted in their midst," Muir recalled. "What a landscape! Only palms as far as the eye could reach! Smooth pillars rising from the grass, each capped with a sphere of leaves, shining in the sun as bright as a star."

Still, he preferred oaks and pines. The palms were "not very graceful." "I have seen grasses waving with far more dignity," he concluded.

Well, then. There would be no climbing to the top of a *palm* tree to experience a windstorm.

He got lost on the way back to Captain Simmons's house. He couldn't find the trail, so he beelined it in the supposed right direction. He pushed through knotty vines, rotted trees, and swampy lagoons "full of dead leaves and alligators" to finally reach the dreaded "jungle of cat-briers." He was soaked, scratched, bloodied, mosquito-bit, and scared. It grew dark. He couldn't find the opening in the "phalanx" of smilax. He considered building a scaffold in a tree for the night. Instead, Muir calmed down, walked the wall of thorns, found the trail and, finally, the captain's home. Ravenous, he dined on fresh venison, Johnnycakes, and milk, and "soon after supper was sleeping the deep sleep of the weary and the safe."

The next morning, Muir went hunting. Simmons's brother flushed a buck that chose not to line up in the hunters' sights, prompting the captain to curse that it was the "d—dest deer that ever ran unshot." To which Muir responded, to himself, that it was the "d—dest work to slaughter God's cattle for sport."

"Let a Christian hunter go to the Lord's woods and kill his well-kept beasts, or wild Indians, and it is well," he wrote. "But let an enterprising specimen of these proper, predestined victims go to houses and fields and kill the most worthless person of the vertical godlike killers,—oh! that is horribly unorthodox."

"If a war of races should occur between the wild beasts and Lord Man," he continued, "I would be tempted to sympathize with the bears."

Even after days trembling before the mere mention of the word *alligator* (he saw only one in Florida), Muir conceded that "the great saurians of an older creation" played a critical role in God's all-welcoming universe. He'd obviously read Jean-Jacques Rousseau, the Enlightenment philosopher, who a century earlier insisted that animals have a right to be free from pain and suffering. "Many good people believe that alligators were created by the Devil," Muir said. "But doubtless these creatures are happy and fill the place assigned them by the great

Creator of us all. Fierce and cruel they appear to us, but beautiful in the eyes of God. They, also, are his children, for He hears their cries, cares for them tenderly, and provides their daily bread." Like Rousseau, Muir became an early animal rights activist. (It was the human species he had trouble with.)

Many consider Muir's Bonaventure-to-Cedar Key stretch as the beginning of the environmental movement in the United States. Yet his impassioned embrace of the alligator could also be considered an opening salvo in the fight to save threatened and endangered species. It took a century, but the almost-extinct alligator was listed under the Endangered Species Preservation Act of 1966, precursor to the Endangered Species Act, alongside the grizzly bear, the Florida manatee, and the bald eagle. But it would take the massacre of the deer, bears, panthers, and otters before public disgust turned into political action. Feather-loving fashionistas in New York and London wiped out the many luminous birds that once strutted along Florida's coasts. Cedar Key was one of the nation's largest green turtle fisheries until a rapacious appetite for soup, meat, and eggs all but killed them off. The Big Bend's oyster industry dried up due to overfishing, drought, and freshwater profligacy by upriver farms and towns. The long-lived longleaf pines succumbed to the woodman's ax and the turpentine still. Prairies were turned into cow pastures and housing tracts. And the rivers, springs, and estuaries were treated like toilets all in the name of Progress.

"I have precious little sympathy for the selfish propriety of civilized man," Muir wrote the day before reaching Cedar Key.

After a few days in the land of the natural springs, I return to Gainesville to pick up State Road 24, which runs parallel to the long-gone Florida Railroad, and finish retracing Muir's journey to the sea. Go-go

Florida quickly gives way to pine-and-pasture Florida, interrupted every eight miles or so by a dying town. Archer. Bronson. Otter Creek. Rosewood.

Rosewood. The name sends shivers down my spine. It's usually followed by *massacre*, or *race riot*. Over several days, in January 1923, White men terrorized the prosperous Black town, killing at least six and burning every building. A married White woman named Fannie Taylor blamed a Black man for a sexual assault and the bruises on her face. That's all it took. Folks later concluded that she made up the story after a White lover did the damage. Rosewood was wiped off the map. Today, only a historic marker remains alongside SR 24. It reads: "Those who survived were forever scarred."

Soon, after miles of uninterrupted pine, the road jogs to the south and crosses little islands and inlets. It passes an RV park, a marina, a tiki bar, and a few motels before ending in still-quaint Cedar Key. For at least two thousand years, the Timucua, Apalachee, or Creek tribes lived here, fishing the rich Gulf waters where the Suwannee River lets out. But the nineteenth-century Seminole Wars either killed or sent packing—to Oklahoma or into the Everglades—the state's Native Americans. During the Civil War, Union troops controlled the dozen keys scattered about the port. Prosperity returned, postwar, with mills on Atsena Otie and Way Keys producing slats from eastern red cedars that were shipped north and turned into pencils. But a rail line in competition with David Yulee's, terminating at the port of Tampa, ninety miles to the south, speeded the region's decline. The 1896 "Cedar Key Hurricane," with its ten-foot storm surge, leveled the town, washed away Yulee's tracks, and killed thirty people. Miles of red cedar were toppled, destroying the town's major industry.

In 1929, President Herbert Hoover turned a few of the barrier islands into the Cedar Key National Wildlife Refuge in order to protect the breeding grounds of pelicans, egrets, ibises, and cormorants from feather-hungry poachers. Nearby the Lower Suwannee National Wildlife Refuge protects the last twenty miles of the famed river as it tumbles into the Gulf.

The state road ends at First Street, near the fishing pier. A block away sits the Cedar Key Historical Museum in the two-story, white-washed, handsomely restored Lutterloh Building, built by a local agent of the Florida Railroad in 1871. I pay the three-dollar entrance fee and inspect the wooden display cases, Indian artifacts, and maritime memorabilia.

Bill Bale, the museum's loquacious docent, welcomes me, asks where I'm from, offers an Atlanta anecdote, and wonders what, in particular, brings me to Cedar Key. I tell him.

"Here's our Muir exhibition," Bill, bearded and bespectacled, announces with flourish.

The glass case contains: a map, highlighted in red, of Muir's Southern route; an original copy of *A Thousand-Mile Walk*; the Hodgson family bible; and other Muir-abilia. Richard Hodgson and family nursed Muir back to health from his malarial stupor. I ask Bill where they lived. West of town, across the marsh, he says. But the house is no more. Only the moss-lined oak tree where Muir supposedly convalesced remains.

"I tell Californians if it wasn't for Cedar Key, California would be one big amusement park," Bill tells me, awaiting a laugh.

And the other visitors?

"Most people who come in here don't know who Muir was," he says.

I thank Bill and head down Second Street to the library, another two-story, white-washed, somewhat restored building hugging the curb.

Lilly Rooks is waiting for me inside. I figure that if anybody could educate me about Cedar Key, where it's been and where it's going, it'd be Lilly. Her daddy's people came from South Carolina at the Civil War's end to fish, mullet mostly. Lilly's first job, at age twelve, was pulling gizzards out of the tasty fish. "I made seven dollars for an entire weekend's work," Lilly recalls. "I thought I was going to be rich."

"Cedar Key was a nice place to grow up in," she continues. "Dock Street was wonderful with all the smells coming out of the kitchens. Oh my gosh, they were frying up seafood and the smell would be just hanging in the air."

Back then, before the bars, restaurants, and T-shirt shops clogged the street, you could see the Gulf from just about anywhere in town. Hundreds of families made a living fishing. Kids wandered all over town, the woods, and the marsh, without worry. Today, Lilly won't let her grandson out of sight. The community has changed, and Lilly doesn't think for the better. She moved into the country, near Rosewood, for the peace, quiet, and stars. But turn her back on Cedar Key? Never.

"The first time I ran for commissioner was 1990 and I didn't know anything about campaigns," Lilly says.

But there was some proposed county ordinance that would restrict who could own what business and where, and Lilly, running her daddy's grocery store (while smoking mullet on the side) was very much opposed to it. So she put up campaign signs and went door to door only to have the men say they couldn't vote for her. "Because I'm a woman," Lilly explains.

She won anyways. Her husband died of cancer three weeks before the next election, which she lost to a cousin. By then the store had closed, and Lilly, with four children including an adopted, badly abused little boy, needed a job. The sheriff hired her to work in the warrant office. She was reelected as a county commissioner in 1998. She lost again in 2010—"because I was a Democrat"—switched parties, and won back her old seat four years later after a second stroke and blood clots in both lungs.

"I love this job. I love being able to help people," Lilly says, deliberately. "I've spent my whole life helping people."

She was an EMT. She worked in a nursing home. A hunter, she shot a wild hog and several deer last year and donated enough meat to feed six families. Now, though, the needs, and the challenges, are greater. Lilly had to get creative.

Like so much of the changing South, Lilly's community faces a particularly insidious threat—sprawl. Not one, but two toll roads were being considered for Levy County when I interviewed Lilly. One would run the county from north to south, thirty miles of bifurcated asphalt. The other would run east–west for maybe twenty miles and hook up with the Florida Turnpike. In all, the state would build 330 miles of new highway right up to the Georgia state line. (Nobody bothered to tell Georgia that a four-lane road would suddenly stop at its two-lane doorstep.) Promoters, none more rah-rah than the Florida Transportation Builders Association, promised jobs, water and sewer lines, broadband connections, and "access to our rural communities." They gave the project an official-sounding name—Multi-Use Corridors of Regional Economic Significance, or M-CORES for short—and lined up a first installment of seven hundred million dollars from the General Assembly, even though 93 percent of Floridians, according to one widely reported survey, opposed the project. The Sierra Club labeled it "the worst bill we have seen for Florida's environment in more than twenty years." And that's saying a lot in a state where Mickey Mouse competes with Billy the Bulldozer for official mascot.

Critics liken the project to other Florida boondoggles, including the environmentally ruinous Cross Florida Barge Canal or the Everglades Jetport. The southernmost toll road would slice across prime Florida panther habitat, where vehicles are already the number-one killer of the big cats. Yet the most widespread damage would be done by the so-called Suncoast Connector running along the Gulf through some of the most pristine marsh, farmland, and forests in the country. In fact, the Big Bend region is the largest stretch of undeveloped coastline in the continental United States. Lilly says the toll road would turn the Big Bend into "another Tampa Bay." In April 2020, she introduced a resolution opposing the toll roads. A majority of commissioners supported it.

"I'm worried about the farmers, the ranchers, the timber people, the watermelon growers. We have a clam industry here that's known worldwide. And most of these people have been here for generations. They're subject to lose everything," says Lilly, leaning forward in her chair. "We have Manatee Springs. We have the Goethe State Forest. We have protected species here that people don't even know about. We have all kinds of natural beauty that, with the signing of one pen stroke, could be turned completely upside down."

Lilly, unlike Muir, is a conservationist. She's not opposed to all growth. She just wants better growth. Muir, on the other hand, was a preservationist who wanted pristine places to remain so in perpetuity. Listen close, though, and the septuagenarian politician and the twenty-something botanist sound awfully alike.

"Even if they build the road nine miles away from the Gulf," Lilly says, "it's going to have an impact on the fish and the clams and the oysters. For every action, there's a reaction. It's like we live for this day and don't think about the future. Are we going to continue to not pay attention?"

In this case, though, the politicians actually listened. The roads package died in the legislature a few months after I first interviewed Lilly. Still, nobody expects it to stay dead. This is Florida, after all, where three hundred thousand newcomers a year demand new subdivisions and the roads to reach them. Sure enough, in 2022, the proposed turnpike through Lilly's neck of the woods is back on the table.

"Have you ever noticed that when someone moves here from somewhere else, supposedly for the slower pace of life, they all of a sudden want to change everything to match where they just came from?" Lilly asks me a few months later. "Are we going to just sit back and let them change the way of life we love?"

Muir had never seen anything like it.

"Today, emerging from a multitude of tropical plants, I behold the Gulf of Mexico stretching away unbounded, except by the sky," he wrote in *A Thousand-Mile Walk*. "What dreams and speculative matter for thought arose as I stood on the strand, gazing out on the burnished, treeless plain!"

Before him lay a watery tableau of a dozen low-slung islands fringed with palm trees, gnarled oaks, longleaf pines, and red cedars. He marveled at beaches and skies filled with brown pelicans, snowy egrets, tricolored herons, "and the multitude of smaller sailors of the air." Great egrets were "old white sages of immaculate feather."

Maybe four hundred people lived in and around the Cedar Keys (as they were then known). They fished, cut trees, and loaded schooners with slats and turpentine destined for factories and shipyards in New York, Texas, and the West Indies. Muir, for the first time in months, didn't know what to do. He'd reached the end of the line. And no steamer sat in the harbor waiting to whisk him to South America. He considered walking to the larger ports of Tampa or Key West. "Or would I wait here, like Crusoe, and pray for a ship?" he wondered.

Muir stopped in a store with shelves of quinine and stacks of alligator and rattlesnake skins, and inquired as to shipping schedules. The proprietor said a schooner bound for Galveston was en route. He steered Muir to the Eagle Pencil Company and its owner, Richard Hodgson, who informed the gangly wanderer that a ship was expected within two weeks. Muir would wait. But he needed a job. Hodgson hired him on the spot and invited his new employee home for the night.

"Mr. Hodgson's family welcomed me with the open, unconstrained cordiality which is characteristic of the better class of Southern people," Muir wrote.

He got right to work the next day. He slept that night in one of the mill's boarding houses.

"The next day I felt a strange dullness and headache while I was botanizing along the coast," Muir wrote.

He took a salubrious swim in the saltwater sea. Hankering for something sour, he bought lemons. For three days he stubbornly tried to slough off the "inexorable leaden numbness" by bathing in the Gulf, searching for plants, and working in the mill. It didn't work.

"Thus and here my long walk was interrupted," Muir said.

He collapsed, unconscious, on a trail surrounded by dwarf palmettos. He awoke hours later with the stars shining and staggered toward the bunkhouse. He fell again, and again, the legs weak, the fever raging. Each time, though, Muir managed to fall with his head pointing in the direction of the bunkhouse. Finally, sometime after midnight, he reached his lodgings only to keel over atop a sawdust pile. A watchman on his rounds refused to help Muir, believing him drunk. Muir crawled up the stairs and into bed, where he "immediately became oblivious to everything."

His first lucid moment, days later, came upon hearing Hodgson's voice ask an attendant if the malarial millworker had spoken. Muir had not, to which the mill owner ordered more quinine. Hodgson had already moved Muir to his spacious house atop a hill with a commanding view of the Gulf.

"I was nursed about three months with unfailing kindness, and to the skill and care of Mr. and Mrs. Hodgson I doubtless owe my life," Muir said.

Slowly he convalesced and was able to stumble outside and sit, day after day, under a moss-draped oak, listening to the winds, marveling at the view, and delighting in the "happy birds." Soon he was sailing from key to key in a little skiff and botanizing his way back to health. "I joyfully return to the immortal truth and immortal beauty of Nature," he wrote.

One January afternoon he climbed to the top of the Hodgson's house to take in the sunset. To the north he saw "the fluttering sails of a Yankee schooner" heading straight for the harbor. Muir's ship had arrived.

The *Island Belle* would've passed Hog Island and Buck Island, Moccasin Creek, and Alligator Pass, as well as the mouth of the mighty Suwannee River. She would've aimed for the lighthouse on Seahorse Key and skirted Deadman's Key for the final jog to shore. All the while, though, the schooner's captain would've been mindful of the oyster reefs that run nearly the length of the sound.

The reefs, today, pose less of a menace to boaters. Obviously, sonar helps. But the reefs have also shrunk—incredibly. They've lost 88 percent of their size in just the last three decades, according to researchers at the University of Florida. The culprit: the Suwannee River. Huh? How can water on the mainland harm offshore limestone ridges?

Just like Apalachicola Bay, at the other end of the Big Bend, the oyster bars of the Suwannee Sound depend upon a healthy mix of fresh and salt water. Salinity levels rise if surges of fresh water don't periodically shoot down the Suwannee and into the Gulf. Oysters die if they get too salty. And reefs, made up of dead oysters, disintegrate into sandbars invisible to unsuspecting boaters.

The reefs, typically long and straight and parallel to the shore, also serve as leaky dams that keep fresh water close to the coast. As they disappear, the estuaries salt up and countless critters suffer. Consider Lone Cabbage Reef, a once-mighty shell bar three miles long and one mile from the mud flats that pass for a shoreline. Lone Cabbage once teemed with American oystercatchers, the bug-eyed, red-beaked shorebirds that use their long snouts to pry open mussels, clams, and oysters. Locals say the oystercatchers disappeared years ago from the Suwannee Sound.

Blame Lord Man. His wanton pursuit of profit, and overall disregard for the natural world, forced oystercatchers to find healthier hunting grounds. Lone Cabbage was overfished. Jacksonville, along with corn and soybean farmers, treats the Suwannee like a bottomless well. Man-caused climate change triggers the droughts that further deplete the river's flow. And, as Muir knew long ago, every upstream action carries downstream consequences. "When we try to pick out anything by itself, we find it hitched to everything else in the Universe," he wrote in *My First Summer in the Sierras*.

So it was only fitting that Muir's journey, and mine, ended in the Big Bend. Just about every environmental ill discovered along the Scotsman's thousand-mile trek is found within a short ride of Cedar Key. Sprawl. Sea-level rise. Air and water pollution. Natural-resource destruction. Water wars. Ever-weirder weather. Threatened and endangered species. Invasive species.

The cedars and longleaf pines disappeared long ago via the wood-cutter's ax. Overfishing of mullet, redfish, snook, and sea trout got so bad that Florida voters passed a constitutional amendment in 1994 outlawing gill-net fishing in state waters. DDT nearly killed off the bald eagles. Alligators were hunted almost to extinction. Manatees, aka sea cows, are a federally listed threatened species succumbing to sewage and fertilizer run-off (and speeding boaters). The Cedar Keys wildlife refuge, in the 1960s and '70s, welcomed two hundred thousand white ibis, brown pelicans, snowy egrets, and tri-colored herons each nesting season. Today, maybe twenty thousand birds raise up their babies on the baker's dozen of islets that make up the refuge. Deer Island, a ninety-acre key adjoining the refuge, is for sale for one and a half million dollars. Buy it quick, though. Half of the island already lies below mean high tide.

"That's Deer Island over there," shouts Brad Ennis over the roar of the airboat.

It's almost 7:00 a.m. and the fog and spitting rain interfere with any lightening of the morning sky. Brad steers the boat over the low-tide mudflats and into the Suwannee Sound on his way to Lone Cabbage Reef. A fat raccoon traipses among clumps of cordgrass in search of breakfast. A pelican, nonplussed by the racket of the airboat, bobs in the shallow water.

Brad's in a race for time. Short-term, he's got three hours until the tide turns and the reef slips underneath the waves. Long term, he's racing the possibility that Lone Cabbage—and the coastal ecosystem itself—will vanish.

"It begs the question," Brad says in a quieter moment. "What can we do?"

He's a saltwater ecologist and the research coordinator in charge of monitoring the health of Lone Cabbage Reef. He works for the Nature Coast Biological Station in Cedar Key, part of the University of Florida. Every other week, from November through February, Brad and a few interns clamber aboard the airboat for a quick ride to one of twenty-two distinct sections of the reef to tally the number of live, and dead, oysters. It's year three of a five-year project to rebuild the reef and restore a way of life. If successful, millions of oysters will recolonize the bar, an industry will be reborn, and, maybe, the estuary will survive anthropomorphic decline. The eight-million-dollar project might also serve as a restoration template for the grossly depleted oyster beds stretching from Florida to Texas.

No pressure, Brad.

Gulf-wide, up to 80 percent of the oyster reefs have suffered dramatic loss of substrate, or the stuff oysters grow on. Reef lengths have shortened while the gaps between them have widened. Lone Cabbage used to lose a couple of inches off the top every year. And it's not just the oysters that have suffered. Mussels, shrimp, blue crabs, anchovies, croaker, sea anemones, and all manner of plankton share the reef habitat.

The National Fish and Wildlife Foundation is paying for the project, appropriately, from the billions of dollars in penalties assessed against BP and Transocean for befouling the Gulf during the 2010 Deepwater Horizon oil spill. In 2018, local oystermen, under the university's guidance, plucked and relocated three thousand bushels of live oysters from Lone Cabbage. Limestone boulders were then plopped onto the eroding reef. Oyster shells were sprinkled an inch deep over the top to mimic the bar's nineteenth-century footprint.

"I think, on the whole, what we're doing is working," says Brad, thirty-three, a blue bandana and black Covid mask covering all but his brown eyes. "I go by the numbers, and the historical data, and I see an increase in oysters growing on the reef."

The GPS atop Brad's cell phone steers the crew to Reef Element No. 17. An intern drops the anchor and the students gets busy. One pounds an H bar into the sand along the edge of the reef. Another unspools bright green string and marches twenty-two meters south where another H bar is implanted. The interns proceed to tally the number of oysters in two-and-a-half-meter increments, then shout their findings to Brad, who keeps track on a clipboard. He shows me how it's done. He picks up a barnacle-encrusted chunk of limestone and feels for an oyster's lips. If open, the oyster is dead. If sealed, it's alive

"Here's a dead one right here. Here's a live one. This one's dead. And this one," Brad says. "Here's a live one. And another. And another. And another."

This particular transect isn't very impressive, mollusk-wise. Brad, though, is pleased with the number of barnacles, a sure sign that a healthy reef is creating habitat for oyster spat.

They repeat the transect count five times, as the fog swirls, then clears, swirls, then clears. By nine-thirty, the tide has reversed course, tugging us landward and topping our knee-high boots. A squall hits. Time to go. Brad turns the airboat toward the Lower Suwannee refuge. Closer to shore, the estuary comes alive. A pelican flies low over the marsh. Herons, egrets, and black skimmers patrol Preacher's Cove. One, two, three oystercatchers head for the reefs. Brad says they're now a common sight, as are bald eagles.

Back on shore, the airboat on its trailer, we empty our boots of water. I've a million questions. Will the restoration work? Can it succeed if the Suwannee River is pumped dry? What's the Big Bend without a fishing industry? Brad, a relative newbie on the decade-old project, defers to his elders.

"Talk to Peter Frederick," he says.

I get Peter off his tractor for a chat. He's a newly retired research professor from the university who spends his days birding, boating, and tending cattle on his farm outside Gainesville. He took to oystering as a hobby a quarter century ago and didn't like what he was seeing.

"There used to be a rule of thumb," Peter says. "The guy in the front of the boat would tong oysters into a tray where the guy culling them would throw the good ones over his shoulder into the back of the boat and the rest into the water. If you had one oyster in the air at all times you were doing pretty well. No one's had oysters flying for a long time."

A decade ago Peter and colleagues began surveying Lone Cabbage Reef from the water and the air. Then came the Gulf spill and the money spigot opened up. The restoration is working, Peter says. "One of the objectives is to get oysters established on a new surface and get that elevation back up to where it ought to be," he says. "That's definitely been accomplished. So we're seeing not just high density of oysters, but some good growth and good structural complexity.

"But we're at a tipping point," he adds. "I'm optimistic about the potential. Am I optimistic we're going to be able to do enough at enough scale to make a difference? That we'll have enough fresh water to do that? That the whole thing will not get wrecked by a Category-5 hurricane? When you work on the coast, the uncertainties are just so manifest. It's sort of like farming in the Dust Bowl."

A day or two later Muir, though still weak, walked to the harbor in search of the captain of the *Island Belle*. The ship was taking on lumber and heading for Cuba. Captain Parsons charged Muir twenty-five dollars for passage and said he'd leave just as soon as a north wind blew. Muir hurried back to the Hodgsons', gathered his plants, "took leave of my kind friends," and returned to the schooner. The wind soon accommodated, and Muir quickly left Florida behind. "This excursion on the sea, the first one after twenty years in the woods, was of course exceedingly interesting, and I was full of hope, glad to be once more on my journey to the South," he wrote.

Upon reaching the Gulf Stream, though, the winds picked up speed. Waves broke across the bow. The captain told his odd passenger to go below.

"I replied," Muir said, "that I hoped the storm would be as violent as his ship could bear, that I enjoyed the scenery of such a sea so much that it was impossible to be sick, that I had long waited in the woods for just such a storm, and that, now that the precious thing had come, I would remain on deck and enjoy it."

He spent a month in Cuba, botanizing by day and returning to the schooner at night. Muir's health remained poor. Nonetheless, he wanted to push on to the Andes and the Amazon. He visited the shipping agencies and—"fortunately"—couldn't find any ships headed for South America. He decided, instead, "to go North to the longed-for cold weather of New York, and thence to the forests and mountains of California." He'd spend a year getting healthy and then revisit his

South American dream. He booked passage on a schooner loaded with oranges and sailed to New York City. After ten days wandering lower Manhattan (he avoided Central Park for fear of getting lost), Muir boarded the *Nebraska* and sailed via the Panama Canal to San Francisco. He arrived in early April, spent one day in town, and then walked to the Yosemite Valley.

Acknowledgments

This book has really been a lifetime in the making. I'd never have become a tree hugger, nor a writer, without the love and encouragement of my parents, Bill and Chris. They turned me on to the mountains and the seas and everywhere in between. Writers both, they bestowed upon me a love of language and a yen for travel.

The kernel for the book took shape a decade ago as I wrote more and more stories about environmental issues bedeviling the South for the *Atlanta Journal-Constitution*. Many of the topics I covered—climate change, ecological degradation, natural-resource battles—evolved into this book's major themes. I am grateful for the many talented *AJC* reporters and editors who educated and inspired me. I also give much credit to colleagues at newspapers and magazines in North Carolina and DC who taught me how to report and write.

I came to the US Fish and Wildlife Service at the cusp of the Trump administration and, boy, did I get an education. Conservation was no longer something somebody else did that I observed with detachment. I was now fully in the nature business, writing about endangered species, fragile ecosystems, and dedicated biologists. I am very thankful for the education and support I received from Jeff Fleming and Daffny Pitchford, in particular. And I'd be remiss in not thanking the countless Fish and Wildlife scientists who patiently explained Southern-style conservation.

And that goes for the biologists, hydrologists, climatologists, and others who work quietly, and faithfully, for the state and federal agencies—DNR, NPS, USFS, USGS—that play such a critical role protecting our public lands and at-risk species. They don't get nearly enough credit. And neither do the myriad nonprofits—the Sierra Club, The Nature Conservancy, the Southern Environmental Law Center (Stacy Shelton, Amanda Garcia), and the riverkeepers (Tonya Bonitatibus, Merrillee Malwitz-Jipson) who willingly shared their time, resources, and insights.

I purposefully shied away from the Sierra Club in writing *Southward*. I didn't want anybody thinking I was shilling for one of the nation's oldest conservation groups, or that I was a Muir hagiographer. I did, though, at first, pore over the John Muir Exhibit, an online library of information and resources sponsored by the Sierra Club and edited by Harold Wood. I've also relied upon the wisdom of Sierra Club members in Georgia for years.

I owe a big thanks to most everybody I interviewed for the book. Some, though, deserve special mention: Mike Wurtz, a University of the Pacific professor and Muir expert; Dick Shore, a Muir "interpreter"; Chris Ulrey, a protector of rare plants; Shannon Hartsfield, an oysterman turned advocate; and Codey Elrod, my favorite marksman. Paul Wolff educated me about the Georgia coast over many years, as did Clark Alexander. Jamie Satterfield is a passionate journalist. Lilly Rooks should be governor of Florida.

The most special sources, to me, are the regular folks who've stories to tell. Tommy and Betty Johnson live a toxic nightmare with grace and determination. Melissa Turner handles disaster with aplomb. Casey Cox's passion for the environment rivals her love of farming.

Chris Manganiello and Katherine Zitsch educated me on water and water wars. Sandy West was a one-of-a-kind environmentalist and philanthropist who saved an island. Charles Seabrook, a former *AJC* colleague, supporter, and sounding-board, is the *éminence grise* of Southern environmental journalism.

I can't thank enough the folks at Island Press who steered *Southward* to fruition, especially David Miller, Sharis Simonian, and Jaime Jennings. A special shout-out to Erin Johnson, my patient, incisive, and compassionate editor who knows more about what I write than I do. And Mike Fleming, who expertly copy edited the manuscript and saved me from myself any number of times.

A book is a selfish endeavor, with all the time spent alone traveling, writing, and thinking ceaselessly about the work at hand. I am guilty of ignoring my boys, Sammy and Naveed, for days on end. I am also guilty of leaving them a world headed in the wrong direction. I've apologized for both of my transgressions and they've absolved me (or at least humored me). My hope is that maybe this book, in some small way, will make the world a better place for them in the future.

I couldn't have written *A Road Running Southward* without the patience, support, and counsel of my wife, Bita. She always encouraged me, and never doubted me, and for that I owe her my sincerest gratitude and everlasting love.

Further Readings

I've cited many books, reports, and articles in this book, so I won't repeat them here. And I read many of John Muir's books, articles, and letters, which are also cited in *A Road Running Southward*. But I would be remiss if I didn't highlight the John Muir Exhibit (https://vault.sierra club.org/john_muir_exhibit/about/site.aspx), wonderfully curated by Harold Wood and hosted by the Sierra Club. It was a great place to start my Muir research.

Here are some other readings that influenced my thinking:

Barry, John M. *Rising Tide: The Great Mississippi Flood of 1927 and How It Changed America*. New York: Simon & Schuster, 1998. An epic social, economic, and scientific accounting of the devastating flood that reverberated far beyond the South's most-famed river.

Bartram, William. *Travels of William Bartram*. Edited by Mark Van Doren. New York: Dover Publications, 2019. An unabridged edition of the 1791 classic detailing the naturalist's travels through Florida, Georgia, and the Carolinas.

Brown, Margaret Lynn. *The Wild East: A Biography of the Great Smoky*

Mountains. Gainesville, FL: University Press of Florida, 2000. A comprehensive history, and natural history, of the southern Appalachians and the making of a national park.

Davis, Jack E. *The Gulf: The Making of an American Sea.* New York: Liveright Publishing, 2017. A sweeping history of the Gulf region.

Jahoda, Gloria. *The Other Florida.* New York: Charles Scribner's Sons, 1967. A purposefully (for me) dated personal and historical account of 1960s life in the Florida Panhandle.

McKibben, Bill. *Wandering Home: A Long Walk Across America's Most Hopeful Landscape.* New York: St. Martin's Press, 2005. A fun and reflective hike through Vermont, New York, and nature.

Stein, Bruce A., Lynn S. Kutner, and Jonathan S. Adams, eds. *Precious Heritage: The Status of Biodiversity in the United States. A Joint Project of The Nature Conservancy and the Association for Biodiversity Information.* New York: Oxford University Press, 2000. A compendium of biodiversity across the United States.

Sutter, Paul S., and Paul M. Pressly, eds. *Coastal Nature, Coastal Culture.* Athens, GA: University of Georgia Press, 2018. A series of environmental and historical essays on Georgia's coast.

Wiedensaul, Scott. *Return to Wild America: A Yearlong Search for the Continent's Natural Soul.* New York: North Point Press, 2005. A nature travelogue that inspired me to follow in Muir's footsteps.

Wilson, Edward O. *Half-Earth: Our Planet's Fight for Life.* New York: W. W. Norton, 2016. A call to arms to save the planet's biodiversity by the South's famed and beloved biologist.

About the Author

Dan Chapman is a longtime writer, reporter, and lover of the outdoors. He grew up in Washington, DC, and Tokyo, the son of a newspaper man and an English teacher. He worked for *Congressional Quarterly*, the *Winston-Salem Journal*, the *Charlotte Observer*, and the *Atlanta Journal-Constitution*. He has also reported from Asia, Europe, and the Middle East. He currently writes stories about conservation in the South for the US Fish and Wildlife Service. He lives in Decatur, Georgia, with his wife, Bita, and their two boys, Samad and Naveed. This is his first (published) book.

Photo credit: Bita Honarvar